ODP.NET Developer's Guide

Oracle Database 10g Development with Visual
Studio 2005 and the Oracle Data Provider for .NET

A practical guide for developers working with the Oracle
Data Provider for .NET and the Oracle Developer Tools
for Visual Studio 2005

Jagadish Chatarji Pulakhandam

Sunitha Paruchuri

BIRMINGHAM - MUMBAI

ODP.NET Developer's Guide

Oracle Database 10g Development with Visual Studio 2005 and the Oracle Data Provider for .NET

First published: June 2007

Production Reference: 1150607

Published by Packt Publishing Ltd.
32 Lincoln Road
Olton
Birmingham, B27 6PA, UK.

ISBN 978-1-847191-96-0

www.packtpub.com

Cover Image by www.visionwt.com

Credits

Authors

Jagadish Chatarji Pulakhandam

Sunitha Paruchuri

Reviewer

Steven M. Swafford

Development Editor

Douglas Paterson

Assistant Development Editor

Mithil Kulkarni

Technical Editor

Divya Menon

Editorial Manager

Dipali Chittar

Project Manager

Patricia Weir

Project Coordinator

Abhijeet Deobhakta

Indexer

Bhushan Pangaonkar

Proofreader

Chris Smith

Production Coordinator

Manjiri Nadkarni

Cover Designer

Manjiri Nadkarni

About the Authors

Jagadish Chatarji Pulakhandam currently works as a .NET Architect and is responsible for analyzing/designing enterprise-level .NET applications. He has worked with Oracle since database version 7.1 and has been in the IT field for about 12 years. Apart from Oracle and .NET, he has a good knowledge of developing corporate software and web applications, designing and implementing databases, designing and implementing data warehouses, and working with enterprise reporting software. During his free time, he contributes technical articles to OTN (Oracle Technology Network) and to the world of developer communities.

I dedicate this book to my mother Dhana Laxmi. Without her patience, support and encouragement, I would never be to this stage. A special thanks to my uncle Ch. Jagadish Kumar, who is the basis for change in my life. And several thanks to all of my relatives and friends who encouraged and supported me at various milestones in my life.

A final thanks to every member of this book project from PACKT Publishing and a special thanks to Douglas Paterson, who offered me the first chance of writing this first book in my life.

Sunitha Paruchuri has been programming with Microsoft tools and Oracle since 1997. She has developed numerous desktop, web, mobile, and distributed applications using Microsoft .NET and has good experience with other Microsoft products like Microsoft SQL Server, Microsoft Sharepoint Portal Server, etc.

I dedicate this book to my parents Harnadha babu and Aruna Kumari and special thanks to my sister (Bhagya Laxmi), all of my relatives and friends who framed, encouraged and supported me in developing my career.

About the Reviewer

Steven M. Swafford began developing software in 1995 while serving in the United States Air Force (USAF). Upon leaving the USAF he continued developing leading edge solutions in support of the America's war fighters as part of the original USAF enterprise portal development team. His roots are now in central Alabama where he works as a senior software engineer developing Java- and .NET-based applications and web services. Steven credits his wife Su Ok and daughter Sarah for supporting and inspiring his ongoing passion for software development and the resultant challenges of life near the bleeding edge. Steven was honored by the Microsoft Corporation in 2006 as a Microsoft ASP.NET Visual Developer MVP. He would like to thank Tim Stewart and Edward Habal who were his professional mentors and to this day remain close friends. Steven's personal website is located at `http://www.radicaldevelopment.net` and his blog is located at `http://aspadvice.com/blogs/sswafford/`.

Table of Contents

Preface

Oracle's ODP.NET is a .NET data provider that can connect to and access Oracle databases with tight integrity. It can be used from any .NET language, including C# and VB.NET. This book will show you how ODP.NET is the best choice for connecting .NET applications with Oracle database. We will be dealing with the concepts of ODP.NET and its requirements, working with SQL, PL/SQL, and XML DB using ODP.NET, looking at application development with ODP.NET: Web Applications, Web Services, and Mobile Applications. We will also learn to manipulate Oracle databases from within Visual Studio using Oracle Developer Tools for Visual Studio.

What This Book Covers

Chapter 1 introduces the concept of Oracle Database Extensions for .NET and provides information about Oracle Developer Tools for Visual Studio.

Chapter 2 introduces the Provider-Independent Model in ADO.NET 2.0, and shows how to connect to Oracle databases from .NET, working with .NET data providers, connection pooling, system privileged connection, and single sign-on etc.

Chapter 3 shows you several methods to retrieve data from an Oracle database. You will work with the core ODP.NET classes like `OracleCommand`, `OracleDataReader`, `OracleDataAdapter`, `OracleParameter`, and ADO.NET classes like `DataSet`, `DataTable`, and `DataRow` etc.

Chapter 4 is about inserting, updating, and deleting data in the database. You will also learn about statement caching, array binding, working with offline data, implementing transactions, and handling errors and exceptions encountered during database work.

Chapter 5 deals with working with PL/SQL blocks, PL/SQL stored procedures, and functions. It also teaches you how to execute routines in PL/SQL packages, how to pass arrays to and receive arrays from the Oracle database, and working with REF CURSOR using ODP.NET.

Chapter 6 is completely dedicated to dealing with large objects in Oracle. This chapter illustrates concepts, configurations, and programming for BFILE, BLOB, and CLOB (or NCLOB) in conjunction with ODP.NET.

Chapter 7 gives details about Oracle XML DB, an add-on feature of Oracle database. It provides information about generating XML from existing rows in tables, manipulating rows in a table using XML, and working with native XML in the Oracle database.

Chapter 8 deals with real-time application development scenarios like Oracle database change notifications, asynchronous application development, web application development using ASP.NET 2.0, web reporting (including grouping, sub-totals, charts, etc.), Object-Oriented development with ODP.NET and ASP.NET, XML web-services development using ODP.NET, and Smart Device Application development (for clients like the Pocket PC).

Chapter 9 introduces you to Oracle Developer Tools for Visual Studio 2005. It teaches you to connect to Oracle from the Visual Studio 2005 environment, retrieve Oracle information from Visual Studio, and work with database objects from Visual Studio. It also provides information about how to create and debug PL/SQL stored procedures and .NET CLR stored procedures in Oracle.

Conventions

In this book, you will find a number of styles of text that distinguish between different kinds of information. Here are some examples of these styles, and an explanation of their meaning.

There are three styles for code. Code words in text are shown as follows: "Connecting to a default Oracle database is purely dependent on the ORACLE_SID key available in your registry."

A block of code will be set as follows:

```
Dim ProviderName As String = _
              "Oracle.DataAccess.Client"
Dim fctry As DbProviderFactory = -
       DbProviderFactories.GetFactory(ProviderName)
```

When we wish to draw your attention to a particular part of a code block, the relevant lines or items will be made bold:

```
Dim dt As DataTable = _
           DbProviderFactories.GetFactoryClasses()
Me.DataGridView1.DataSource = dt
```

New terms and **important words** are introduced in a bold-type font. Words that you see on the screen, in menus or dialog boxes for example, appear in our text like this: "clicking the **Next** button moves you to the next screen".

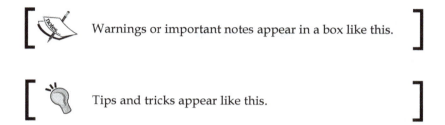

Warnings or important notes appear in a box like this.

Tips and tricks appear like this.

Reader Feedback

Feedback from our readers is always welcome. Let us know what you think about this book, what you liked or may have disliked. Reader feedback is important for us to develop titles that you really get the most out of.

To send us general feedback, simply drop an email to feedback@packtpub.com, making sure to mention the book title in the subject of your message.

If there is a book that you need and would like to see us publish, please send us a note in the **SUGGEST A TITLE** form on www.packtpub.com or email suggest@packtpub.com.

If there is a topic that you have expertise in and you are interested in either writing or contributing to a book, see our author guide on www.packtpub.com/authors.

Customer Support

Now that you are the proud owner of a Packt book, we have a number of things to help you to get the most from your purchase.

Downloading the Example Code for the Book

Visit http://www.packtpub.com/support, and select this book from the list of titles to download any example code or extra resources for this book. The files available for download will then be displayed.

 The downloadable files contain instructions on how to use them.

Errata

Although we have taken every care to ensure the accuracy of our contents, mistakes do happen. If you find a mistake in one of our books—maybe a mistake in text or code—we would be grateful if you would report this to us. By doing this you can save other readers from frustration, and help to improve subsequent versions of this book. If you find any errata, report them by visiting http://www.packtpub.com/support, selecting your book, clicking on the **Submit Errata** link, and entering the details of your errata. Once your errata are verified, your submission will be accepted and the errata added to the list of existing errata. The existing errata can be viewed by selecting your title from http://www.packtpub.com/support.

Questions

You can contact us at questions@packtpub.com if you are having a problem with some aspect of the book, and we will do our best to address it.

Introduction to ODP.NET
1

In the early days of databases, developers used to have knowledge on only one data access technology as they would usually concentrate on a single database. Later, numerous database products advanced quickly, leaving programmers in a confused state when selecting a particular data access methodology. The era of evolving architectures like client/server (two tier), three tier, and multi-tier (which includes web-enabled) has dramatically changed the way of accessing databases.
The paradigm got shifted from simple "connection-oriented" applications to connection-less or disconnected (or offline) applications to meet the demands of devices like PDAs/Handhelds, Smart Phones, Pocket PCs etc.

Introduction to ODP.NET

We now have several types of data access methodologies to develop applications. Choosing the best data access methodology is totally dependent on the type of application you are working on.

ADO.NET is a rock-solid technology and a proof of Microsoft's commitment to the UDA (Universal Data Access) strategy. The ADO.NET layer in the .NET architecture internally contains a few .NET data components (or .NET data providers), which can be used to connect to and access any database.

The data access through ADO.NET is shown in the following figure (along with other data access methodologies available prior to .NET):

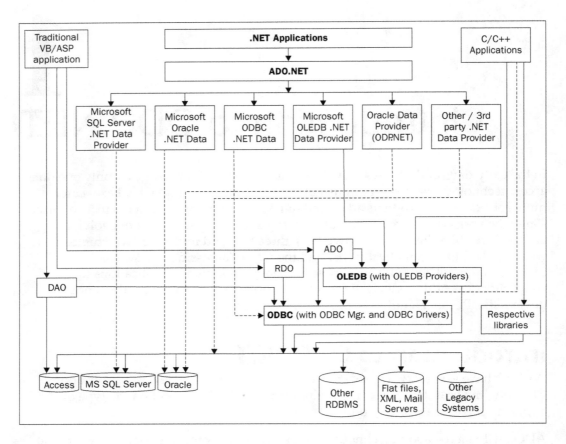

Even though Microsoft designed its own .NET data providers, it has also opened its doors (specification) to the public and is encouraging other database companies to develop their own .NET data providers. Microsoft made the data access model consistent among all of the .NET data providers and thus any .NET data provider should definitely conform to the standards and architecture of ADO.NET. One of those is Oracle's ODP.NET, a .NET data provider that can connect to and access Oracle databases with tight integrity.

The ODP.NET features optimized data access to the Oracle database from a .NET environment. It is one of the several data access methods to connect to and access Oracle databases. Oracle didn't simply stop giving support to Microsoft platform with only ODP.NET. Instead, it has extended its commitment for Microsoft .NET by adding **Oracle database extensions for .NET** and **Oracle Developer Tools for Visual Studio.**

The upcoming sections will give you a solid understanding of ODP.NET along with its features.

Why Use ODP.NET?

Can't we access Oracle without ODP.NET? Yes, we can. It is not compulsory for you to work with ODP.NET. As mentioned in the following section, we can still connect to and access Oracle using other alternative methods. But, in terms of features and performance, ODP .NET is your best choice for connecting .NET applications with Oracle database. Let us see how!

 I am limiting the discussion to only .NET applications or clients that are trying to access Oracle databases. I will not be discussing application development prior to .NET.

Oracle Database Access from .NET Applications

There exist four main methodologies to access Oracle database from a .NET application:

- Microsoft's .NET data provider for ODBC (or ODBC.NET)
- Microsoft's .NET data provider for OLEDB (or OLEDB.NET)
- Microsoft's .NET data provider for Oracle
- Oracle's data provider for .NET (or ODP.NET)

Before discussing each of the above methodologies, let us understand their nature from the following figure:

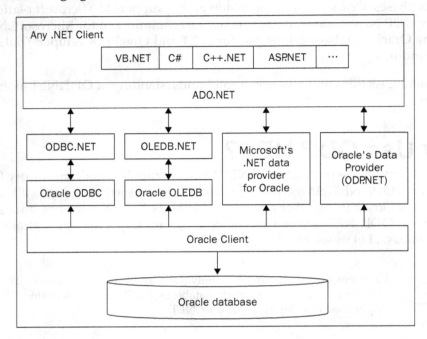

Microsoft's .NET data providers for ODBC and OLEDB are *not* intentionally developed exclusively for Oracle database. Those are generic .NET data providers mainly targeted for most of the common data sources. If you plan to use either of those two .NET data providers, you are likely to face performance problems.

From the above figure, you can observe that there exists a separate layer for each of those .NET data providers. In other words, ODBC.NET or OLEDB.NET would not directly execute the queries or commands. Those operations would be carried to another intermediate layer (or data access bridge) and further get executed at Oracle database. The existence of this intermediate layer really kills the performance (or response time) of execution. So, if you are trying to access Oracle database from a .NET application, neither of those would be a good choice.

Coming to the next choice, it is somewhat promising. Microsoft contributed a separate .NET Framework data provider (or Microsoft's Data Provider for Oracle) to connect to and access Oracle. It enables data access to Oracle data sources through Oracle client connectivity software without having any intermediate layers. This really improves performance over the previous two choices. Before using this provider in your .NET applications, you should install and configure Oracle client software (version 8.1.7 or later) on the development machine and test it.

The **Oracle Data Provider for .NET (ODP.NET)** features optimized data access to the Oracle database from any .NET client. It is the best in performance together with great flexibility. It allows developers to take advantage of native Oracle data types (including XML data type), XML DB, binding array parameters, Multiple Active Result Sets (MARS), Real Application Clusters (RAC), advanced security, etc.

What Do We Require to Work with ODP.NET?

As we are trying to develop .NET applications with access to Oracle database, we must have .NET Framework installed on our machine. Any Windows Operating System (preferably Windows Server 2003 or Windows XP Professional) supporting .NET can be used to work with ODP.NET.

At the time of this writing, .NET Framework 3.0 is the latest in market; but Oracle hasn't released ODP.NET compatible with that version yet. Not only that, Visual Studio 2008 (or "Orcas") supporting .NET Framework 3.0/3.5 is still in its beta version. For our purpose .NET Framework 2.0 is the latest in market, and you can download it free from Microsoft's website.

Even though .NET Framework (including SDK and .NET runtime) alone is enough to develop .NET-based applications, it is better to have some GUI-based RAD environment (or IDE) installed, so that we can develop .NET applications in no time. Microsoft Visual Studio 2005 Professional Edition is the preferred GUI to develop .NET 2.0-based applications. If you install Microsoft Visual Studio 2005 Professional Edition, all the necessary components (including .NET Framework SDK and runtime) get automatically installed.

The next is Oracle database. It is preferred to have at least Oracle 8.1 on your machine (or on a separate server). If you want to test with the latest version of Oracle on your own machine, you can download it free from Oracle's website for your development purposes. The lightest Oracle database version available (free) at the time of this writing is Oracle Database 10g Express Edition (or XE). Certain of the features like .NET CLR extensions (for .NET CLR-based stored procedure development) for Oracle are available only from Oracle 10g version 2.0 (Oracle 10.2) onwards. If you want to have distributed transaction support (like COM+ or Enterprise Services, etc.), then you may have install and configure Oracle Services for MTS.

If you install Oracle database version 9i release 2 or later on your own system, no special Oracle client is necessary to work with ODP.NET. If your database is at some other location, then you may have to install and configure Oracle 9i Release 2 or higher client on your machine to work with ODP.NET. Oracle Net Services get automatically installed when Oracle 9i Release 2 or higher client is installed on your machine. This may be required when you try to access an Oracle database on a network.

Another important optional component is Oracle Developer Tools for Visual Studio 2005. This is a wonderful add-in, which gets injected right into Visual Studio 2005. Using this add-in (called Oracle Explorer), you can connect to any Oracle database and work with schema or data without leaving the Visual Studio 2005 environment. It is particularly useful if you are likely to deal with .NET CLR extensions for Oracle. I strongly recommend having it installed on your machine, if you are working with Visual Studio Environment.

If you are developing ASP.NET applications, it is better to have IIS configured on your machine, to test web applications over the network. If you are developing Smart Phone or Pocket PC applications, you may need to install Smart Device Extensions for Visual Studio (which automatically installs .NET Compact Framework for Smart Devices).

Introduction to Oracle Database Extensions for .NET

The Oracle Database Extensions for .NET is a new feature of Oracle Database 10g Release 2 on Windows that makes it easy to develop, deploy, and run stored procedures and functions written in any .NET-compliant language.

Oracle Database Extensions for .NET

Oracle Database Extensions for .NET makes it possible to build and run any .NET-based stored procedures or functions with Oracle Database for Microsoft Windows. This feature is supported only from Oracle 10g version 2 (on Windows) onwards or Oracle 10g Express Edition (or Oracle 10g XE).

How does .NET Work within Oracle Database?

How come Oracle understands .NET? Oracle database doesn't need to understand .NET at all. It simply hosts the Microsoft .NET Common Language Runtime (CLR) in an external process, outside of the Oracle database process, but on the same computer. The integration of Oracle database with the Microsoft Common Language Runtime (CLR) enables applications to run .NET stored procedures or functions on Oracle database without any hurdles.

Application developers can write stored procedures and functions using any .NET-compliant language, such as C# and VB.NET, and use these .NET stored procedures in the database, in the same manner as other PL/SQL or Java stored procedures. .NET stored procedures can be used from PL/SQL packages, procedures, functions, and triggers.

Once the caller (or other PL/SQL stored procedures, packages, etc.) calls any of these .NET routines (stored procedures or functions), they get executed by the Oracle hosted Microsoft CLR and the results are automatically picked up by the Oracle PL/SQL engine. Once the control comes back to PL/SQL engine, it proceeds with the normal and traditional the PL/SQL process flow of execution.

Processing of .NET Stored Procedure with Oracle

To develop .NET CLR-based stored procedures or functions, you may need to have Oracle 10g version 2 or higher (for Windows) or at least Oracle 10g Express Edition together with Oracle Database Extensions for .NET installed. If you use Oracle 10g Express Edition, the extensions get automatically installed. But, if you install Oracle 10g version 2 (for Windows), you may have to go to custom install and select the extensions. Apart from the extensions, you also need to download Oracle Developer Tools for Visual Studio (with appropriate version) to develop and deploy .NET CLR-based routines in Oracle database.

Application developers build .NET stored procedures or functions using any .NET compliant language, such as C# and VB.NET, into a .NET assembly (generally a DLL), typically using Microsoft Visual Studio .NET 2003/2005. Obviously, we use Oracle Data Provider for .NET (ODP.NET) in .NET stored procedures and functions for Oracle data access. After building .NET procedures and functions into a .NET assembly, developers deploy them in Oracle database, using the **Oracle Deployment Wizard for .NET**, a component of the Oracle Developer Tools for Visual Studio .NET.

Once the .NET stored procedure gets deployed, the PL/SQL wrappers for all of those routines get automatically created within the schema. The user invokes a .NET stored procedure or function through this PL/SQL wrapper (which would be the same as for normal PL/SQL stored procedures or functions). Oracle Deployment Wizard for .NET determines the probable mappings between Oracle data types and .NET data types, which the user can override. The mappings are handled seamlessly by the PL/SQL wrapper.

Introduction to Oracle Developer Tools for Visual Studio

Oracle Developer Tools for Visual Studio is an add-in for Microsoft Visual Studio that tightly integrates the Visual Studio environment with Oracle database. You will be able to manipulate Oracle databases from within Visual Studio and without leaving Visual Studio.

At the time of this writing, Oracle Developer Tools for Visual Studio is available for both Microsoft Visual Studio.NET 2003 and Microsoft Visual Studio.NET 2005 versions. If you have both versions on your computer, you can install for both of those IDEs by installing Oracle Developer Tools for Visual Studio 2005.

Once you install Oracle Developer Tools for Visual Studio, **Oracle Explorer** automatically shows up in the **View** menu of Visual Studio as shown in the following figure:

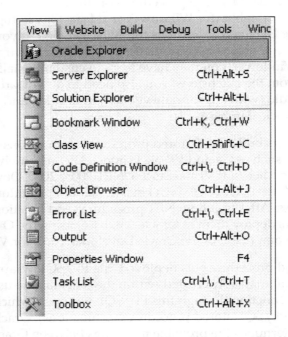

Using **Oracle Explorer** in the Visual Studio environment, you can browse through your entire Oracle schema, launch several designers and wizards to work with different schema objects (like tables, views, etc.), execute queries directly against your schema (using SQL Query Window), automatically generate .NET code, and several more. The following is a small glimpse of **Oracle Explorer**:

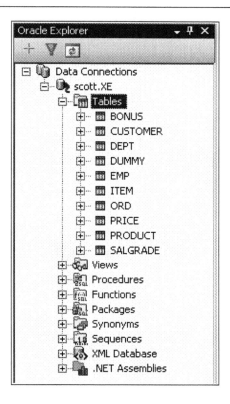

To work with database tables (for example inserting, updating, etc.) you can keep yourself tied with Oracle Data Window. It also gives you the flexibility to run and test your PL/SQL stored procedures. **Oracle Explorer** also includes a fully integrated PL/SQL debugger (for Visual Studio 2005).

Apart from all of the above, you can easily develop and deploy .NET stored procedures and functions using .NET Deployment Wizard.

Summary

In this chapter, we have covered the concepts of ODP.NET, requirements to work with ODP.NET, Oracle Database Extensions for .NET, and finally concluded with an introduction to Oracle Developer Tools for Visual Studio.NET

2

Connecting to Oracle

From this chapter on, we will start programming with ODP.NET. This chapter mainly concentrates on the following:

- Introducing the Provider-Independent Model in ADO.NET 2.0
- Working with .NET data providers
- Different ways to connect to Oracle database from ADO.NET 2.0
- Connection pooling, system privileged connection, Windows authentication

Provider-Independent Model in ADO.NET 2.0

ADO.NET internally works with .NET data providers (or .NET data bridge provider) to connect to and access data from different kinds of data sources (including databases). The same data provider model existing in ADO.NET 1.1 is further enhanced in ADO.NET 2.0 (with new factory classes) to leverage the flexibility of developing database-independent applications.

What exactly is a factory class? The purpose of a factory class is to provide an interface for creating families of related objects, with or without specifying their concrete (method implementation) classes. If the factory class is created without one or more implementations of methods, we call it as an *abstract* factory class.

The provider-independent programming model in ADO.NET 2.0 revolves around the classes in the `System.Data.Common` namespace. There are mainly two new factory classes that implement the provider-independent model (within the same namespace):

- `DbProviderFactories`
- `DbProviderFactory`

Listing All Installed .NET Data Providers

Now, let us start our programming with listing all .NET data providers installed on your machine. All .NET data provider-related information gets listed in the `machine.config` file on your machine. Each provider is generally identified with its *invariant name*. The invariant name (in most cases) is the same as its namespace.

The following code gives out the list of all .NET data providers installed on your machine:

```
Imports System.Data.Common

Public Class Form1

    Private Sub btnProviders_Click(ByVal sender As
        System.Object, ByVal e As System.EventArgs) Handles
        btnProviders.Click

        Dim dt As DataTable = _
                DbProviderFactories.GetFactoryClasses()
        Me.DataGridView1.DataSource = dt

    End Sub

End Class
```

Within the above code, the `DbProviderFactories` class is mainly used to enumerate all .NET data providers installed on your machine. Using the same class, we can also create instances related to a specific provider (to access databases specific to that provider). To list all the .NET data providers installed on your machine, we can use a `GetFactoryClasses()` method available in the `DbProviderFactories` class.

The highlighted line of code finds and lists all the .NET data providers installed on your machine (and populates them into a data table). When that code gets executed, the output should look similar to the following:

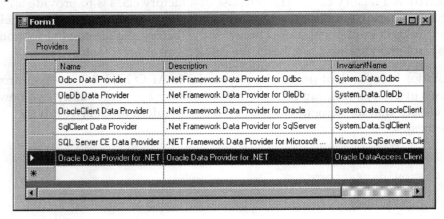

According to the preceding figure, you can see that the machine has six .NET data providers installed. The third column represents the invariant names to identify each of those providers.

Enumerating all Oracle Data Sources Available

In the previous section, we enumerated the list of all .NET data providers installed on the machine. In the previous screenshot, you should observe that the machine in this example has the **Oracle Data Provider for .NET** installed, which is identified with invariant name **Oracle.DataAccess.Client**.

In this section, we shall enumerate the list of all Oracle data sources available. Let us go through the following code first:

```
Imports System.Data.Common

Public Class Form2

    Private Sub btnDataSources_Click(ByVal sender As
        System.Object, ByVal e As System.EventArgs) Handles
        btnDataSources.Click

        Dim ProviderName As String = _
              "Oracle.DataAccess.Client"
        Dim fctry As DbProviderFactory = _
              DbProviderFactories.GetFactory(ProviderName)
        If (fctry.CanCreateDataSourceEnumerator) Then
          Dim dsenum As DbDataSourceEnumerator = _
                  fctry.CreateDataSourceEnumerator()
          Dim dt As DataTable = dsenum.GetDataSources()
          Me.DataGridView1.DataSource = dt
        Else
          MessageBox.Show("No datasources found")
        End If

    End Sub

    End Class
```

Let us go through the above code step by step.

The following is the statement that selects the ODP.NET data provider:

```
Dim ProviderName As String = "Oracle.DataAccess.Client"
```

The .NET data provider name is nothing but the invariant name available for the respective .NET data provider. In the previous screenshot, you can observe that there is a special column named **InvariantName** to identify the respective .NET data provider.

The following statement creates a factory instance of the data provider selected:

```
Dim fctry As DbProviderFactory = _
  DbProviderFactories.GetFactory(ProviderName)
```

Once the factory instance is created, we need to determine whether the provider (or instance) supports enumerating of data sources or not. This is easily accomplished with the CanCreateDataSourceEnumerator() method (which returns a Boolean).

If the underlying .NET data provider supports enumerating the data sources, we can find and retrieve all the data sources for respective .NET data provider using the following code:

```
If (fctry.CanCreateDataSourceEnumerator) Then
  Dim dsenum As DbDataSourceEnumerator = _
    fctry.CreateDataSourceEnumerator()
  Dim dt As DataTable = dsenum.GetDataSources()
  Me.DataGridView1.DataSource = dt
Else
  MessageBox.Show("No datasources found")
End If
```

The CreateDataSourceEnumerator() method simply creates an enumerator. The method GetDataSources() enumerates through all existing Oracle data sources.

When the above code gets executed, the output should look similar to the following:

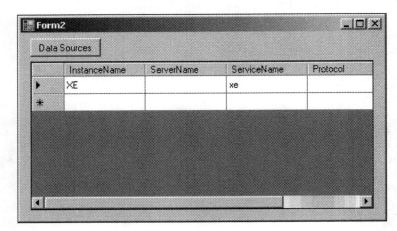

Here, the **XE** is nothing but the name of the Oracle instance (SID) running on the system, which has Oracle 10g Express Edition installed.

So far we have just enumerated all the .NET data providers installed on our machine and the list of Oracle data sources. We haven't connected to an Oracle database yet in the preceding code.

Connecting to Oracle Databases from .NET

There are several ways to connect to Oracle database from within .NET. Each of those methods has its own pros and cons as described in Chapter 1. Now, we will explore the most popular methodologies to connect to Oracle database through .NET.

To connect to Oracle, we need to have proper connection descriptors configured on the system. This is usually taken care by the tnsnames.ora file. **TNS** stands for **Transparent Network Substrate**. It provides a uniform application interface to enable network applications to access the underlying network protocols. tnsnames. ora is simply a text file that provides SQL*Net with the Oracle server location and the necessary connection strings to connect to Oracle databases. This file always resides in the Oracle home's Network\Admin folder.

If the Oracle client (or SQL*Plus) is already able to connect to the Oracle database server, the tnsnames.ora file is already correctly configured and you need not disturb it. But, it is beneficial for you to look at the content of tnsnames.ora to have a better understanding of the connection descriptors. The following is an example entry available in the tnsname.ora file on a machine to get connected to Oracle (yours could be different):

```
XE =
  (DESCRIPTION =
    (ADDRESS_LIST =
      (ADDRESS = (PROTOCOL = TCP)(HOST = 127.0.0.1)
                                   (PORT = 1521))
    )
    (CONNECT_DATA =
      (SERVICE_NAME = xe)
    )
  )
```

The above configuration script shows that the Oracle database server is available at 127.0.0.1 (local machine) and listening at port 1521. The service name (or SID) to connect to the server is xe. The whole description is assigned to a name XE.

We will make use of the above specification in most of the connection strings available in the examples.

> Before building the connection strings, make sure that you configured
> and tested `tnsnames.ora` properly and can connect to the Oracle
> database. If you can already connect to the Oracle database server,
> you need not modify further. But you should know to which host
> you are going to connect. This is essential, as an Oracle client could
> be configured to connect to more than one Oracle database server
> simultaneously. You can also configure and test these connections
> using a graphical wizard, **Net Configuration Assistant**.

Connecting Using .NET Data Provider Factory Classes

The previous topic introduced .NET data provider factory classes and this section
will use those classes to connect to an Oracle database.

The following code demonstrates how to connect to an Oracle database using the
.NET data provider factory classes:

```
Imports System.Data.Common

Public Class Form3

    Private Sub btnConnect_Click(ByVal sender As
        System.Object, ByVal e As System.EventArgs) Handles
        btnConnect.Click

        'specify provider's invariant name
        Dim ProviderName As String = _
                "Oracle.DataAccess.Client"
        'create factory instance for the provider
        Dim fctry As DbProviderFactory = _
            DbProviderFactories.GetFactory(ProviderName)
        'create connection based on the factory
        Dim Connection As Data.Common.DbConnection
        Connection = fctry.CreateConnection
        'specify connection string
        Connection.ConnectionString = _
                        "Data Source=xe;user id=scott;password=tiger"
        Try
           'try connecting to oracle
           Connection.Open()
           'close the connection before exiting
           Connection.Close()
           MessageBox.Show("Succesfully connected")
```

```
      Catch ex As Exception
        'display error message if not connected
        MessageBox.Show("Unable to connect. " & ex.Message)
      End Try

   End Sub

End Class
```

From the preceding code we have the following statements that are used to create a factory instance for the .NET data provider selected (in this case it is `Oracle.DataAccess.Client`).

```
      Dim ProviderName As String = _
                  "Oracle.DataAccess.Client"
      Dim fctry As DbProviderFactory = _
          DbProviderFactories.GetFactory(ProviderName)
```

Further moving down, we have the following:

```
      Dim Connection As Data.Common.DbConnection
      Connection = fctry.CreateConnection
```

`Data.Common.DbConnection` can simply hold any type of database connection irrespective of the data source or data provider. To create a database connection object from the factory instance, we can make use of the `CreateConnection()` method, which in turn returns an object of the type `Data.Common.DbConnection`. Once the `DbConnection` object is created (for the respective .NET data provider through the factory instance), it needs to be provided with database connection string information as follows:

```
   Connection.ConnectionString = _
                      "Data Source=xe;user id=scott;password=tiger"
```

Once the `DbConnection` object is ready, we can open the connection to connect and work with the database. It is always suggested to open a database connection as late as possible and close it as early as possible. The following code fragment tries to open the connection using the `Open()` method and closes using the `Close()` method:

```
      Try
        'try connecting to oracle
        Connection.Open()
        'close the connection before exiting
        Connection.Close()
        MessageBox.Show("Succesfully connected")
      Catch ex As Exception
        'display error message if not connected
        MessageBox.Show("Unable to connect. " & ex.Message)
      End Try
```

This model (and method) of connectivity is mostly preferred when you are trying to develop database-independent applications.

Connecting Using .NET Data Provider for OLEDB

This method is mostly preferred when you are trying to develop database-independent applications based on ADO.NET 1.1. If you are trying to develop a database-independent application based on ADO.NET 2.0, the method provided in the previous section is preferred.

The following is the code to connect to Oracle database using .NET data provider for OLEDB:

```
Imports System.Data.OleDb

Public Class Form4

  Private Sub btnConnect_Click(ByVal sender As
    System.Object, ByVal e As System.EventArgs) Handles
    btnConnect.Click

    Dim cn As New OleDbConnection
    cn.ConnectionString = "Provider=msdaora;
                    Data Source=xe;User Id=scott;Password=tiger;"
    Try
       'try connecting to oracle
       cn.Open()
       'close the connection before exiting
       cn.Close()
       MessageBox.Show("Succesfully connected")
    Catch ex As Exception
       'display error message if not connected
       MessageBox.Show("Unable to connect. " & ex.Message)
    End Try

  End Sub
End Class
```

In the above code, the System.Data.oleDb namespace is used to deal with *.NET Data Provider for OLEDB*. When we are working with OLEDB data sources, we need to connect through the OleDbConnection class. The connection string information would also be different when we deal with .NET Data Provider for OLEDB to connect to Oracle.

The following is the new connection string used to get connected to Oracle database using .NET Data Provider for OLEDB:

```
cn.ConnectionString = "Provider=msdaora;
                  Data Source=xe;User Id=scott;Password=tiger;"
```

Connecting Using .NET Data Provider for ODBC

This method is used when you are trying to develop multi-platform database-independent applications using ADO.NET. This method is preferable, if you want to connect to legacy systems or database systems existing on other platforms.

The following is the code to connect to Oracle database using .NET data provider for ODBC:

```
Imports System.Data.odbc

Public Class Form5

    Private Sub btnConnect_Click(ByVal sender As
        System.Object, ByVal e As System.EventArgs) Handles
        btnConnect.Click

        Dim cn As New OdbcConnection
        cn.ConnectionString =
                        "Driver={Microsoft ODBC for Oracle};
                        Server=xe;Uid=scott;Pwd=tiger;"

        Try
            'try connecting to oracle
            cn.Open()
            'close the connection before exiting
            cn.Close()
            MessageBox.Show("Succesfully connected")
        Catch ex As Exception
            'display error message if not connected
            MessageBox.Show("Unable to connect. " & ex.Message)
        End Try

    End Sub
End Class
```

In the preceding code, the `System.Data.odbc` namespace is used to deal with *.NET Data Provider for ODBC*. When we are working with ODBC data sources, we need to connect through the `OdbcConnection` class. The connection string information would also be different when we deal with .NET Data Provider for ODBC to connect to Oracle. The following is the new connection string used to get connected to Oracle database using .NET Data Provider for ODBC:

```
cn.ConnectionString = "Driver={Microsoft ODBC for Oracle};
                                Server=xe;Uid=scott;Pwd=tiger;"
```

Connecting using Microsoft's .NET Data Provider for Oracle

This provider is added by Microsoft to facilitate developers connecting and accessing Oracle databases. This method is mostly preferred when you are trying to access only Oracle databases and when you don't have ODP.NET installed on your machine.

Before you start working with this provider, you need to add a reference to the assembly `System.Data.OracleClient` as shown in following figure:

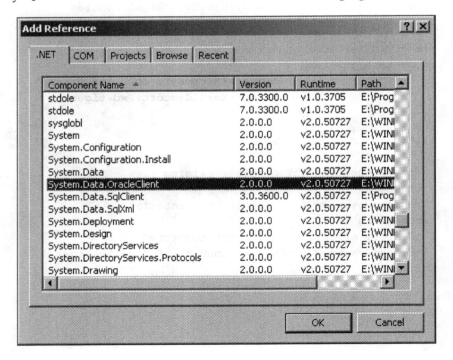

Once you add a reference as shown in the preceding figure, you can proceed with the following code to connect to Oracle database using Microsoft's .NET data provider for Oracle:

```
Imports System.Data.OracleClient

Public Class Form6

    Private Sub btnConnect_Click(ByVal sender As
        System.Object, ByVal e As System.EventArgs) Handles
        btnConnect.Click

        Dim cn As New OracleConnection
        cn.ConnectionString = _
                        "Data Source=xe; User Id=scott;Password=tiger;"

        Try
            'try connecting to oracle
            cn.Open()
            'close the connection before exiting
            cn.Close()
            MessageBox.Show("Succesfully connected")
        Catch ex As Exception
            'display error message if not connected
            MessageBox.Show("Unable to connect. " & ex.Message)
        End Try

    End Sub
End Class
```

In the above code, we are making use of the `System.Data.OracleClient` namespace to deal with Microsoft's *.NET Data Provider for Oracle*. The `OracleConnection` class used in the above code is available as part of the same namespace (and not to be confused with the same class available in `Oracle.DataAccess.Client`).

Connecting Using Oracle Data Provider for .NET (ODP.NET)

This provider is contributed by Oracle to facilitate developers connecting and accessing Oracle databases with tight integration (along with best performance) and advanced features. This method is the best even when you are trying to access Oracle, as ODP.NET has tight integration with Oracle database. To use this method, you must have ODP.NET downloaded (available free) and installed on your machine.

Once you have ODP.NET installed on your machine, you need to add a reference to the assembly `Oracle.DataAccess`. If you have more than one version installed, you may have to choose the right one. If you are using Visual Studio 2005 and ODP.NET 10.2.0.2.20 (with support for ADO.NET 2.0) choose as shown in following figure:

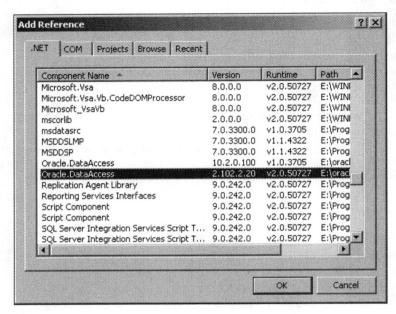

Once you add a reference as shown in the above figure, you can proceed with the following code to connect to Oracle database using ODP.NET:

```
Imports oracle.DataAccess.Client

Public Class Form7

    Private Sub btnConnect_Click(ByVal sender As
        System.Object, ByVal e As System.EventArgs) Handles
        btnConnect.Click

        Dim cn As New OracleConnection
        cn.ConnectionString = _
                        "Data Source=xe;User Id=scott;Password=tiger;"

        Try
            'try connecting to oracle
            cn.Open()
            'close the connection before exiting
            cn.Close()
            MessageBox.Show("Succesfully connected")
        Catch ex As Exception
```

```
        'display error message if not connected
        MessageBox.Show("Unable to connect. " & ex.Message)
      End Try
    End Sub

End Class
```

In the above code, the namespace `Oracle.DataAccess.Client` is used to deal with *Oracle Data Provider for .NET (ODP.NET)*. The `OracleConnection` class used in the above code is available as part of the same namespace (and not to be confused with the same class available in `System.data.OracleClient`). The connection string information for this data provider and .NET data provider factory classes could be the same (as both of them deal with the namespace internally).

Connecting with Connection Pooling

Opening and maintaining a database connection for each client (or application/ user) is expensive and wastes lots of resources. This is true especially during web application development. To overcome such scenarios, Connection Pooling can be implemented.

A Connection Pool is simply a cache of database connections. These connections can be reused when the database receives future requests from clients (or applications) for data. The clients (or applications) will feel as if each of them has a separate connection to the database.

Connection Pooling is enabled by default and it is not only limited to ODP.NET but also available with other .NET data providers. You can simply add `pooling=false` to your connection string to disable Connection Pooling. You can customize pooling with your own specification within the connection string.

The following is a simple demonstration of customizing the Connection Pooling as part of the connection string:

```
Imports oracle.DataAccess.Client

Public Class Form7

  Private Sub btnConnect_Click(ByVal sender As
    System.Object, ByVal e As System.EventArgs) Handles
    btnConnect.Click

    Dim cn As New OracleConnection
    cn.ConnectionString = "Data Source=xe;
                         User id=scott;Password=tiger;
                         Min Pool Size= 5;
                         Connection Lifetime=120;
```

```
                          Connection Timeout=60;
                          Incr Pool size=2;
                          Decr Pool size=1"
      Try
         'try connecting to oracle
         cn.Open()
         'close the connection before exiting
         cn.Close()
         MessageBox.Show("Succesfully connected")
      Catch ex As Exception
         'display error message if not connected
         MessageBox.Show("Unable to connect. " & ex.Message)
      End Try
    End Sub

  End Class
```

The connection string in the code above is defined with several parameters. Connection Lifetime sets the maximum duration in seconds of the connection object in the pool. Connection Timeout is the maximum number of seconds to wait for the connection to the server (before raising an error). Min Pool Size is the number of connection objects it needs to hold at any time (similarly Max Pool Size is also available). Based on the demands of requests and activity, the number of connections in the pool gets decreased or increased based on the specification of Incr Pool size and Decr Pool size.

Connecting with System-Level Privileges or DBA Privileges

DBA-level privileges are primarily focussed on database object-level access of a particular user. *System-level* privileges are more special when compared with ordinary database-level (or even object-level) privileges. When connecting with system-level privileges, you have the opportunity to administer the database, even before it starts up.

The two main system-level privileges are **SYSDBA** and **SYSOPER**. When you log in as SYSDBA, the default schema is SYS, whereas with SYSOPER the default schema is PUBLIC. SYSDBA is a superset of SYSOPER.

While connecting with system-level privileges, it is obvious to work with DBA privileges as well. If you don't need to work at system level, and simply want to access few of the DBA objects, it is not really necessary to connect using system-level privileges.

If you need .NET applications to connect to Oracle with system-level privileges, you just need to add connection parameters to the existing connection string as follows:

```
Imports oracle.DataAccess.Client

Public Class Form7

  Private Sub btnConnect_Click(ByVal sender As
    System.Object, ByVal e As System.EventArgs) Handles
    btnConnect.Click

    Dim cn As New OracleConnection

    cn.ConnectionString = "Data Source=xe;
                          User id=system;Password=manager;
                          DBA Privilege=SYSOPER"
    Try
      'try connecting to oracle
      cn.Open()
      'close the connection before exiting
      cn.Close()
      MessageBox.Show("Succesfully connected")
    Catch ex As Exception
      'display error message if not connected
      MessageBox.Show("Unable to connect. " & ex.Message)
    End Try
  End Sub

End Class
```

In the above statement, you can observe that the user name is system (which is a DBA user) and privilege is SYSDBA.

Dynamic Connecting String Using OracleConnectionStringBuilder and app.config

You can dynamically build a connection string using the OracleConnectionStringBuilder class available in ODP.NET 10.2.0.2. This is very helpful if you have any Oracle connectivity parameters in the .NET configuration files like app.config or web.config.

Now, let us add few of the Oracle connectivity parameters to the app.config file by using solution properties as follows:

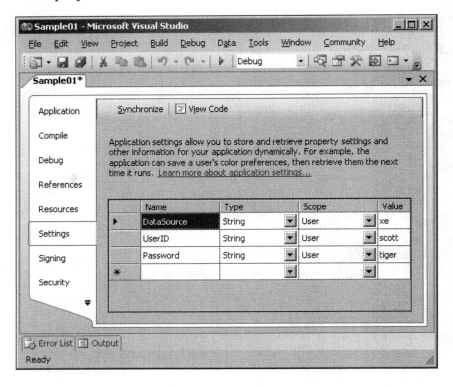

Once you add the parameters as shown in the above figure, you can develop the code as follows to dynamically create a connection string using OracleConnectionStringBuilder (explained later):

```
Imports Oracle.DataAccess.Client

Public Class Form9

    Private Function getConnectionString() As String
        Dim cnBuilder As New OracleConnectionStringBuilder
        With cnBuilder
            .DataSource = My.Settings.DataSource
            .UserID = My.Settings.UserID
            .Password = My.Settings.Password
        End With
        Return cnBuilder.ConnectionString
    End Function
```

```
Private Sub btnConnect_Click(ByVal sender As
    System.Object, ByVal e As System.EventArgs) Handles
    btnConnect.Click
    Dim cn As New OracleConnection
    cn.ConnectionString = getConnectionString()
    Try
      'try connecting to oracle
      cn.Open()
      'close the connection before exiting
      cn.Close()
      MessageBox.Show("Succesfully connected")
    Catch ex As Exception
      'display error message if not connected
      MessageBox.Show("Unable to connect. " & ex.Message)
    End Try
  End Sub
End Class
```

From the above code, you can observe that we are trying to retrieve all the connection parameters from the app.config file using the My object introduced in .NET Framework 2.0. The OracleConnectionStringBuilder object simply needs to have a few properties (like DataSource, UserID, Password etc.) set. Once the properties are set, it automatically frames a connection string internally and returns this when used with the ConnectionString property.

Embedding a "tnsnames.ora" Entry-like Connection String

In all of the above examples, we directly used the specification available in the tnsnames.ora file. You can even define your own entry in the style of tnsnames.ora, directly within the connection string. The following is the code for a *tnsnames.ora-less* connection:

```
Imports oracle.DataAccess.Client

Public Class Form7

  Private Sub btnConnect_Click(ByVal sender As
    System.Object, ByVal e As System.EventArgs) Handles
    btnConnect.Click

    Dim cn As New OracleConnection
    Dim ConnStr As String
```

```
ConnStr = "Data Source = "
ConnStr &= "(DESCRIPTION = "
ConnStr &= "   (ADDRESS_LIST ="
ConnStr &= "      (ADDRESS = (PROTOCOL = TCP)
                     (HOST = 127.0.0.1)(PORT = 1521))"
ConnStr &= "   )"
ConnStr &= "   (CONNECT_DATA ="
ConnStr &= "      (SERVICE_NAME = xe)"
ConnStr &= "   )"
ConnStr &= ");"
ConnStr &= "User Id=scott;"
ConnStr &= "password=tiger;"
cn.ConnectionString = ConnStr

Try
   'try connecting to oracle
   cn.Open()
   'close the connection before exiting
   cn.Close()
   MessageBox.Show("Succesfully connected")
Catch ex As Exception
   'display error message if not connected
   MessageBox.Show("Unable to connect. " & ex.Message)
   End Try
End Sub

End Class
```

In the above code, we simply copied and pasted the entry available in tnsnames.ora and it worked like a charm. You can also make the above connection string dynamic (say, if you want to connect to different data sources at different times), by adding text boxes to your form and concatenating those values with the above connection string.

Connecting to a Default Oracle Database

In all of the previous methods, within the connection string, we specified the data source or server values to connect to an Oracle instance (using SID). Sometimes, it may be necessary for us to get connected to the default Oracle database existing on the same machine as of the .NET application (but not on any other network server).

Connecting to a default Oracle database is purely dependent on the ORACLE_SID key available in your registry (as shown in the following). You can even add it manually if it is not available in your Oracle home. Once that is added, you can define connection strings without the specification of data source or server.

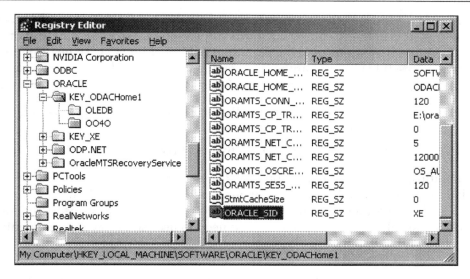

 Even though you can add this ORACLE_SID using the "Environment Variables" dialog box, this method is not suggested if you have multiple versions of Oracle installed on the same machine.

Once you set up the default Oracle database using the ORACLE_SID registry key in your registry, the connection string could be modified and made simple (without specifying any data source or server specification) as follows:

```
cn.ConnectionString = "User Id=scott;Password=tiger;"
```

Connecting Using Windows Authentication (Single Sign-On)

This is totally a different scenario from any of the previous types of connectivity to Oracle databases. A *Windows Authentication* is simply a process of authenticating against Oracle database using the Windows-user credentials. A *Single Sign-on* is the process of authenticating against Oracle database even without providing any credentials (by taking into the account of existing Windows-user credentials).

There exists no direct solution to achieve 100% single sign-on to authenticate against Oracle database. However, we need to provide the user ID as "/", which automatically carries our current Windows-user credentials to authenticate against Oracle database. By using this facility, we can develop .NET applications implementing 100% single sign-on against Oracle databases.

Primarily, a Windows Authentication to an Oracle database is not a straight process. Even though, it is not very complicated process, we do have some configuration, which needs to be set up using database administrator privileges. To get a Windows user for a successful Windows authentication (or single sign-on) against Oracle database, we must start by finding two important values as follows:

- Operating System Authentication Prefix (os_authent_prefix parameter in the init.ora file)
- Windows user name (along with either host name or domain name)

The Operating System Authentication Prefix gets configured during Oracle installation and is available as an os_authent_prefix parameter in the init.ora file. We need to use this value as a prefix to the Windows-user credentials. To retrieve the value of that parameter, you need to use the following statement:

```
SQL> show parameter os_authent_prefix
```

You may need to have DBA privileges (or log in as *system/sysdba/sysoper* user) to carry out these tasks.

You can easily get your complete user name (along with your host name or domain name) from your login dialog box. You can even get it dynamically using the following VB.NET code:

```
Private Sub btnWindowsUser_Click(ByVal sender As
    System.Object, ByVal e As System.EventArgs) Handles
    btnWindowsUser.Click

    Dim WindowsUser As String = My.User.Name
    MessageBox.Show(WindowsUser)

End Sub
```

Once you find out those two values, you need to create a user in Oracle with the same Windows user name (along with host/domain name) preceded with the value of os_authent_prefix and grant enough privileges to get the user connected.

 Sometimes, the value of os_authent_prefix could be empty (or no value). In such scenarios, you need not prefix the Windows user with any value.

You can issue the following statements to create and grant privileges to the Windows user in Oracle:

```
SQL> CREATE USER "PS$LAPTOP2K3\ADMINISTRATOR"
                        IDENTIFIED EXTERNALLY;
SQL> GRANT connect, resource TO
                "PS$LAPTOP2K3\ADMINISTRATOR"
```

In the above commands, PS$ is the parameter value of os_authent_prefix on my machine and LAPTOP2K3\ADMINISTRATOR is the Windows user. If there is no value (or empty) for *os_authent_prefix*, you need not prefix the Windows user with any value. Once the above setup is perfectly configured, you must be able to connect to that user using the following command at the SQL prompt:

```
SQL> connect /
```

You can observe that it is quite simple to connect to Oracle database using "/", which informs it to use a Windows authentication. In the same manner, you can modify your connection string in .NET as follows to achieve a single sign-on authentication (with Windows authentication) to Oracle database:

```
Dim cn As New OracleConnection
cn.ConnectionString = "Data Source=xe;User Id=/;"
```

Summary

In this chapter, we have reviewed the strategy of the Provider-Independent Model in ADO.NET 2.0, used this model to list installed .NET data providers and data sources, and finally developed code to connect to Oracle database from .NET using all the available methods.

3

Retrieving Data from Oracle Using ODP.NET

We have several methodologies to retrieve information from Oracle using ODP.NET. Sometimes, we may have to use few of the ODP.NET classes together with few of the ADO.NET classes to develop .NET applications efficiently.

In this chapter, we will concentrate on the following:

- Executing queries with `OracleCommand`
- Retrieving data using `OracleDataReader`
- Retrieving data using `OracleDataAdapter`
- Working with `DataTable` and `Dataset` when offline (disconnected mode)
- Using `DataTableReader` with `DataTable`
- Bind variables using `OracleParameter`
- Performance techniques

If you would like to work with stored procedures to retrieve data, you should skip to Chapter 5 (provided you are familiar with all the concepts discussed here).

Fundamental ODP.NET Classes to Retrieve Data

To retrieve data from an Oracle database using ODP.NET, we need to work with a few of the ODP.NET classes. At this point, we will discuss the most fundamental classes available in ODP.NET for retrieving data.

The following is the list of fundamental ODP.NET classes:

- `OracleConnection`
- `OracleCommand`
- `OracleParameter`
- `OracleDataReader`
- `OracleDataAdapter`

The `OracleConnection` class provides the means to connect to the Oracle database. We have already used this class several number of times in the previous chapter. It connects to Oracle database and performs all the operations we need to carry out. Without this class, we would never be able to perform any database operation. It also manages transactions and connection pooling.

The `OracleCommand` class is mainly used to execute commands against Oracle database. It supports the execution of SQL commands (like SELECT, INSERT, and CREATE), stored procedures, etc. We can even specify table or view names (without even providing a SELECT statement) to retrieve the rows available through them. It works in conjunction with `OracleConnection` to connect to Oracle database.

The `OracleParameter` class is complementary to the `OracleCommand` class to provide run-time parameters along with their values to SQL queries or stored procedures. You can even work with different types of stored-procedure parameters like IN, OUT, or IN OUT. It is also mostly used whenever you want to execute the same SQL command frequently or continuously.

The `OracleDataReader` class is simply a read-only and forward-only result set. As the data retrieved using this class is non-updatable and only forward-navigable, this is the fastest retrieval mechanism available. The most important point to remember while using `OracleDataReader` is that it needs a dedicated connection to Oracle database while it retrieves information. It is best used to fill in drop-down lists, data grids, etc. It works in conjunction with `OracleCommand` to connect to and retrieve information from Oracle database.

The `OracleDataAdapter` class is mainly used to populate datasets or data tables for offline use (disconnected use). The `OracleDataAdapter` simply connects to the database, retrieves the information (or data), populates that information into datasets or data tables, and finally disconnects the connection to the database. It works with `OracleConnection` to connect to Oracle database. It can also work with `OracleCommand` if necessary.

A data table is very similar to a disconnected result set (or record set). A dataset is simply a set of data tables along with their relations (if available). A dataset is a kind of small scale in-memory RDBMS, which gets created on demand.

DataTable and DataSet are the two classes for these in ADO.NET that are used in combination with OracleDataAdapter. The data in a dataset (or data table) can be modified offline (in disconnected mode) and later can be updated back to the database using the same OracleDataAdapter. In simple words, OracleDataAdapter works as a bridge between offline data (or a dataset) and Oracle database.

Retrieving Data Using OracleDataReader

OracleDataReader is simply a read-only and forward-only result set. It works only if the database connection is open and it makes sure that the connection is open while you are retrieving data. As the data that it retrieves is read-only, it is a bit faster than any other method to retrieve data from Oracle.

You need to work with OracleCommand together with OracleConnection to get access to OracleDataReader. There is an ExecuteReader method in the OracleCommand class, which gives you the OracleDataReader.

Retrieving a Single Row of Information

Let us start by retrieving a single row from Oracle database using ODP.NET and populate the data into few textboxes on a WinForm.

To connect to and work with Oracle database, we need to start with OracleConnection. Once a connection to the database is established, we need to issue a SELECT statement to retrieve some information from the database. A query (or any SQL command) can be executed with the help of an OracleCommand object. Once the SELECT statement gets executed, we can use OracleDataReader to retrieve the information.

The following code accepts an employee number from the user and gives you the details of that employee:

```
Imports Oracle.DataAccess.Client

Public Class Form1

  Private Sub btnGetEmployee_Click(ByVal sender As
    System.Object, ByVal e As System.EventArgs) Handles
    btnGetEmployee.Click
    'create connection to db
    Dim cn As New OracleConnection("Data Source=xe; _
                      User Id=scott;Password=tiger")
    Try
      Dim SQL As String
      'build the SELECT statement
```

```
        SQL = String.Format("SELECT ename, sal, job FROM
                 emp WHERE empno={0}", Me.txtEmpno.Text)
        'create command object to work with SELECT
        Dim cmd As New OracleCommand(SQL, cn)
        'open the connection
        cmd.Connection.Open()
        'get the DataReader object from command object
        Dim rdr As OracleDataReader = _
        cmd.ExecuteReader(CommandBehavior.CloseConnection)
        'check if it has any rows
        If rdr.HasRows Then
          'read the first row
          rdr.Read()
          'extract the details
          Me.txtEname.Text = rdr("ename")
          Me.txtSal.Text = rdr("sal")
          Me.txtJob.Text = rdr("job")
        Else
          'display message if no rows found
          MessageBox.Show("Not found")
        End If
        'clear up the resources
        rdr.Close()
      Catch ex As Exception
      'display if any error occurs
      MessageBox.Show("Error: " & ex.Message)
        'close the connection if it is still open
        If cn.State = ConnectionState.Open Then
          cn.Close()
        End If
      End Try
    End Sub

  End Class
```

As explained earlier, the above program creates an `OracleConnection` object
as follows:

```
Dim cn As New OracleConnection("Data Source=xe; _
                    User Id=scott;Password=tiger")
```

Next, we need to create an `OracleCommand` object by providing a SELECT query and the connection object (through which it can connect to the database):

```
Dim SQL As String
SQL = String.Format("SELECT ename, sal, job FROM
            emp WHERE empno={0}", Me.txtEmpno.Text)
Dim cmd As New OracleCommand(SQL, cn)
```

Once the `OracleCommand` object is created, it is time to open the connection and execute the SELECT query. The following does this:

```
cmd.Connection.Open()
Dim rdr As OracleDataReader = _
        cmd.ExecuteReader(CommandBehavior.CloseConnection)
```

You must observe that the query gets executed using the `ExecuteReader` method of `OracleCommand` object, which in turn returns an `OracleDataReader` object. In the above statement, the `ExecuteReader` method is specified with `CommandBehavior.CloseConnection`, which simply closes the database connection once the `OracleDataReader` and `OracleCommand` are disposed.

We can use the `HasRows` property of `OracleDataReader` to test whether the reader retrieved any rows or not. If any rows are retrieved, we can read each successive row using the `Read` method of `OracleDataReader`. The `Read` method returns a `Boolean` value to indicate whether it has successfully read a row or not. Once the `Read` succeeds, we can retrieve each value in the row with the column name as follows:

```
If rdr.HasRows Then
    'read the first row
    rdr.Read()
    'extract the details
    Me.txtEname.Text = rdr("ename")
    Me.txtSal.Text = rdr("sal")
    Me.txtJob.Text = rdr("job")
Else
    'display message if no rows found
    MessageBox.Show("Not found")
End If
```

Finally, we close the `OracleDataReader` object using the `Close` method as follows:

```
rdr.Close()
```

If it could read successfully, the output for this code would look similar to the following figure:

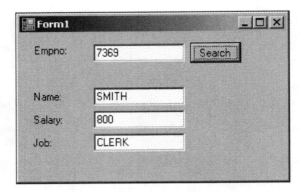

Using "Using" for Simplicity

The above program can be made simple by using the Using statement together with ODP.NET classes as follows:

```
Using cn As New OracleConnection("Data Source=xe;
                    User Id=scott;Password=tiger")
  Try
    cn.Open()
    Dim SQL As String
    SQL = String.Format("SELECT ename, sal,
     job FROM emp WHERE empno={0}", Me.txtEmpno.Text)
    Using cmd As New OracleCommand(SQL, cn)
    Using rdr As OracleDataReader = cmd.ExecuteReader
        If rdr.HasRows Then
          'read the first row
          rdr.Read()
          'extract the details
          Me.txtEname.Text = rdr("ename")
          Me.txtSal.Text = rdr("sal")
          Me.txtJob.Text = rdr("job")
        Else
          'display message if no rows found
          MessageBox.Show("Not found")
        End If
    End Using
    End Using
  Catch ex As Exception
    MessageBox.Show("Error: " & ex.Message)
    If cn.State = ConnectionState.Open Then
```

```
        cn.Close()
      End If
    End Try
  End Using
```

The `Using` keyword is new in Visual Basic 2005, which internally generates `try` and `finally` blocks around the object being allocated and calls `Dispose()` for you saving you the hassle of manually creating it.

The objects created using the `Using` keyword are automatically erased (and respective resources would be automatically cleared) from the memory once it is out of `using` scope. Even though it is very flexible to use the `Using` statement, for the sake of clarity, we will go without using it in the examples of this book.

Retrieving Multiple Rows on to the Grid

In the previous section, we tried to retrieve only one row using `OracleDataReader`. In this section, we will try to retrieve more than one row (or a result set) and populate a `DataGridView` on a WinForm.

The following code lists out the details of all employees available in the `emp` table:

```
Imports Oracle.DataAccess.Client

Public Class Form2
  Private Sub btnGetEmployees_Click(ByVal sender As
    System.Object, ByVal e As System.EventArgs) Handles
    btnGetEmployees.Click
    'create connection to db
    Dim cn As New OracleConnection("Data Source=xe;
                      User Id=scott;Password=tiger")
    Try
      Dim SQL As String
      'build the SELECT statement
      SQL = String.Format("SELECT empno, ename, job,
          mgr, hiredate, sal, comm, deptno FROM emp")
      'create command object to work with SELECT
      Dim cmd As New OracleCommand(SQL, cn)
      'open the connection
      cmd.Connection.Open()
      'get the DataReader object from command object
      Dim rdr As OracleDataReader = _
      cmd.ExecuteReader(CommandBehavior.CloseConnection)
      'check if it has any rows
      If rdr.HasRows Then
```

```vb
        With Me.DataGridView1
          'remove existing rows from grid
          .Rows.Clear()
          'get the number of columns
          Dim ColumnCount As Integer = rdr.FieldCount
          'add columns to the grid
          For i As Integer = 0 To ColumnCount - 1
            .Columns.Add(rdr.GetName(i), rdr.GetName(i))
          Next
          .AutoSizeColumnsMode =
          DataGridViewAutoSizeColumnsMode.ColumnHeader
          'loop through every row
          While rdr.Read
            'get all row values into an array
            Dim objCells(ColumnCount - 1) As Object
            rdr.GetValues(objCells)
            'add array as a row to grid
            .Rows.Add(objCells)
          End While
        End With
      Else
        'display message if no rows found
        MessageBox.Show("Not found")
        Me.DataGridView1.Rows.Clear()
      End If
      'clear up the resources
      rdr.Close()
    Catch ex As Exception
      'display if any error occurs
      MessageBox.Show("Error: " & ex.Message)
      'close the connection if it is still open
      If cn.State = ConnectionState.Open Then
        cn.Close()
      End If
    End Try
  End Sub
End Class
```

Except the highlighted section, the rest of the code is already explained as part of the previous section. You can observe that the SELECT statement now tries to retrieve all rows from emp as follows:

```vb
SQL = String.Format("SELECT empno, ename, job, mgr,
             hiredate, sal, comm, deptno FROM emp")
```

Once the `OracleDataReader` is ready with rows, we need to start with clearing the rows already displayed in the `DataGridView` with the help of the following code:

```
With Me.DataGridView1
  'remove existing rows from grid
  .Rows.Clear()
```

Once the rows are cleared, the first issue is the header of the grid. The moment we add columns to the grid, the header row gets automatically populated (with the column names). Before adding columns to the header, we should know the number of columns being added (just for the loop iterations) with the `FieldCount` property of `DataGridView`. The following is the code fragment that finds the number of columns and adds the columns to `DataGridView`:

```
Dim ColumnCount As Integer = rdr.FieldCount
For i As Integer = 0 To ColumnCount - 1
  .Columns.Add(rdr.GetName(i), rdr.GetName(i))
Next
```

All the columns get auto-sized based on the column header with the following statement:

```
.AutoSizeColumnsMode =
      DataGridViewAutoSizeColumnsMode.ColumnHeader
```

Once the columns are added, we need to read every successive row from the `OracleDataReader` and add it to the `DataGridview`. To add all column values at a time, we make use of the `GetValues()` method of `OracleDataReader` to push all the values in to an array and finally add the array itself as a row to the `DataGridView`. The following code fragment accomplishes this.

```
While rdr.Read
  'get all row values into an array
  Dim objCells(ColumnCount - 1) As Object
  rdr.GetValues(objCells)
  'add array as a row to grid
  .Rows.Add(objCells)
End While
```

The output for this code would look similar to the following figure:

Pulling Information Using Table Name

In all of the previous examples, the SELECT statement was used to retrieve a set of rows. The SELECT statement is a good choice if you would like to retrieve only specific columns or to include some complex combinations using sub-queries, joins etc. You can also retrieve a complete table (without using a SELECT statement) by setting the CommandType of OracleCommand to TableDirect. The following code demonstrates the use of TableDirect:

```
Imports Oracle.DataAccess.Client

Public Class Form2
  Private Sub btnGetEmployees_Click(ByVal sender As
    System.Object, ByVal e As System.EventArgs) Handles
    btnGetEmployees.Click
    'create connection to db
    Dim cn As New OracleConnection("Data Source=xe; _
      User Id=scott;Password=tiger")
    Try
      Dim SQL As String
      'build the SELECT statement
```

```
Dim cmd As New OracleCommand("emp", cn)
cmd.CommandType = CommandType.TableDirect
cmd.Connection.Open()
...
   End Sub
End Class
```

The default `CommandType` is `Text`, which accepts any SQL statement. When we change it to `TableDirect`, it accepts only a table name. Another command type available is `StoredProcedure`. It is mainly used when you want to execute stored procedures using an `OracleCommand` object. (Working with PL/SQL stored procedures is covered in Chapter 5.)

Retrieving Typed Data

While retrieving values from `OracleDataReader`, we can extract information available in individual columns (of a particular row) either by using column ordinal (position) values or column names.

Retrieving Typed Data Using Ordinals

ODP.NET provides data-specific enumerations through the namespace `oracle.DataAccess.types`. This is specially useful if you are trying to retrieve very specific data from the `OracleDataReader`.

For example, you can modify the code given previously to work with specific data types as following:

```
Me.txtEname.Text = rdr.GetOracleString(1)
Me.txtSal.Text = rdr.GetFloat(5)
Me.txtJob.Text = rdr.GetOracleString(2)
```

Here we provide ordinal values (column numbers starting from 0) to retrieve the data in a specific column. Apart from above data types, you also have the full support of every native data type existing in ODP.NET!

Retrieving Typed Data Using Column Names

The strategy of working with column ordinals will not be an issue as long as we know with what columns we are dealing with. But, sometimes, it is very dangerous to play with it. If the underlying table structure gets modified, our application becomes out of synch with the column ordinals. At the same time, using column ordinals can make your code very difficult to follow. It is always suggested not to go for column ordinals (unless we use it for looping purposes).

However, the typed methods only accept column ordinals as parameters. Fortunately, we can use the `GetOrdinal()` method to find the ordinal corresponding to a particular column name as demonstrated in the following:

```
Me.txtEname.Text =
   rdr.GetOracleString(rdr.GetOrdinal("ename"))
Me.txtSal.Text = rdr.GetFloat(rdr.GetOrdinal("sal"))
Me.txtJob.Text =
   rdr.GetOracleString(rdr.GetOrdinal("job"))
```

Working with Data Tables and Data Sets

The `OracleDataAdapter` class is mainly used to populate data sets or data tables for offline use. The `OracleDataAdapter` simply connects to the database, retrieves the information, populates that information into datasets or data tables, and finally disconnects the connection to the database. You can navigate through any of those rows in any manner. You can modify (add or delete) any of those rows in disconnected mode and finally update them back to the database using the same `OracleDataAdapter`.

A set of rows can be populated into a data table and a set of data tables can be grouped into a data set. Apart from grouping, a data set can also maintain offline relationships (using `DataRelation` between data tables existing in it).

`OracleDataAdapter` primarily works with `OracleConnection` to connect to Oracle database. It can also work with `OracleCommand` if necessary.

Retrieving Multiple Rows into a DataTable Using OracleDataAdapter

Now that we understand about `OracleDataAdapter`, let us try to use it to retrieve all the employees available in the `emp` table:

```
Imports Oracle.DataAccess.Client
Public Class Form4

  Private Sub btnGetEmployees_Click(ByVal sender As
  System.Object, ByVal e As System.EventArgs) Handles
btnGetEmployees.Click
    'create connection to db
    Dim cn As New OracleConnection("Data Source=xe; _
                          User Id=scott;Password=tiger")
    Try
      Dim SQL As String
```

```
'build the SELECT statement
SQL = String.Format("SELECT empno, ename, job,
mgr, hiredate, sal, comm, deptno FROM emp")
'create the dataadapter object
Dim adp As New OracleDataAdapter(SQL, cn)
'create the offline datatable
Dim dt As New DataTable
'fill the data table with rows
adp.Fill(dt)
'clear up the resources and work offline
adp.Dispose()
'check if it has any rows
If dt.Rows.Count > 0 Then
  'simply bind datatable to grid
  Me.DataGridView1.DataSource = dt
Else
  'display message if no rows found
  MessageBox.Show("Not found")
  Me.DataGridView1.Rows.Clear()
End If
Catch ex As Exception
'display if any error occurs
MessageBox.Show("Error: " & ex.Message)
'close the connection if it is still open
If cn.State = ConnectionState.Open Then
  cn.Close()
End If
End Try
End Sub
End Class
```

Once the `OracleConnection` is established, we need to start with the
`OracleDataAdapter` object as follows:

```
SQL = String.Format("SELECT empno, ename, job,
    mgr, hiredate, sal, comm, deptno FROM emp")
Dim adp As New OracleDataAdapter(SQL, cn)
```

You can understand from the above that `OracleDataAdapter` can be used directly
with a SELECT statement. You can also specify an `OracleCommand` object in place of a
SELECT statement if necessary.

To place data offline, we need to either work with `DataSet` or `DataTable` objects. In
this scenario, we will deal with a `DataTable` object, and it is created as follows:

```
Dim dt As New DataTable
```

Once the `DataTable` object is created, we need to fill up all the rows using the `OracleDataAdapter` object as follows:

```
adp.Fill(dt)
```

Once all the rows are available in the `DataTable` object (which will always be in memory), we can close (`dispose`) the `OracleDataAdapter` using the following statement:

```
adp.Dispose()
```

The `DataTable` object contains a collection of `DataRow` objects corresponding to each row populated into it. We can retrieve the number of rows available in the `DataTable` object using the `DataTable.Rows.Count` property as follows:

```
If dt.Rows.Count > 0 Then
        'simply bind datatable to grid
        Me.DataGridView1.DataSource = dt
    Else
        'display message if no rows found
        MessageBox.Show("Not found")
        Me.DataGridView1.Rows.Clear()
End If
```

In the above code fragment, we are assigning the `DataTable` object as `DataSource` to `DataGridView`. This would automatically populate entire `DataGridView` with all the column names (as part of the header) and all rows.

The output for the above code would look similar to the following figure:

EMPNO	ENAME	JOB	MGR	HIREDATE	SAL	COMM	DEPTNO
7839	KING	PRESI...		11/17/1981 1...	5000		10
7698	BLAKE	MANA...	7839	5/1/1981 12:0...	2850		30
7782	CLARK	MANA...	7839	6/9/1981 12:0...	2450		10
7566	JONES	MANA...	7839	4/2/1981 12:0...	2975		20
7654	MARTIN	SALES...	7698	9/28/1981 12:...	1250	1400	30
7499	ALLEN	SALES...	7698	2/20/1981 12:...	1600	300	30
7844	TURNER	SALES...	7698	9/8/1981 12:0...	1500	0	30
7900	JAMES	CLERK	7698	12/3/1981 12:...	950		30
7521	WARD	SALES...	7698	2/22/1981 12:...	1250	500	30
7902	FORD	ANALY...	7566	12/3/1981 12:...	3000		20
7369	SMITH	CLERK	7902	12/17/1980 1...	800		20
7788	SCOTT	ANALY...	7566	12/9/1982 12:...	3000		20
7876	ADAMS	CLERK	7788	1/12/1983 12:...	1100		20
7934	MILLER	CLERK	7782	1/23/1982 12:...	1300		10

Filling a DataTable Using OracleDataReader

So far, we have been filling data tables using `OracleDataAdapter`. ADO.NET 2.0 gives us the flexibility to fill a data table using `OracleDataReader` as well. The following code gives you the details of all employees available in the `emp` table by filling a data table using an `OracleDataReader`:

```vb
Dim cn As New OracleConnection("Data Source=xe; _
                  User Id=scott;Password=tiger")
    Try
       Dim SQL As String
       Dim dt As New DataTable
       'build the SELECT statement
       SQL = String.Format("SELECT empno, ename, job, _
            mgr, hiredate, sal, comm, deptno FROM emp")
       'create command object to work with SELECT
       Dim cmd As New OracleCommand(SQL, cn)
       'open the connection
       cmd.Connection.Open()
       'get the DataReader object from command object
       Dim rdr As OracleDataReader = _
        cmd.ExecuteReader(CommandBehavior.CloseConnection)
       'check if it has any rows
       If rdr.HasRows Then
          'simply bind datatable to grid
          dt.Load(rdr, LoadOption.OverwriteChanges)
          Me.DataGridView1.DataSource = dt
       Else
          'display message if no rows found
          MessageBox.Show("Not found")
          Me.DataGridView1.Rows.Clear()
       End If
       rdr.Close()
    Catch ex As Exception
       'display if any error occurs
       MessageBox.Show("Error: " & ex.Message)
       'close the connection if it is still open
       If cn.State = ConnectionState.Open Then
          cn.Close()
       End If
    End Try
```

Once the `OracleConnection` and `OracleDataReader` are created, we need to create and fill a `DataTable` object using `OracleDataReader` itself. The following is the statement that creates a `DataTable` object:

```vb
Dim dt As New DataTable
```

To fill the above `DataTable` object with respect to `OracleDataReader`, we can directly use the `Load` method of `DataTable`, which accepts a `DataReader` object and the type of `LoadOption`. The following statement loads the content of an `OracleDataReader` into a `DataTable` object with a `LoadOption` as `OverwriteChanges` (overwrites all the modifications that are available as part of the `DataTable` object):

```
dt.Load(rdr, LoadOption.OverwriteChanges)
```

Retrieving a Single Row of Information Using OracleDataAdapter

In the previous example, we worked with a set of rows in the `DataTable` object. Now, we shall work with a particular row using the `DataTable` object. The following code accepts an employee number from the user and gives you the details of that employee:

```
Imports Oracle.DataAccess.Client

Public Class Form3

    Private Sub btnGetEmployee_Click(ByVal sender As
    System.Object, ByVal e As System.EventArgs) Handles
    btnGetEmployee.Click
      'create connection to db
      Dim cn As New OracleConnection("Data Source=xe; _
                      User Id=scott;Password=tiger")
      Try
        Dim SQL As String
        'build the SELECT statement
        SQL = String.Format("SELECT ename, sal, job FROM
                  emp WHERE empno={0}", Me.txtEmpno.Text)
        'create the dataadapter object
        Dim adp As New OracleDataAdapter(SQL, cn)
        'create the offline datatable
        Dim dt As New DataTable
        'fill the data table with rows
        adp.Fill(dt)
        'clear up the resources and work offline
        adp.Dispose()

        'check if it has any rows
```

```
      If dt.Rows.Count > 0 Then
        'extract the details
        Me.txtEname.Text = dt.Rows(0)("ename")
        Me.txtSal.Text = dt.Rows(0)("sal")
        Me.txtJob.Text = dt.Rows(0)("job")
      Else
        'display message if no rows found
        MessageBox.Show("Not found")
      End If

    Catch ex As Exception
      'display if any error occurs
      MessageBox.Show("Error: " & ex.Message)
      'close the connection if it is still open
      If cn.State = ConnectionState.Open Then
        cn.Close()
      End If
    End Try
  End Sub
End Class
```

Once the `DataTable` object is filled using `OracleDataAdapter`, we can directly retrieve a particular row using the row index. Once the row is fetched, we extract column values by providing column names for the rows as follows:

```
Me.txtEname.Text = dt.Rows(0)("ename")
Me.txtSal.Text = dt.Rows(0)("sal")
Me.txtJob.Text = dt.Rows(0)("job")
```

The output for the above code would look similar to the following figure:

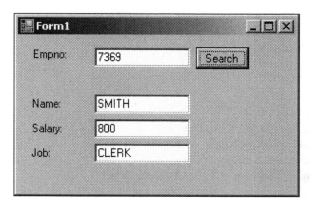

Working with DataTableReader

DataTableReader is complementary to a DataTable object, and is mainly used as a type of *Data Reader* in the disconnected mode. The following is the modified code:

```
'create connection to db
Dim cn As New OracleConnection("Data Source=xe; _
                        User Id=scott;Password=tiger")
Try
  Dim SQL As String
  'build the SELECT statement
  SQL = String.Format("SELECT ename, sal, job FROM emp
                  WHERE empno={0}", Me.txtEmpno.Text)
  'create the DataAdapter object
  Dim adp As New OracleDataAdapter(SQL, cn)
  'create the offline datatable
  Dim dt As New DataTable
  'fill the data table with rows
  adp.Fill(dt)
  'clear up the resources and work offline
  adp.Dispose()
  Dim dtr As DataTableReader = dt.CreateDataReader

  'check if it has any rows
  If dtr.HasRows Then
    'read the first row
    dtr.Read()
    'extract the details
    Me.txtEname.Text = dtr("ename")
    Me.txtSal.Text = dtr("sal")
    Me.txtJob.Text = dtr("job")
  Else
    'display message if no rows found
    MessageBox.Show("Not found")
  End If

Catch ex As Exception
  'display if any error occurs
  MessageBox.Show("Error: " & ex.Message)
  'close the connection if it is still open
  If cn.State = ConnectionState.Open Then
    cn.Close()
  End If
End Try
```

You can observe the highlighted code, which creates a `DataTableReader` object by calling the `CreateDataReader` method related to the `DataTable` object. Once the `DataTableReader` is created, we can directly retrieve the column values with the specified column names as follows:

```
Me.txtEname.Text = dtr("ename")
Me.txtSal.Text = dtr("sal")
Me.txtJob.Text = dtr("job")
```

Populating a Dataset with a Single Data Table

A dataset is simply a group of data tables. These data tables can be identified with their own unique names within a dataset. You can also add relations between data tables available in a dataset.

The following code gives you the details of all employees available in the `emp` table by populating a dataset with only a single data table using `OracleDataAdapter`:

```
Imports Oracle.DataAccess.Client
Public Class Form6

    Private Sub btnGetEmployees_Click(ByVal sender As
    System.Object, ByVal e As System.EventArgs) Handles
    btnGetEmployees.Click
      'create connection to db
      Dim cn As New OracleConnection("Data Source=xe; _
                            User Id=scott;Password=tiger")
      Try
        Dim SQL As String
        'build the SELECT statement
        SQL = String.Format("SELECT empno, ename, job,
              mgr, hiredate, sal, comm, deptno FROM emp")
        'create the dataadapter object
        Dim adp As New OracleDataAdapter(SQL, cn)
        'create the offline datatable
        Dim ds As New DataSet
        'fill the data set with a data table named emp
        adp.Fill(ds, "emp")
        'clear up the resources and work offline
        adp.Dispose()
        'check if it has any rows
        If ds.Tables("emp").Rows.Count > 0 Then
          'simply bind datatable to grid
          Me.DataGridView1.DataSource = ds.Tables("emp")
```

```
          Else
            'display message if no rows found
            MessageBox.Show("Not found")
            Me.DataGridView1.Rows.Clear()
          End If
        Catch ex As Exception
          'display if any error occurs
          MessageBox.Show("Error: " & ex.Message)
          'close the connection if it is still open
          If cn.State = ConnectionState.Open Then
            cn.Close()
          End If
        End Try
      End Sub
    End Class
```

If you can observe the highlighted code in the above script, we are creating a new `DataSet` object, populating it with a `DataTable` named "emp" (which contains all the rows) and finally assigning the same `DataTable` to the grid. The output for the above code would look similar to the figure in the section *Retrieving Multiple Rows into a Data Table Using OracleDataAdapter*.

Populating a Dataset with Multiple Data Tables

Now, let us add more than one data table into a dataset. The following code retrieves a list of department details into a data table named `Departments` and another list of employee details into a data table named `Employees`:

```
Imports Oracle.DataAccess.Client
Public Class Form7

    Private Sub btnData_Click(ByVal sender As
    System.Object, ByVal e As System.EventArgs) Handles
    btnData.Click
      'create connection to db
      Dim cn As New OracleConnection("Data Source=xe; _
                         User Id=scott;Password=tiger")
      Try
        Dim ds As New DataSet
        Dim adp As OracleDataAdapter

        adp = New OracleDataAdapter("SELECT deptno,
                            dname, loc FROM Dept", cn)
        adp.Fill(ds, "Departments")
```

```
        adp.Dispose()
        adp = New OracleDataAdapter("SELECT empno, ename,
                job, mgr, hiredate, sal, comm, deptno FROM
                Emp", cn)
        adp.Fill(ds, "Employees")
        adp.Dispose()

        Me.DataGridView1.DataSource = ds
        Me.DataGridView1.DataMember = "Departments"

        Me.DataGridView2.DataSource =
                                    ds.Tables("Employees")
    Catch ex As Exception
      'display if any error occurs
      MessageBox.Show("Error: " & ex.Message)
      'close the connection if it is still open
      If cn.State = ConnectionState.Open Then
        cn.Close()
      End If
    End Try
  End Sub
End Class
```

From the above highlighted code, you can easily observe that we are retrieving two different result sets (identified by `Departments` and `Employees`) into the same dataset. The following code fragment creates the `Departments` data table:

```
adp = New OracleDataAdapter("SELECT deptno, dname,
                            loc FROM Dept", cn)
adp.Fill(ds, "Departments")
adp.Dispose()
```

The following code fragment creates the `Employees` data table:

```
adp = New OracleDataAdapter("SELECT empno, ename, job,
        mgr, hiredate, sal, comm, deptno FROM Emp", cn)
adp.Fill(ds, "Employees")
adp.Dispose()
```

Those two result sets are automatically created as two data tables within the same dataset. Once the dataset is populated, we can present them with two different grids (two different methods) as follows:

```
Me.DataGridView1.DataSource = ds
Me.DataGridView1.DataMember = "Departments"
Me.DataGridView2.DataSource = ds.Tables("Employees")
```

The output for this code would look similar to the following figure:

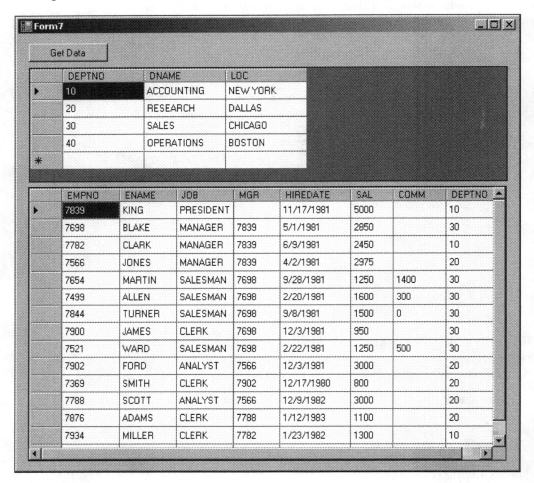

Presenting Master-Detail Information Using a Dataset

As mentioned before, a `DataSet` object can have its own relations between data tables existing in it. We can add these relations dynamically at the client side (within an application), to represent master-detail (or hierarchical) information. The following code gives the list of employees (in the bottom grid) based on the department you choose in the top grid:

```vb
Imports Oracle.DataAccess.Client
Public Class Form8

    Private Sub btnData_Click(ByVal sender As
    System.Object, ByVal e As System.EventArgs) Handles
    btnData.Click
        'create connection to db
        Dim cn As New OracleConnection("Data Source=xe; _
                            User Id=scott;Password=tiger")
        Try
            Dim ds As New DataSet
            Dim adp As OracleDataAdapter

            adp = New OracleDataAdapter("SELECT deptno,
                                dname, loc FROM Dept", cn)
            adp.Fill(ds, "Departments")
            adp.Dispose()

            adp = New OracleDataAdapter("SELECT empno, ename,
                    job, mgr, hiredate, sal, comm, deptno FROM
                    Emp", cn)
            adp.Fill(ds, "Employees")
            adp.Dispose()

            ds.Relations.Add(New DataRelation("FK_Emp_Dept",
                    ds.Tables("Departments").Columns("Deptno"),
                    ds.Tables("Employees").Columns("Deptno")))
            Dim bsMaster As New BindingSource(ds, _
                                        "Departments")
            Dim bsChild As New BindingSource(bsMaster, _
                                        "FK_Emp_Dept")
            Me.DataGridView1.DataSource = bsMaster
            Me.DataGridView2.DataSource = bsChild

        Catch ex As Exception
            'display if any error occurs
            MessageBox.Show("Error: " & ex.Message)
            'close the connection if it is still open
            If cn.State = ConnectionState.Open Then
                cn.Close()
            End If
        End Try
    End Sub
End Class
```

Once the `DataSet` is filled with data tables (`Departments` and `Employees`), we can add an in-memory relation using the following statement:

```
ds.Relations.Add(New DataRelation("FK_Emp_Dept",
    ds.Tables("Departments").Columns("Deptno"),
    ds.Tables("Employees").Columns("Deptno")))
```

The above statement simply adds a new relation (named `FK_Emp_Dept`) between two `DataTable` objects (`Departments` and `Employees`) based on the column `Deptno` (available in both `DataTable` objects).

To present the information in a master-detail fashion, we can make use of the `BindingSource` object as follows:

```
Dim bsMaster As New BindingSource(ds, "Departments")
Dim bsChild As New BindingSource(bsMaster, "FK_Emp_Dept")
```

In the above code fragment, we used two `BindingSource` objects corresponding to master and child data tables respectively. The child `BindingSource` object is created based on the master `BindingSource` object together with the specification of `DataRelation`. Once the `BindingSource` objects are ready, we can assign them as data sources to the `DataGridView` controls as following:

```
Me.DataGridView1.DataSource = bsMaster
Me.DataGridView2.DataSource = bsChild
```

The output for the above code would look similar to the following figure:

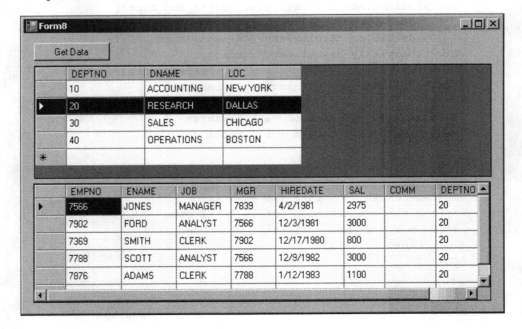

You can observe that this screen displays only the employees working in department number 20 as that is selected in the top grid.

More About the OracleCommand Object

Till now, we have seen OracleCommand working with OracleDataReader. OracleCommand is not simply meant for OracleDataReader. It has got a lot of functionality for itself. Let us see few of the most commonly used features of OracleCommand in this section. We will further go into depth in subsequent sections and chapters.

Retrieving a Single Value from the Database

As we already covered working with single or multiple rows, we need to work on retrieving a single value from database very effectively. We have already retrieved row values in our previous examples, but those examples are more suitable when you are trying to deal with entire rows.

OracleCommand is equipped with a method called ExecuteScalar, which is mainly used to retrieve single values from the database very efficiently thus improving the performance. The following example focuses on this:

```
Imports Oracle.DataAccess.Client

Public Class Form9
    Private Sub btnEmployeeCount_Click(ByVal sender As
    System.Object, ByVal e As System.EventArgs) Handles
    btnEmployeeCount.Click
       'create connection to db
       Dim cn As New OracleConnection("Data Source=xe; _
                        User Id=scott;Password=tiger")
       Try
          'create the command object
          Dim cmd As New OracleCommand("SELECT COUNT(*) _
                                   FROM emp", cn)
          'open the connection from command
          cmd.Connection.Open()
          'execute the command and get the single value
          'result
          Dim result As String = cmd.ExecuteScalar
          'clear the resources
          cmd.Connection.Close()
          cmd.Dispose()
          'display the output
```

```
            MessageBox.Show("No. of Employees: " & result)
        Catch ex As Exception
            'display if any error occurs
            MessageBox.Show("Error: " & ex.Message)
            'close the connection if it is still open
            If cn.State = ConnectionState.Open Then
                cn.Close()
            End If
        End Try
    End Sub
End Class
```

The highlighted line in the above code simply executes the SELECT command, which retrieves the number of rows from the emp table and assigns this value to the result variable.

Handling Nulls when Executing with ExecuteScalar

The most important issue to remember is that ExecuteScalar simply returns an object type of data. The object refers to any data type within .NET. If the data type of your variable matches with the type of object returned by ExecuteScalar, an implicit (automatic) conversion takes place. There would not be a problem as long as the data types match. However, it would be a problem if the result is NULL. Let us have an example that accepts an employee number from the user and gives his or her commission:

```
Imports Oracle.DataAccess.Client

Public Class Form12

    Private Sub btnGetCommission_Click(ByVal sender As
    System.Object, ByVal e As System.EventArgs) Handles
    btnGetCommission.Click
        'create connection to db
        Dim cn As New OracleConnection("Data Source=xe; _
                        User Id=scott;Password=tiger")
        Try
            'create the command object
            Dim cmd As New OracleCommand("SELECT comm FROM _
                    emp WHERE empno=" & Me.txtEmpno.Text, cn)
            'open the connection from command
            cmd.Connection.Open()
            'execute the command and get the single value
            'result
            Dim result As Double = cmd.ExecuteScalar
            cmd.Connection.Close()
```

```
        cmd.Dispose()
        'display the output
        MessageBox.Show("Commission: " & result)
      Catch ex As Exception
        'display if any error occurs
        MessageBox.Show("Error: " & ex.Message)
        'close the connection if it is still open
        If cn.State = ConnectionState.Open Then
          cn.Close()
        End If
      End Try
    End Sub
```

In the highlighted statement above, we are expecting a numeric (or double) value as the result. If the ExecuteScalar returns a double value, it would never be a problem. What if it returns a NULL? The following is the error you would receive:

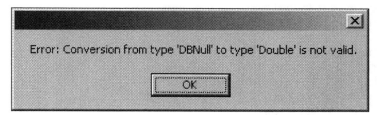

To deal with the above error, we may have to include our own condition to test against nulls in the output. Just replace the highlighted code above with the following two statements and it should work fine now:

```
Dim result As Object = cmd.ExecuteScalar
If IsDBNull(result) Then result = 0
```

You can observe from the above two lines that we are receiving the value in the form of an object and assigning a value zero if it is null.

Handling Nulls when Working with OracleDataReader

When we work with OracleDataReader (or for that matter, even with data rows in a data table), we may come across nulls. The following is the efficient way to deal in with such scenarios:

```
'create connection to db
Dim cn As New OracleConnection("Data Source=xe; _
                    User Id=scott;Password=tiger")
Try
```

```
'create the command object
Dim cmd As New OracleCommand("SELECT comm FROM _
          emp WHERE empno=" & Me.txtEmpno.Text, cn)
'open the connection from command
cmd.Connection.Open()
'create the data reader
Dim rdr As OracleDataReader = _
  cmd.ExecuteReader(CommandBehavior.CloseConnection)
'check if it has any rows
If rdr.HasRows Then
  'read the first row
  rdr.Read()
  'extract the details
  Dim result As Double = IIf(IsDBNull(rdr("comm")), _
                                  0, rdr("comm"))
  MessageBox.Show("Commission: " & result)
Else
  'display message if no rows found
  MessageBox.Show("Not found")
End If
rdr.Dispose()
Catch ex As Exception
  'display if any error occurs
  MessageBox.Show("Error: " & ex.Message)
  'close the connection if it is still open
  If cn.State = ConnectionState.Open Then
    cn.Close()
  End If
End Try
```

You can observe that we are making use of the IIF function in Visual Basic.NET to make the inline comparison. We can also use the rdr.isDBNull method to achieve the same.

Working with Bind Variables together with OracleParameter

With the help of OracleParameter, you can include bind variables within any SQL statement. These bind variables are nothing but run-time query parameters. The values in the SQL statement are bound at run time when we use bind variables.

If the same SQL statement is being continuously used (with different values), it is recommended to work with bind variables. When you use bind variables in SQL statements, the statements would automatically cache at server level to improve performance during repeated database operations of the same type.

Following is a simple example that includes a bind variable in a SELECT statement followed by OracleParameter, which fills the bind variable with a value:

```
Imports Oracle.DataAccess.Client

Public Class Form11

  Private Sub btnGetEmployee_Click(ByVal sender As
  System.Object, ByVal e As System.EventArgs) Handles
  btnGetEmployee.Click
    'create connection to db
    Dim cn As New OracleConnection("Data Source=xe; _
                 User Id=scott;Password=tiger")
    Try
      'create command object to work with SELECT

      Dim cmd As New OracleCommand("SELECT empno, _
      ename, sal, job FROM emp WHERE empno=:empno", cn)
      cmd.Parameters.Add(New OracleParameter(":empno",
                           Me.txtEmpno.Text))

      'open the connection
      cmd.Connection.Open()
      'get the DataReader object from command object
      Dim rdr As OracleDataReader = _
      cmd.ExecuteReader(CommandBehavior.CloseConnection)
      'check if it has any rows
      If rdr.HasRows Then
        'read the first row
        rdr.Read()
        'extract the details
        Me.txtEmpno.Text = rdr("empno")
        Me.txtEname.Text = rdr("ename")
        Me.txtSal.Text = rdr("sal")
        Me.txtJob.Text = rdr("job")
      Else
        'display message if no rows found
        MessageBox.Show("Not found")
      End If
      'clear up the resources
      rdr.Close()
    Catch ex As Exception
      'display if any error occurs
      MessageBox.Show("Error: " & ex.Message)
      'close the connection if it is still open
```

```
        If cn.State = ConnectionState.Open Then
           cn.Close()
        End If
      End Try
   End Sub
End Class
```

Within the above highlighted code, :empno is the bind variable. We are placing (or assigning) a value into that bind variable using OracleParameter.

If you want to provide a very clear OracleParameter, you can even write something like the following code:

```
Dim cmd As New OracleCommand("SELECT empno, ename, _
        sal, deptno FROM emp WHERE ename=:ename", cn)
Dim pEmpno As New OracleParameter
With pEmpno
  .ParameterName = ":ename"
  .OracleDbType = OracleDbType.Varchar2
  .Size = 20
  .Value = Me.txtEname.Text
End With
cmd.Parameters.Add(pEmpno)
```

In the above code fragment, we are working with a bind variable :ename, which is of type VARCHAR2 and size 20. We will deal with OracleParemeter in more detail in subsequent chapters.

Working with OracleDataAdapter together with OracleCommand

In the previous examples, we worked with OracleDataAdapter by directly specifying SQL statements. You can also pass OracleCommand to OracleDataAdapter. This is very useful if you deal with stored procedures (covered in Chapter 5) or bind variables together with OracleDataAdapter.

The following is a simple example that uses OracleCommand together with OracleDataAdapter:

```
Imports Oracle.DataAccess.Client

Public Class Form10

   Private Sub btnGetEmployees_Click_1(ByVal sender As
```

```
System.Object, ByVal e As System.EventArgs) Handles
btnGetEmployees.Click
    'create connection to db
    Dim cn As New OracleConnection("Data Source=xe; _
                        User Id=scott;Password=tiger")
    Try
        'create command object to work with SELECT
        Dim cmd As New OracleCommand("SELECT empno, _
            ename, job, mgr, hiredate, sal, comm, deptno _
            FROM emp", cn)
        'create DataAdapter from command
        Dim adp As New OracleDataAdapter(cmd)
        'create the offline data table
        Dim dt As New DataTable
        'fill the data table with data and clear resources
        adp.Fill(dt)
        adp.Dispose()
        'display the data
        Me.DataGridView1.DataSource = dt
    Catch ex As Exception
        'display if any error occurs
        MessageBox.Show("Error: " & ex.Message)
        'close the connection if it is still open
        If cn.State = ConnectionState.Open Then
            cn.Close()
        End If
    End Try

    End Sub
End Class
```

You can observe from the above highlighted code that we created an OracleCommand object, and the OracleDataAdapter can accept OracleCommand as a parameter.

Techniques to Improve Performance while Retrieving Data

Performance tuning is a great subject in Oracle. Volumes of books would not be enough to cover every aspect of performance tuning in Oracle. However, in this section, we will only discuss the fundamental performance techniques while working with ODP.NET.

Some of the frequently used techniques to achieve greater performance with ODP. NET are as follows:

- Connection pooling
- Choosing a proper retrieval methodology for every data retrieval task
- Choosing a proper `CommandType` (when using an `OracleCommand` object)
- Controlling the amount of data returned to the client (or middle tier)
- SQL statement caching
- Developing object pooling components (like COM+ etc.)

We have already mentioned Connection Pooling earlier in this chapter. Working with a physical database connection for every SQL statement could be very expensive in terms of performance. Try to figure out the best strategy to implement connection pooling in your applications based on factors like heavy data consumption, server resources utilization, frequent access to database, continuous (or long) operations on data, mission-critical scenarios, etc.

As discussed previously, the only way to retrieve data from Oracle in ODP.NET is by using the core `OracleCommand`, `OracleDataReader`, or `OracleDataAdapter`. An application would be made with several simple to complex tasks. Be wise and select the best option between those three, based on every respective task and its complexity. Do not try to take a decision on using only one of them throughout the application, which really kills performance in several scenarios. For example, to retrieve a single value from the database, it is always the best to use `ExecuteScalar` (of the `OracleCommand` object) directly, rather than using the other two.

Never retrieve a whole table unnecessarily. Never use "SELECT *"; always fully qualify an SQL statement. Using "SELECT *" would not only slow down your application performance but also can be a bit dangerous. Imagine a few more new columns are added to the table. All those columns would also be retrieved automatically in the .NET application (whether required or not).

Try to be selective when choosing `CommandType`. It is suggested to use the `StoredProcedure` command type (if you implement stored procedures) or `Text` rather than `TableDirect`. Working with PL/SQL stored procedures is covered in Chapter 5.

Another very common mistake is retrieving too many rows unnecessarily. Imagine a table exists with one million rows and you are trying to retrieve all of them for the user. Any user would never want to view million rows in his or her life time. Not only that, pulling one million of rows from the server really consumes huge memory resources and also makes the network too busy.

In any case, ODP.NET by default fetches only 64K at a time. So, even though you try to execute a SELECT statement that retrieves all rows in a table, it retrieves only chunks of 64K based on demand. You can customize this fetch size by issuing the following statement:

```
cmd.FetchSize = cmd.RowSize * 25
```

The above makes sure that it retrieves a maximum of 25 rows per round-trip to the server. You can observe that the FetchSize is completely based on RowSize and not simply on the number of rows. Apart from modifying the FetchSize, try to provide filters in your user interface to minimize the data fetching from server.

If you are working continuously with a similar set of SQL statements (like INSERT in a loop etc.) in a routine, it is always suggested to take advantage of statement caching. A cache is nothing but some high-performance memory at server. If you cache the frequently used SQL statements, a copy of such SQL statements gets stored at that high-performance memory and gets executed (with different values) every time you issue the same SQL statement. This removes the burden at the server of parsing and preparing an execution plan for every SQL statement and improves the performance tremendously. Generally, when you use the concept of bind variables together with OracleParameter, the statement caching automatically takes place.

Finally, when developing business logic, it is suggested to design scalable business components, which can take advantage of features like automatic object pooling, loosely coupled behavior, caching, persistence, accessibility permissions (security), transactions etc. Designing and implementing business components (like COM+, MSMQ, Windows Services, Web Services, .NET Remoting, etc.) are very common in enterprise applications. Selecting a proper approach for implementing a business component is the main backbone at the middle tier (if you are developing multi-tier applications).

Summary

In this chapter, we have seen several methods to retrieve data from Oracle database. We worked with the core ODP.NET classes like OracleCommand, OracleDataReader, OracleDataAdapter, OracleParameter, etc., and the most important ADO.NET classes like Dataset, DataTable, DataRow, etc.

4

Manipulating Data in Oracle Using ODP.NET

The most common manipulations for any database are inserting or adding, updating, and deleting of data. The fundamental life-cycle of a database purely depends on these three manipulations. In this chapter, we will mainly cover the following:

- Inserting, updating, and deleting rows in a database
- Working with DDL statements
- Statement caching
- Array binding
- Working with offline data
- Dealing with transactions
- Handling Oracle errors (exception handling)

Executing DML or DDL Statements Using OracleCommand

The most commonly used DML (Data Manipulation Language) commands to manipulate data at Oracle are INSERT, UPDATE, and DELETE. I assume that you are already familiar with the syntax and usage of those commands. Let us see how to get those statements executed through OracleCommand.

Using INSERT with OracleCommand

Let us start with inserting data into Oracle database using `OracleCommand`. For the sake of executing DML statements that do not return any result sets, `OracleCommand` offers a method called `ExecuteNonQuery`. This is the most important method that is used to execute any Oracle commands (including stored procedures), which do not return any result set.

The following code inserts a new row into the `emp` table:

```
Private Sub btnAdd_Click(ByVal sender As System.Object,
  ByVal e As System.EventArgs) Handles btnAdd.Click
    'create connection to db
    Dim cn As New OracleConnection("Data Source=xe; _
                  User Id=scott;Password=tiger")
    Try
      Dim SQL As String
      'build the INSERT statement
      Dim sb As New System.Text.StringBuilder
      sb.Append(" INSERT INTO emp")
      sb.Append(" (empno, ename, sal, deptno)")
      sb.Append(" VALUES")
      sb.Append(" ({0},'{1}',{2},{3})")
      SQL = String.Format(sb.ToString, Me.txtEmpno.Text,
        Me.txtEname.Text, Me.txtSal.Text,
        Me.txtDeptno.Text)
      'create command object
      Dim cmd As New OracleCommand(SQL, cn)
      'open the connection
      cmd.Connection.Open()
      'execute the command
      Dim result As Integer = cmd.ExecuteNonQuery()
      'close the connection
      cmd.Connection.Close()
      'display the result
      If result = 0 Then
        MessageBox.Show("No rows inserted")
      Else
        MessageBox.Show("Succesfully inserted")
      End If
    Catch ex As Exception
      'display if any error occurs
      MessageBox.Show("Error: " & ex.Message)
      'close the connection if it is still open
      If cn.State = ConnectionState.Open Then
        cn.Close()
      End If
```

```
        End Try
    End Sub
```

If you observe the highlighted statement in the above code, we are making use of
ExecuteNonQuery to execute the INSERT command. It is necessary as INSERT is not a
query that returns any information. However, ExecuteNonQuery returns the number
of rows affected by the DML statement provided to it. In this case, if the INSERT
statement adds only one row, the value of result would be 1. Once the above code
gets executed, you are likely to see the following output:

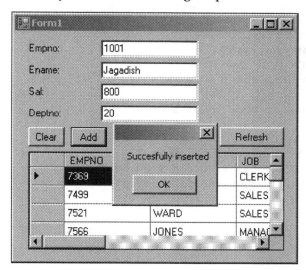

Using UPDATE with OracleCommand

The code for using the UPDATE statement is almost identical to the code for the
INSERT statement, except we use the UPDATE statement!

```
Private Sub btnSave_Click(ByVal sender As System.Object, _
    ByVal e As System.EventArgs) Handles btnSave.Click
    'create connection to db
    Dim cn As New OracleConnection("Data Source=xe; _
                        User Id=scott;Password=tiger")
    Try
        Dim SQL As String
        'build the UPDATE statement
        Dim sb As New System.Text.StringBuilder
        sb.Append(" UPDATE emp SET")
        sb.Append(" ename = '{1}'")
        sb.Append(",sal = {2}")
        sb.Append(",deptno = {3}")
```

```
        sb.Append(" WHERE empno = {0}")
        SQL = String.Format(sb.ToString, Me.txtEmpno.Text,
         Me.txtEname.Text, Me.txtSal.Text,
         Me.txtDeptno.Text)
        'create command object
        Dim cmd As New OracleCommand(SQL, cn)
        'open the connection
        cmd.Connection.Open()
        'execute the command
        Dim result As Integer = cmd.ExecuteNonQuery()
        'close the connection
        cmd.Connection.Close()
        'display the result
        If result = 0 Then
          MessageBox.Show("No rows updated")
        Else
          MessageBox.Show("Succesfully updated")
        End If
      Catch ex As Exception
        'display if any error occurs
        MessageBox.Show("Error: " & ex.Message)
        'close the connection if it is still open
        If cn.State = ConnectionState.Open Then
          cn.Close()
        End If
      End Try
    End Sub
```

Once the above code gets executed, you are likely to see the following output:

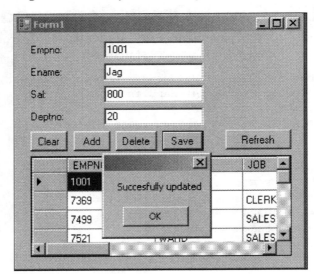

Using DELETE with OracleCommand

The code for DELETE is almost the same as listed previously except that we will replace UPDATE with DELETE as shown below:

```
Private Sub btnDelete_Click(ByVal sender As
   System.Object, ByVal e As System.EventArgs) Handles
   btnDelete.Click
      'create connection to db
      Dim cn As New OracleConnection("Data Source=xe; _
                      User Id=scott;Password=tiger")
    Try
      Dim SQL As String
      'build the DELETE statement
      Dim sb As New System.Text.StringBuilder
      sb.Append(" DELETE FROM emp")
      sb.Append(" WHERE empno = {0}")
      SQL = String.Format(sb.ToString, Me.txtEmpno.Text)
      'create command object
      Dim cmd As New OracleCommand(SQL, cn)
      'open the connection
      cmd.Connection.Open()
      'execute the command
      Dim result As Integer = cmd.ExecuteNonQuery()
      'close the connection
      cmd.Connection.Close()
      'display the result
      If result = 0 Then
        MessageBox.Show("No rows deleted")
      Else
        MessageBox.Show("Succesfully deleted")
      End If
    Catch ex As Exception
      'display if any error occurs
      MessageBox.Show("Error: " & ex.Message)
      'close the connection if it is still open
      If cn.State = ConnectionState.Open Then
        cn.Close()
      End If
    End Try
  End Sub
```

Once the above code gets executed, you are likely to see the following output:

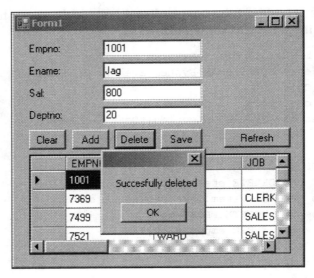

Multiple Inserts Using Statement Caching

When you are trying to execute the same type of SQL commands repeatedly with different values, it is better to implement *statement caching* to improve performance. In this example, I would like to insert eight sample rows using a loop. We will generate all the values of each row dynamically within the same loop and implement statement caching to improve performance.

When dealing with statement caching, we must use bind variables and fill the values of those bind variables using `OracleParameter` (as already discussed in Chapter 3). The highlighted statements in the code below achieve this.

The following is the code:

```
Private Sub btnMultipleInserts_Click(ByVal sender As
   System.Object, ByVal e As System.EventArgs) Handles
   btnMultipleInserts.Click
     'create connection to db
     Dim cn As New OracleConnection("Data Source=xe; _
                     User Id=scott;Password=tiger")
     Try
       Dim SQL As String
       'build the INSERT statement
       Dim sb As New System.Text.StringBuilder
```

```
                sb.Append(" INSERT INTO emp")
                sb.Append(" (empno, ename, sal, deptno)")
                sb.Append(" VALUES")
                sb.Append(" (:empno, :ename, :sal, :deptno)")
                SQL = sb.ToString
                'create command object
                Dim cmd As New OracleCommand(SQL, cn)
                'open the connection
                cmd.Connection.Open()
                For i As Integer = 1 To 8
                  cmd.Parameters.Clear()
                  cmd.Parameters.Add(New OracleParameter(":empno",
                                                    i + 1000))
                  cmd.Parameters.Add(New OracleParameter(":ename",
                                                  "dummy " & i))
                  cmd.Parameters.Add(New OracleParameter(":sal",
                                                    i * 1000))
                  cmd.Parameters.Add(New
                                OracleParameter(":deptno", 20))
                  cmd.ExecuteNonQuery()
                Next
                'close the connection
                cmd.Connection.Close()
                'display the result
                MessageBox.Show("Succesfully inserted")
            Catch ex As Exception
                'display if any error occurs
                MessageBox.Show("Error: " & ex.Message)
                'close the connection if it is still open
                If cn.State = ConnectionState.Open Then
                    cn.Close()
                End If
            End Try
        End Sub
```

We started with building an INSERT statement with bind variables as shown below:

```
Dim sb As New System.Text.StringBuilder
sb.Append(" INSERT INTO emp")
sb.Append(" (empno, ename, sal, deptno)")
sb.Append(" VALUES")
sb.Append(" (:empno, :ename, :sal, :deptno)")
```

To fill the values of each bind variable, we use the `OracleParameter` class, which accepts both bind variable name and value as following:

```
cmd.Parameters.Add(New OracleParameter(":empno",
                                       i + 1000))
cmd.Parameters.Add(New OracleParameter(":ename",
                                       "dummy " & i))
cmd.Parameters.Add(New OracleParameter(":sal",
                                       i * 1000))
cmd.Parameters.Add(New OracleParameter(":deptno", 20))
```

Multiple Inserts Using Array Binding

Another method to insert rows repeatedly is *array binding*. Using this technique, you can store all the values (based on the number of rows to be inserted) of each column in different arrays. The maximum size of all the arrays (indirectly columns) would be the maximum rows you are trying to insert. Once you fill all the arrays with values (treat each array as a column of data), you can directly bind them as parameters to `OracleCommand`. The rest would be automatically taken care of by the `OracleCommand`.

The following example code uses array binding to achieve multiple inserts:

```
Private Sub btnArrayBind_Click(ByVal sender As
   System.Object, ByVal e As System.EventArgs) Handles
   btnArrayBind.Click
   'create connection to db
   Dim cn As New OracleConnection("Data Source=xe; _
                      User Id=scott;Password=tiger")
   Try
     Dim SQL As String
     'build the INSERT statement
     Dim sb As New System.Text.StringBuilder
     sb.Append(" INSERT INTO emp")
     sb.Append(" (empno, ename, sal, deptno)")
     sb.Append(" VALUES")
     sb.Append(" (:empno, :ename, :sal, :deptno)")
     SQL = sb.ToString
     'create array structures to hold 8 rows
     Dim ar_empno(7) As Integer
     Dim ar_ename(7) As String
     Dim ar_sal(7) As Integer
     Dim ar_deptno(7) As Integer
```

```
      'fill the array structures with rows
      For i As Integer = 0 To 7
        ar_empno(i) = i + 1000
        ar_ename(i) = "dummy " & i
        ar_sal(i) = i * 1000
        ar_deptno(i) = 20
      Next
      'define parameters
      Dim p_empno As New OracleParameter
      p_empno.OracleDbType = OracleDbType.Int16
      p_empno.Value = ar_empno
      Dim p_ename As New OracleParameter
      p_ename.OracleDbType = OracleDbType.Varchar2
      p_ename.Value = ar_ename
      Dim p_sal As New OracleParameter
      p_sal.OracleDbType = OracleDbType.Double
      p_sal.Value = ar_sal
      Dim p_deptno As New OracleParameter
      p_deptno.OracleDbType = OracleDbType.Int16
      p_deptno.Value = ar_deptno
      'create command object
      Dim cmd As New OracleCommand(SQL, cn)
      cmd.ArrayBindCount = 8
      'rows to insert through binding
      'add parameters to command
      cmd.Parameters.Add(p_empno)
      cmd.Parameters.Add(p_ename)
      cmd.Parameters.Add(p_sal)
      cmd.Parameters.Add(p_deptno)
      'open the connection
      cmd.Connection.Open()
      Dim result As Integer = cmd.ExecuteNonQuery()
      'close the connection
      cmd.Connection.Close()
      'display the result
      MessageBox.Show("Succesfully inserted " &
                                  result & " rows")
    Catch ex As Exception
      'display if any error occurs
      MessageBox.Show("Error: " & ex.Message)
      'close the connection if it is still open
      If cn.State = ConnectionState.Open Then
        cn.Close()
      End If
    End Try
  End Sub
```

Now we will take a detailed look at this code. As we would like to insert eight rows (using array binding), we need to create arrays that can hold eight values each for each column. That is achieved as follows:

```
Dim ar_empno(7) As Integer
Dim ar_ename(7) As String
Dim ar_sal(7) As Integer
Dim ar_deptno(7) As Integer
```

Now, we need to fill in the arrays with some values. We will use a loop to fill up the arrays as in the following snippet:

```
For i As Integer = 0 To 7
  ar_empno(i) = i + 1000
  ar_ename(i) = "dummy " & i
  ar_sal(i) = i * 1000
  ar_deptno(i) = 20
  Next
```

Once the arrays are filled, we need to assign each of these arrays to different `OracleParameter` objects (one `OracleParameter` object for each column). The following code fragment creates an `OracleParameter` object for the empno column and assigns the array for it:

```
Dim p_empno As New OracleParameter
p_empno.OracleDbType = OracleDbType.Int16
p_empno.Value = ar_empno
```

Once the `OracleParameter` objects are ready, we need to add all of these parameters to an `OracleCommand` object as shown in the following code:

```
Dim cmd As New OracleCommand(SQL, cn)
cmd.ArrayBindCount = 8 'rows to insert through binding
'add parameters to command
cmd.Parameters.Add(p_empno)
cmd.Parameters.Add(p_ename)
cmd.Parameters.Add(p_sal)
cmd.Parameters.Add(p_deptno)
```

Observe the highlighted statement in the above code fragment; that is to inform the `OracleCommand` object that the arrays are made up of eight values.

Creating an Oracle Table Dynamically Using ODP.NET

You can work with almost any DDL command using the same method you used previously i.e. ExecuteNonQuery with OracleCommand. We can just replace the DML command we used earlier with a DDL command.

The following example creates a table in Oracle database dynamically from within .NET:

```
Private Sub btnCreateTable_Click(ByVal sender As
    System.Object, ByVal e As System.EventArgs) Handles
    btnCreateTable.Click
        'create connection to db
        Dim cn As New OracleConnection("Data Source=xe; _
                        User Id=scott;Password=tiger")
    Try
        Dim SQL As String
        'build the CREATE TABLE statement
        Dim sb As New System.Text.StringBuilder
        sb.Append(" CREATE TABLE MyEmp")
        sb.Append(" (")
        sb.Append("    empno NUMBER(4),")
        sb.Append("    ename VARCHAR2(20) ")
        sb.Append(" ) ")
        SQL = sb.ToString
        'create command object
        Dim cmd As New OracleCommand(SQL, cn)
        'open the connection
        cmd.Connection.Open()
        'execute the DDL command
        cmd.ExecuteNonQuery()
        'close the connection
        cmd.Connection.Close()
        'display the result
        MessageBox.Show("Succesfully created")
    Catch ex As Exception
        'display if any error occurs
        MessageBox.Show("Error: " & ex.Message)
        'close the connection if it is still open
        If cn.State = ConnectionState.Open Then
            cn.Close()
        End If
    End Try
End Sub
```

Updating Offline Data to the Database Using OracleDataAdapter

When you use `OracleDataAdapter`, you will generally fill information into either a dataset or data table. A dataset or data table resides in client memory (offline) without having any connection to Oracle database. You can make changes to the data available at the client (in offline mode) and finally update all of those modifications to the database using the `Update` method of `OracleDataAdapter`.

The following is a demonstration, which adds a new row to a data table (in offline mode) and later updates it to the database using the `Update` method:

```
Private Sub btnDatasetUpdate_Click(ByVal sender As
   System.Object, ByVal e As System.EventArgs) Handles
   btnDatasetUpdate.Click
     'create connection to db
     Dim cn As New OracleConnection("Data Source=xe; _
                       User Id=scott;Password=tiger")
     Try

         'build the INSERT statement
         Dim sb As New System.Text.StringBuilder
         sb.Append(" INSERT INTO emp")
         sb.Append(" (empno, ename, sal, deptno)")
         sb.Append(" VALUES")
         sb.Append(" (:empno, :ename, :sal, :deptno)")
         Dim sqlInsert As String = sb.ToString

         'build the SELECT statement
         sb = New System.Text.StringBuilder
         sb.Append(" SELECT")
         sb.Append(" empno, ename, sal, deptno")
         sb.Append(" FROM emp")
         Dim sqlSelect As String = sb.ToString

         'create command objects
         Dim cmdSelect As New OracleCommand(sqlSelect, cn)
         Dim cmdInsert As New OracleCommand(sqlInsert, cn)
         'attach parameters to insert command object
         With cmdInsert.Parameters
           .Add(New OracleParameter(":empno",
                       OracleDbType.Int16, 4, "empno"))
           .Add(New OracleParameter(":ename",
                     OracleDbType.Varchar2, 12, "ename"))
           .Add(New OracleParameter(":sal",
                     OracleDbType.Decimal, 0, "sal"))
```

```
               .Add(New OraceParameter(":deptno",
                        OracleDbType.Int16, 4, "deptno"))
        End With

        'create data adapter
        Dim da As New OracleDataAdapter
        'assign command objects to data adapter
        da.SelectCommand = cmdSelect
        da.InsertCommand = cmdInsert
        'create and fill the datatable
        Dim dt As New DataTable
        da.Fill(dt)
        'modify data in datatable by adding
        'a new offline row
        Dim dr As DataRow = dt.NewRow
        dr("empno") = 1001
        dr("ename") = "Jagadish"
        dr("sal") = 1300
        dr("deptno") = 20
        dt.Rows.Add(dr)
        'update the offline row back to database
        da.Update(dt)
        'clear resources
        da.Dispose()
        'display the result
        MessageBox.Show("Updated succesfully")
    Catch ex As Exception
        'display if any error occurs
        MessageBox.Show("Error: " & ex.Message)
        'close the connection if it is still open
        If cn.State = ConnectionState.Open Then
            cn.Close()
        End If
    End Try
End Sub
```

`OracleDataAdapter` doesn't know any commands by itself. It is our responsibility to let `OracleDataAdapter` know about how to retrieve, insert, update, or delete data. In the above case, we just assigned two command objects (one each for retrieving and inserting) to `OracleDataAdapter`. This is done as follows:

```
'create data adapter
Dim da As New OracleDataAdapter
'assign command objects to data adapter
da.SelectCommand = cmdSelect
da.InsertCommand = cmdInsert
```

If you wish to update or delete existing rows when offline, you may have to add UPDATE and DELETE statements to OracleDataAdapter using OracleCommand objects. As well as INSERT, UPDATE, or DELETE, you can also specify stored procedures directly to work with OracleDataAdapter to update the offline data (covered in subsequent chapters).

Once the data is filled into the DataTable object, we can add a new row offline as follows:

```
Dim dr As DataRow = dt.NewRow
dr("empno") = 1001
dr("ename") = "Jagadish"
dr("sal") = 1300
dr("deptno") = 20
dt.Rows.Add(dr)
```

We can not only add information, we can even opt for modifying or deleting rows in the data table and finally update the changes back to the database with a simple statement as follows:

```
da.Update(dt)
```

Working with OracleCommandBuilder and OracleDataAdapter

Now that you have understood how to work with offline data tables (or datasets) and get them updated to the database using OracleDataAdapter, it is time to deal with OracleCommandBuilder now.

Specifying INSERT, UPDATE, and DELETE manually to every OracleDataAdapter is very problematic (or even error prone due to syntax or database changes). OracleCommandBuilder offers you the mechanism to automatically generate all those statements internally for OracleDataAdapter.

The modified code for the previous example is as follows:

```
Private Sub btnUpdDSusingCB_Click(ByVal sender As
    System.Object, ByVal e As System.EventArgs) Handles
    btnUpdDSusingCB.Click
    'create connection to db
    Dim cn As New OracleConnection("Data Source=xe; _
                    User Id=scott;Password=tiger")
    Try

        'build the SELECT statement
```

```
       Dim sb As New System.Text.StringBuilder
       sb.Append(" SELECT")
       sb.Append(" empno, ename, sal, deptno")
       sb.Append(" FROM emp")
       Dim sqlSelect As String = sb.ToString

       'create command objects
       Dim cmdSelect As New OracleCommand(sqlSelect, cn)

       'create data adapter
       Dim da As New OracleDataAdapter
       'assign command objects to data adapter
       da.SelectCommand = cmdSelect
       Dim CommBuilder As New OracleCommandBuilder(da)
       'create and fill the datatable
       Dim dt As New DataTable
       da.Fill(dt)
       'modify data in datatable by adding
       'a new offline row
       Dim dr As DataRow = dt.NewRow
       dr("empno") = 2001
       dr("ename") = "Sunitha"
       dr("sal") = 1300
       dr("deptno") = 20
       dt.Rows.Add(dr)
       'update the offline row back to database
       da.Update(dt)
       'clear resources
       da.Dispose()
       'display the result
       MessageBox.Show("Updated succesfully")
     Catch ex As Exception
       'display if any error occurs
       MessageBox.Show("Error: " & ex.Message)
       'close the connection if it is still open
       If cn.State = ConnectionState.Open Then
         cn.Close()
       End If
     End Try
   End Sub
```

The highlighted statement in the above code does the entire magic of generating automatic INSERT, UPDATE, and DELETE statements internally for the OracleDataAdapter.

Working with Transactions Using ODP.NET

A *transaction* is simply a set of data operations (like some inserts, updates, or deletes, or combinations of them), where all of the operations must be successfully executed or none of them will be successful. To work with transactions using ODP.NET, we need to use the `OracleTransaction` class.

To demonstrate a transaction example, I added two sample tables: `stock` and `sales`. The `stock` table looks as follows:

ITEMID	NAME	QTY
1001	Camera	10
1002	Ipod	8
1003	MP3 Player	12

The `sales` table looks something like the following:

ORDERNO	ORDERDATE	CUSTOMERNAME	ITEMID	QTY
201	25-JUN-78	Jagadish	1002	1

The following code adds a row into the `sales` table and updates a row in the `stock` table as part of a transaction. We are trying to do two operations in a single transaction. If any part of the operation fails, the whole transaction must be canceled.

```
Private Sub btnGenTransaction_Click(ByVal sender As
   System.Object, ByVal e As System.EventArgs) Handles
   btnGenTransaction.Click
   'create connection to db
   Dim cn As New OracleConnection("Data Source=xe; _
                    User Id=scott;Password=tiger")
   'create transaction object
   Dim trans As OracleTransaction = Nothing
   Try
      Dim sqlInsertSales As String
      Dim sb As New System.Text.StringBuilder
      sb.Append(" INSERT INTO sales")
      sb.Append(" (orderno, customername, itemid, qty)")
      sb.Append(" VALUES")
      sb.Append(" ({0},'{1}',{2},{3})")
      sqlInsertSales = String.Format(sb.ToString,
                       202, "Winner", 1002, 3)
      Dim sqlUpdateStock As String
      sb = New System.Text.StringBuilder
```

```
        sb.Append(" UPDATE stock SET")
        sb.Append(" qty = qty - {1}")
        sb.Append(" WHERE")
        sb.Append(" itemid = {0}")
        sqlUpdateStock = String.Format(sb.ToString,
                                            1002, 3)

        'open the connection
        cn.Open()
        'begin the transaction
        trans = cn.BeginTransaction
        'create command objects
        Dim cmdInsertSales As New _
                    OracleCommand(sqlInsertSales, cn)
        Dim cmdUpdateStock As New _
                    OracleCommand(sqlUpdateStock, cn)
        'execute the commands
        cmdInsertSales.ExecuteNonQuery()
        cmdUpdateStock.ExecuteNonQuery()
        'commit the transaction
        trans.Commit()
        'close the connection
        cn.Close()
        'display the result
        MessageBox.Show("Transaction Succesful")
    Catch ex As Exception
        If Not trans Is Nothing Then
          'rollback the transaction
          trans.Rollback()
        End If

        'display if any error occurs
        MessageBox.Show("Error: " & ex.Message)
        'close the connection if it is still open
        If cn.State = ConnectionState.Open Then
          cn.Close()
        End If
    End Try
End Sub
```

For any transaction, we must first begin it, do a sequence of operations, and then commit it. If any error occurs, the transaction needs to be rolled back. This is achieved by using the highlighted statements in the above code. If you really want to check the transaction, try modifying the UPDATE statement above with a syntax error (simply replace stock with stock2). After execution, you will observe that the sales table did not get inserted with any new row (even though that is the first command issued to execute).

Handling Oracle Errors and Exceptions

In all of the previous examples, we simply used only the Exception class, which is the ancestral error handling class in .NET. ODP.NET also includes its own exception class OracleException, to deal with errors (received from Oracle database) in detail.

Displaying a Single or First Error

The following code gives you the error details when we try to execute the INSERT statement (which is wrong):

```
Private Sub btnSingleError_Click(ByVal sender As
   System.Object, ByVal e As System.EventArgs) Handles
   btnSingleError.Click
     'create connection to db
     Dim cn As New OracleConnection("Data Source=xe; _
                       User Id=scott;Password=tiger")
     Try
       Dim SQL As String
       'build the INSERT statement
       Dim sb As New System.Text.StringBuilder
       sb.Append(" INSERT INTO emp2")
       sb.Append(" (empno, ename, sal, deptno)")
       sb.Append(" VALUES")
       sb.Append(" ({0},'{1}',{2},{3})")
       SQL = String.Format(sb.ToString, 1001,
                           "Jagadish", 1300, 20)
       'create command object
       Dim cmd As New OracleCommand(SQL, cn)
       'open the connection
       cmd.Connection.Open()
       'execute the command
       Dim result As Integer = cmd.ExecuteNonQuery()
       'close the connection
       cmd.Connection.Close()
       'display the result
       If result = 0 Then
         MessageBox.Show("No rows inserted")
       Else
         MessageBox.Show("Succesfully inserted")
       End If
     Catch ex As OracleException
       'display if any error occurs
       Dim sb As New System.Text.StringBuilder
```

```
            sb.Append("Error occurred at:" &
                                ControlChars.NewLine)
            sb.Append("------------------------------
                    --------" & ControlChars.NewLine)
            sb.Append("Source: " & ex.Source &
                                ControlChars.NewLine)
            sb.Append("Data Source: " & ex.DataSource &
                                ControlChars.NewLine)
            sb.Append("Error Number: " & ex.Number &
                                ControlChars.NewLine)
            sb.Append("Procedure: " & ex.Procedure &
                                ControlChars.NewLine)
            sb.Append("Message: " & ex.Message)
            MessageBox.Show(sb.ToString)
            'close the connection if it is still open
            If cn.State = ConnectionState.Open Then
                cn.Close()
            End If
        End Try
    End Sub
```

You can observe the above highlighted code, which makes use of the
`OracleException` class. It contains the entire information of the error raised during
execution (run time). The output for the above code looks like the following:

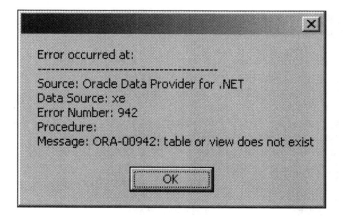

Displaying Multiple Errors

`OracleException` maintains an `OracleErrorCollection` (a collection of
`OracleError` instances) to deal with more errors. If an `OracleException` contains
more than one error message, you can retrieve all of them using the error collection
as follows:

```vb
Private Sub btnMultipleErrors_Click(ByVal sender As
  System.Object, ByVal e As System.EventArgs) Handles
  btnMultipleErrors.Click
    'create connection to db
    Dim cn As New OracleConnection("Data Source=xe; _
      User Id=scott;Password=tiger")
    Try
      Dim SQL As String
      'build the INSERT statement
      Dim sb As New System.Text.StringBuilder
      sb.Append(" INSERT INTO emp")
      sb.Append(" (empno, ename, sal, deptno)")
      sb.Append(" VALUES")
      sb.Append(" (:empno, :ename, :sal, :deptno)")
      SQL = sb.ToString
      'create array structures to hold 8 rows
      Dim ar_empno(7) As Integer
      Dim ar_ename(7) As String
      Dim ar_sal(7) As Integer
      Dim ar_deptno(7) As Integer
      'fill the array structures with rows
      For i As Integer = 0 To 7
        ar_empno(i) = i + 1000
        ar_ename(i) = "too many number of chars here " _
                                                    & i
        ar_sal(i) = i * 1000
        ar_deptno(i) = 20
      Next
      'define parameters
      Dim p_empno As New OracleParameter
      p_empno.OracleDbType = OracleDbType.Int16
      p_empno.Value = ar_empno
      Dim p_ename As New OracleParameter
      p_ename.OracleDbType = OracleDbType.Varchar2
      p_ename.Value = ar_ename
      Dim p_sal As New OracleParameter
      p_sal.OracleDbType = OracleDbType.Double
      p_sal.Value = ar_sal
      Dim p_deptno As New OracleParameter
      p_deptno.OracleDbType = OracleDbType.Int16
      p_deptno.Value = ar_deptno
      'create command object
      Dim cmd As New OracleCommand(SQL, cn)
      cmd.ArrayBindCount = 8 'rows to insert
        through binding
      'add parameters to command
      cmd.Parameters.Add(p_empno)
```

```
        cmd.Parameters.Add(p_ename)
        cmd.Parameters.Add(p_sal)
        cmd.Parameters.Add(p_deptno)
        'open the connection
        cmd.Connection.Open()
        Dim result As Integer = cmd.ExecuteNonQuery()
        'close the connection
        cmd.Connection.Close()
        'display the result
        MessageBox.Show("Succesfully inserted "
           & result & " rows")
     Catch ex As OracleException
        'display if any error occurs
        Dim sb As New System.Text.StringBuilder
        For Each er As OracleError In ex.Errors
           sb.Append("-->" & er.Message &
              ControlChars.NewLine)
        Next
        MessageBox.Show(sb.ToString)
        'close the connection if it is still open
        If cn.State = ConnectionState.Open Then
           cn.Close()
        End If
     End Try
  End Sub
```

You can observe the highlighted code, which gives you all the error messages related to a single exception. The output for the above program looks like the following:

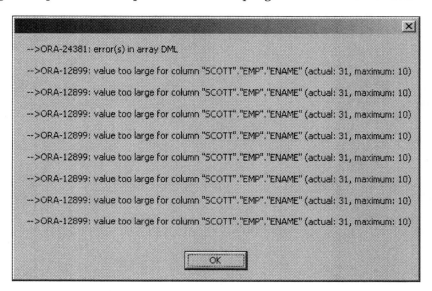

Summary

In this chapter, we completely dealt with inserting, updating, and deleting data at the database. Along with that, we also covered other concepts like statement caching, array binding, working with offline data, implementing transactions, and finally handling errors.

5
Programming ODP.NET with PL/SQL

In previous chapters, we learned about connecting to Oracle databases, retrieving and manipulating information together with error handling. In this chapter, we will explore the following capabilities using ODP.NET:

- Working with PL/SQL blocks, stored procedures, and user-defined functions
- Working with PL/SQL packages, and PL/SQL tables
- Taking advantage of Ref Cursors and MARS (Mutiple Active Result Sets)

 This chapter does not explain PL/SQL. It explains working with PL/SQL together with ODP.NET. Explanation of PL/SQL programming (in this or successive chapters) is beyond the scope of this book.

Working with Anonymous PL/SQL Blocks

Let us start with simple PL/SQL anonymous blocks. A simple PL/SQL block starts with a BEGIN statement and ends with an END statement. You may also have to work with a DECLARE section if you would like to declare or initialize variables.

Executing Anonymous PL/SQL Blocks

Now, let us execute a simple PL/SQL block using ODP.NET. The following code increases the salaries of all employees by 500:

```
Private Sub btnExecuteDML_Click(ByVal sender As
   System.Object, ByVal e As System.EventArgs) Handles
   btnExecuteDML.Click
     'create connection to db
     Dim cn As New OracleConnection("Data Source=xe; _
                     User Id=scott;Password=tiger")
     Try
       'build the anonymous PL/SQL
       Dim sb As New System.Text.StringBuilder
       sb.Append(" BEGIN")
       sb.Append("    UPDATE emp SET sal = sal + 500;")
       sb.Append("    COMMIT;")
       sb.Append(" END;")
       'create command object
       Dim cmd As New OracleCommand(sb.ToString, cn)
       'open the connection
       cmd.Connection.Open()
       'execute the PL/SQL
       cmd.ExecuteNonQuery()
       'close the connection
       cmd.Connection.Close()
       'dispose the command
       cmd.Dispose()
       'display the message
       MessageBox.Show("Succesfully executed")
     Catch ex As Exception
       'display if any error occurs
       MessageBox.Show("Error: " & ex.Message)
       'close the connection if it is still open
       If cn.State = ConnectionState.Open Then
         cn.Close()
       End If
     End Try
   End Sub
```

In the above code, a `StringBuilder` object is used to define the PL/SQL block. It is not compulsory to use it, but it provides better flexibility to work with long strings and also provides better performace over string concatenation. The highlighted section in the above code generates a dynamic anonymous PL/SQL block. The PL/SQL block in the above code fragment (starting with BEGIN and ending with END) simply increases the salaries of all employees by 500 and finally commits it.

To execute this anonymous PL/SQL block, we simply made use of the
ExecuteNonQuery method of OracleCommand.

Passing Information to Anonymous PL/SQL Blocks

Now that you have seen the execution of an anonymous PL/SQL block, we need to
concentrate on sending values to anonymous blocks in the form of parameters.

The following code increases the salaries of all employees by the value (500) passed
as a parameter to it:

```
Private Sub btnExecuteDML_Click(ByVal sender As
   System.Object, ByVal e As System.EventArgs) Handles
   btnExecuteDML.Click
      'create connection to db
      Dim cn As New OracleConnection("Data Source=xe;_
                     User Id=scott;Password=tiger")
      Try
         'build the anonymous PL/SQL
         Dim sb As New System.Text.StringBuilder
         sb.Append(" DECLARE")
         sb.Append("    amt NUMBER;")
         sb.Append(" BEGIN")
         sb.Append("    amt := :1;")
         sb.Append("    UPDATE emp SET sal = sal + :1;")
         sb.Append("    COMMIT;")
         sb.Append(" END;")
         'create command object
         Dim cmd As New OracleCommand(sb.ToString, cn)
         'provide parameter details
         Dim p_amt As New OracleParameter
         p_amt.ParameterName = ":1"
         p_amt.OracleDbType = OracleDbType.Int32
         p_amt.Direction = ParameterDirection.Input
         p_amt.Value = 500
         cmd.Parameters.Add(p_amt)
         'open the connection
         cmd.Connection.Open()
         'execute the PL/SQL
         cmd.ExecuteNonQuery()
         'close the connection
         cmd.Connection.Close()
         'dispose the command
         cmd.Dispose()
```

```
            'display the message
            MessageBox.Show("Succesfully executed")
        Catch ex As Exception
            'display if any error occurs
            MessageBox.Show("Error: " & ex.Message)
            'close the connection if it is still open
            If cn.State = ConnectionState.Open Then
                cn.Close()
            End If
        End Try
    End Sub
```

From the highlighted code, it can be seen that a PL/SQL variable amt is declared as part of the block and provided with a value using a bind variable :1. The value for the bind variable gets populated using OracleParameter. Bind variables and OracleParameter were explained in the previous chapter. In this case, an OracleParameter object is created using the following statement:

```
Dim p_amt As New OracleParameter
```

Once the OracleParameter object is created, we need to specify the bind variable to which it belongs, along with data type and parameter direction as following:

```
p_amt.ParameterName = ":1"
p_amt.OracleDbType = OracleDbType.Int32
p_amt.Direction = ParameterDirection.Input
```

The value for the bind variable is specified using the following statement:

```
p_amt.Value = 500
```

At run time, :1 in the PL/SQL block gets replaced with 500 automatically.

> When you pass values to an anonymous block, the parameters must be of type Input. When you retrieve values from an anonymous block, the parameters must be of Output type. You can also use the Input/Output type of parameter, when you want to deal with both passing and retrieving information using a single parameter.

Retrieving Information from Anonymous Blocks

In the previous example, we simply executed the PL/SQL block, which doesn't return any value or information back to the application. But, it may be necessary for us to retrieve the information from a PL/SQL block using our .NET application. The easiest way to achieve this is by using bind variables with Output parameters.

The following code retrieves and displays the highest salary returned by a PL/SQL block:

```
Private Sub btnGetSingleValue_Click(ByVal sender As
    System.Object, ByVal e As System.EventArgs) Handles
    btnGetSingleValue.Click
    'create connection to db
    Dim cn As New OracleConnection("Data Source=xe; _
                      User Id=scott;Password=tiger")
    Try
      'build the anonymous PL/SQL
      Dim sb As New System.Text.StringBuilder
      sb.Append(" BEGIN")
      sb.Append("   SELECT MAX(sal) INTO :1 FROM emp;")
      sb.Append(" END;")
      'create command object
      Dim cmd As New OracleCommand(sb.ToString, cn)
      cmd.Parameters.Add(New OracleParameter(":1",
        OracleDbType.Double,
        ParameterDirection.Output))
      'open the connection
      cmd.Connection.Open()
      'execute the PL/SQL
      cmd.ExecuteNonQuery()
      'gather the result
      Dim result As String = _
        cmd.Parameters(":1").Value.ToString
      'close the connection
      cmd.Connection.Close()
      'dispose the command
      cmd.Dispose()
      'display the result
      MessageBox.Show("Succesfully executed with
                          result: " & result)
    Catch ex As Exception
      'display if any error occurs
      MessageBox.Show("Error: " & ex.Message)
      'close the connection if it is still open
      If cn.State = ConnectionState.Open Then
        cn.Close()
      End If
    End Try
End Sub
```

From this code, it can be observed that :1 is the bind variable used to retrieve information from the PL/SQL block. As :1 is used to retrieve information, it must be defined as an Output type of parameter as follows:

```
cmd.Parameters.Add(New OracleParameter(":1",
    OracleDbType.Double, ParameterDirection.Output))
```

Once the OracleCommand executes the block, the value from the PL/SQL block can be retrieved into a result variable using the following statement:

```
Dim result As String = _
                cmd.Parameters(":1").Value.ToString
```

 To retrieve multiple values as a single row, you may have to use multiple bind variables. To retrieve a result set, you may have to use Ref Cursor or Associative Arrays (covered in later sections).

Working with PL/SQL Stored Procedures and Functions

A PL/SQL stored procedure is simply a PL/SQL block that gets stored physically within Oracle database. It has tremendous benefits in terms of maintainability, accessibility, complex logic, performance, portability, and scalability.

To help us build powerful database applications, stored procedures provide several advantages including better performance and higher productivity. Stored procedures typically contain a group of logical SQL statements with (or without) complex logic. They are compiled once and stored in executable form. This gives a quick and efficient execution when any user tries to execute it. Executable code is automatically cached and shared among several users reducing the consumption of memory and processing resources.

PL/SQL user-defined functions are very much similar to stored procedures except that they return values back to the execution environment (or applications calling them). No enterprise solution really exists without implementing stored procedures or user-defined functions!

Executing a PL/SQL Stored Procedure

The following is a simple PL/SQL stored procedure, which increments the salaries of all employees by 500:

```
CREATE OR REPLACE PROCEDURE p_Increment_Salary IS
  BEGIN
    UPDATE emp SET sal = sal + 500;
    COMMIT;
  END;
```

When the above script is executed, it creates a stored procedure named
p_Increment_Salary. The stored procedure simply increases the salary of all
employees by 500 and finally commits it.

Now, let us try to execute the above stored procedure using ODP.NET.

```
Private Sub btnExecute_Click(ByVal sender As
    System.Object, ByVal e As System.EventArgs) Handles
    btnExecute.Click
    'create connection to db
    Dim cn As New OracleConnection("Data Source=xe; _
                    User Id=scott;Password=tiger")
    Try
      'create command object
      Dim cmd As New OracleCommand
      With cmd
        'specify that you are working with stored
        'procedure
        .CommandType = CommandType.StoredProcedure
        'provide the name of stored procedure
        .CommandText = "p_Increment_Salary"
        'proceed with execution
        .Connection = cn
        .Connection.Open()
        .ExecuteNonQuery()
        .Connection.Close()
        .Dispose()
      End With
      MessageBox.Show("Succesfully executed")
    Catch ex As Exception
      'display if any error occurs
      MessageBox.Show("Error: " & ex.Message)
      'close the connection if it is still open
      If cn.State = ConnectionState.Open Then
        cn.Close()
      End If
    End Try
End Sub
```

From the highlighted code, it can be seen that the CommandType property is set to StoredProcedure. This is necessary, when you are dealing with stored procedures. The name of the stored procedure is specified as part of the CommandText property. And finally, the stored procedure is executed using ExecuteNonQuery().

Passing Parameter Values to a PL/SQL Stored Procedure

Not every stored procedure works by itself. Sometimes, it may be necessary for us to pass some values (as arguments/parameters) from our application to stored procedures. The same old OracleParameter needs to be used for this purpose.

The following is a simple PL/SQL stored procedure, which increments the salaries of all employees by the amount passed to it (in the form of a parameter):

```
CREATE OR REPLACE PROCEDURE p_Increment_Salary
  (
    amt IN NUMBER
  )
  IS
  BEGIN
    UPDATE emp SET sal = sal + amt;
    COMMIT;
  END;
```

The above stored procedure (p_Increment_Salary) accepts a parameter amt (input type of parameter) of type NUMBER. The salaries of all employees get increased based on the value passed to it.

Now, let us try to execute the above stored procedure using ODP.NET.

```
Private Sub btnExecuteWithParameters_Click(ByVal sender
  As System.Object, ByVal e As System.EventArgs) Handles
  btnExecuteWithParameters.Click
    'create connection to db
    Dim cn As New OracleConnection("Data Source=xe; _
                  User Id=scott;Password=tiger")
    Try
      'create command object
      Dim cmd As New OracleCommand
      With cmd
        'specify that you are working with
        'stored procedure
```

```
      .CommandType = CommandType.StoredProcedure
      'provide the name of stored procedure
      .CommandText = "p_Increment_Salary"
      'provide parameter details
      Dim p_amt As New OracleParameter
      p_amt.ParameterName = "amt"
      p_amt.OracleDbType = OracleDbType.Int32
      p_amt.Direction = ParameterDirection.Input
      p_amt.Value = 500
      .Parameters.Add(p_amt)
      'proceed with execution
      .Connection = cn
      .Connection.Open()
      .ExecuteNonQuery()
      .Connection.Close()
      .Dispose()
    End With
    MessageBox.Show("Succesfully executed")
  Catch ex As Exception
    'display if any error occurs
    MessageBox.Show("Error: " & ex.Message)
    'close the connection if it is still open
    If cn.State = ConnectionState.Open Then
      cn.Close()
    End If
  End Try
End Sub
```

For every existing parameter of a stored procedure, a separate OracleParameter object must be defined corresponding to it. In the highlighted code above, we created an OracleParameter and assigned a few properties according to the needs.

It is very similar to working with bind variables except that the bind variables are replaced with parameter names. Make sure that you always specify the parameter's Direction property.

When a stored procedure is likely to receive a value through a parameter from an application (or during execution), it is called an input (or IN) parameter. When a stored procedure is likely to send a value back through a parameter to an application, it is called an output (or OUT) parameter. When a stored procedure is likely to receive a value and return back some value based on the same parameter (two-way parameter), it is called an input/output (or IN OUT) parameter. If no direction (IN, OUT, or IN OUT) is specified, it defaults to IN.

Using an Anonymous PL/SQL Block to Execute a PL/SQL Stored Procedure

In previous sections, we executed stored procedures directly without using any other PL/SQL logic. Sometimes, it may be necessary to embed our own PL/SQL logic in an anonymous PL/SQL block and then execute the stored procedure.

The following code executes the same stored procedure given in the previous section, with a custom anonymous PL/SQL block:

```
Private Sub btnExecuteWithAnanymousBlock_Click(ByVal
    sender As System.Object, ByVal e As System.EventArgs)
    Handles btnExecuteWithAnanymousBlock.Click
    'create connection to db
    Dim cn As New OracleConnection("Data Source=xe; _
                    User Id=scott;Password=tiger")
    Try
      'build the anonymous PL/SQL
      Dim sb As New System.Text.StringBuilder
      sb.Append(" DECLARE")
      sb.Append("    amt NUMBER;")
      sb.Append(" BEGIN")
      sb.Append("    amt := :1;")
      sb.Append("    p_increment_salary(amt => amt);")
      sb.Append(" END;")
      'create command object
      Dim cmd As New OracleCommand(sb.ToString, cn)
      'provide parameter details
      Dim p_amt As New OracleParameter
      p_amt.ParameterName = ":1"
      p_amt.OracleDbType = OracleDbType.Int32
      p_amt.Direction = ParameterDirection.Input
      p_amt.Value = 500
      cmd.Parameters.Add(p_amt)
      'open the connection
      cmd.Connection.Open()
      'execute the PL/SQL
      cmd.ExecuteNonQuery()
      'close the connection
      cmd.Connection.Close()
      'dispose the command
      cmd.Dispose()
```

```
      'display the result
      MessageBox.Show("Succesfully executed")
    Catch ex As Exception
      'display if any error occurs
      MessageBox.Show("Error: " & ex.Message)
      'close the connection if it is still open
      If cn.State = ConnectionState.Open Then
        cn.Close()
      End If
    End Try
  End Sub
```

In the highlighted code, we created our own anonymous PL/SQL block, which directly executes the stored procedure as part of the same script. The PL/SQL block is defined as follows:

```
DECLARE
    amt NUMBER;
BEGIN
    amt := :1;
    p_increment_salary(amt => amt);
END;
```

The most important line from the above PL/SQL block is the following statement:

```
    p_increment_salary(amt => amt);
```

The above statement simply executes the existing stored procedure (p_increment_salary) by passing the value available in the amt variable to the parameter amt of the stored procedure.

You can also observe that we are passing values to the anonymous block using an OracleParameter. Another most important issue is that we did not specify the CommandType as StoredProcedure anymore! This is not necessary, as you are executing an anonymous block (and not a stored procedure) from the point of application.

Retrieving Output Parameters from a PL/SQL Stored Procedure

Not only can a stored procedure receive a value, but also can return a value back to the application or any other execution environment. This is possible if you are using output parameters as part of stored procedures.

The following is a simple PL/SQL stored procedure, which retrieves the name of the highest earning employee:

```
CREATE OR REPLACE PROCEDURE p_Highest_Earned_Employee
(
    HighestEarned OUT VARCHAR2
)
IS
BEGIN
    SELECT ename INTO HighestEarned
    FROM emp
    WHERE sal = (SELECT MAX(sal) FROM emp);
END;
```

From the highlighted code above, you can observe that we are making use of an output parameter to return some value back to the application. In the above case, the stored procedure simply returns the name of the highest earning employee back to the application through `HighestEarned` variable (which is an output parameter).

Now, let us try to execute the above stored procedure using ODP.NET.

```
Private Sub btnOutParameter_Click(ByVal sender As
    System.Object, ByVal e As System.EventArgs) Handles
btnOutParameter.Click
    'create connection to db
    Dim cn As New OracleConnection("Data Source=xe; _
                    User Id=scott;Password=tiger")
    Try
        'create command object
        Dim cmd As New OracleCommand
        With cmd
            'specify that you are working with
            'stored procedure
            .CommandType = CommandType.StoredProcedure
            'provide the name of stored procedure
            .CommandText = "p_Highest_Earned_Employee"
            .Parameters.Add("HighestEarned",
                OracleDbType.Varchar2, 20, Nothing,
                ParameterDirection.Output)
            'proceed with execution
            .Connection = cn
            .Connection.Open()
            .ExecuteNonQuery()
            Dim Result As String = _
```

```
          cmd.Parameters("HighestEarned").Value.ToString
        .Connection.Close()
        .Dispose()
        MessageBox.Show("Succesfully executed with
                             result: " & Result)
      End With
    Catch ex As Exception
      'display if any error occurs
      MessageBox.Show("Error: " & ex.Message)
      'close the connection if it is still open
      If cn.State = ConnectionState.Open Then
        cn.Close()
      End If
    End Try
  End Sub
```

In the highlighted code above, we created an `OracleParameter` named
`HighestEarned` and specified it as of type `Output` parameter as follows:

```
.Parameters.Add("HighestEarned",
   OracleDbType.Varchar2, 20, Nothing,
   ParameterDirection.Output)
```

You can also define the above output parameter as follows:

```
Dim p_ename As New OracleParameter
p_ename.ParameterName = "HighestEarned"
p_ename.OracleDbType = OracleDbType.Varchar2
p_ename.Size = 20
p_ename.Direction = ParameterDirection.Output
cmd.Parameters.Add(p_ename)
```

It is simply a matter of convenience!

The value returned by the stored procedure as part of the `Output` parameter gets
received into the variable `Result` using the following statement:

```
Dim Result As String = _
   cmd.Parameters("HighestEarned").Value.ToString
```

Passing IN and Getting OUT Simultaneously

Now that we have seen how to deal with input and output parameters, it is time
to work with both simultaneously. Let us declare a parameter that is capable of
handling both input and output directions.

The following is a simple PL/SQL stored procedure, which accepts employee number (input) and increment of salary (input) as parameters and returns back (output) the updated salary of the same employee:

```
CREATE OR REPLACE PROCEDURE p_Increment_Salary
  (
    eno IN NUMBER,
    inc_sal IN OUT NUMBER
  )
  IS
  BEGIN
    UPDATE emp SET sal = sal + inc_sal
    WHERE empno = eno;
    SELECT sal INTO inc_sal
    FROM emp
    WHERE empno = eno;
  END;
```

From the highlighted code above, you can observe that we are trying to make use of a parameter inc_sal, which is of type both input and output. That means, we can pass a value and retrieve a value from the same parameter.

Now, let us try to execute the above stored procedure using ODP.NET.

```
Private Sub btnINOUTDemo_Click(ByVal sender As
  System.Object, ByVal e As System.EventArgs) Handles
  btnINOUTDemo.Click
    'create connection to db
    Dim cn As New OracleConnection("Data Source=xe; _
                    User Id=scott;Password=tiger")
    Try
      'create command object
      Dim cmd As New OracleCommand
      With cmd
        'specify that you are working with
        'stored procedure
        .CommandType = CommandType.StoredProcedure
        'provide the name of stored procedure
        .CommandText = "p_Increment_Salary"
        'provide parameter details
        cmd.Parameters.Add("eno", OracleDbType.Decimal,
                Nothing, 7369, ParameterDirection.Input)
        cmd.Parameters.Add("inc_sal",
                OracleDbType.Decimal, Nothing, 500,
                ParameterDirection.InputOutput)
        'proceed with execution
        .Connection = cn
```

```
    .Connection.Open()
    .ExecuteNonQuery()
    Dim Result As String = _
        cmd.Parameters("inc_sal").Value.ToString
    .Connection.Close()
    .Dispose()
    MessageBox.Show("Salary Succesfully increased to:
                                    " & Result)
  End With
Catch ex As Exception
  'display if any error occurs
  MessageBox.Show("Error: " & ex.Message)
  'close the connection if it is still open
  If cn.State = ConnectionState.Open Then
    cn.Close()
  End If
End Try
End Sub
```

In the first piece of highlighted code, we created an `OracleParameter` named `inc_sal` and specified it as of type `InputOutput` parameter. The value returned by the stored procedure (as part of the `InputOutput` parameter) gets received into the variable `Result` using the following statement:

```
Dim Result As String = _
  cmd.Parameters("inc_sal").Value.ToString
```

Handling User-Defined Application Errors

PL/SQL is equipped with its own error handling or exception handling capabilities. Apart from that, it also gives us the flexibility to raise our own errors during the execution of PL/SQL. When these errors get raised, our .NET application gets into an abnormal termination. Now, let us handle these types of errors effectively from within our application.

The following is a simple PL/SQL stored procedure, which accepts employee number (input) and increment of salary (input) as parameters and returns back (output) the updated salary of the same employee:

```
CREATE OR REPLACE PROCEDURE p_Increment_Salary
  (
    eno IN NUMBER,
    inc_sal IN NUMBER
  )
  IS
  BEGIN
```

```
    IF inc_sal > 1000 THEN
     RAISE_APPLICATION_ERROR(-20000,'Invalid update to
                                              salary);
    END IF;
    UPDATE emp SET sal = sal + inc_sal
    WHERE empno = eno;
  END;
```

The highlighted code above represents a custom error raised within the stored procedure when the application tries to provide a value more than 1000 to the inc_sal parameter.

Now, let us try to execute the above stored procedure using ODP.NET.

```
Private Sub btnErrorDemo_Click(ByVal sender As
  System.Object, ByVal e As System.EventArgs) Handles
  btnErrorDemo.Click
    'create connection to db
    Dim cn As New OracleConnection("Data Source=xe; _
                     User Id=scott;Password=tiger")
    Try
      'create command object
      Dim cmd As New OracleCommand
      With cmd
         'specify that you are working with
         'stored procedure
         .CommandType = CommandType.StoredProcedure
         'provide the name of stored procedure
         .CommandText = "p_Increment_Salary"
         'provide parameter details
         cmd.Parameters.Add("eno", OracleDbType.Decimal,
                 Nothing, 7369, ParameterDirection.Input)
         cmd.Parameters.Add("inc_sal",
                 OracleDbType.Decimal, Nothing, 1500,
                 ParameterDirection.Input)
         'proceed with execution
         .Connection = cn
         .Connection.Open()
         .ExecuteNonQuery()
         .Connection.Close()
         .Dispose()
         MessageBox.Show("Salary Succesfully increased")
      End With
    Catch oex As OracleException
      If oex.Number = 20000 Then
         MessageBox.Show("Please provide valid increment.
         It should be less than 1000")
```

```
      Else
        MessageBox.Show("Error: " & oex.Message)
      End If
   Catch ex As Exception
      'display if any error occurs
      MessageBox.Show("Error: " & ex.Message)
   Finally
      'close the connection if it is still open
      If cn.State = ConnectionState.Open Then
         cn.Close()
      End If
   End Try
End Sub
```

From the highlighted code, you can observe that the error is being handled using OracleException. Within the Catch block, we are checking if the error belongs to 20000 (our custom error number) and displaying a convincing message to the user.

Executing a PL/SQL User-Defined Function

A PL/SQL stored procedure is simply a set of PL/SQL statements (bundled as a single unit) to get executed at the database server. A PL/SQL user-defined function is very similar to a PL/SQL stored procedure except that it will certainly return a value to the calling application or environment. The main value being returned from a user-defined function is handled using a RETURN statement within the function.

> Do not confuse output parameters with RETURN values. Both of these return values to the calling application. Output parameters are logical ways of returning values. RETURN exists only with PL/SQL user-defined functions. You can also have IN, OUT or IN OUT parameters along with a RETURN statement as part of user-defined functions.

The following is a simple PL/SQL stored procedure, which accepts employee number (input) parameter and returns back (output) the employee's department:

```
CREATE OR REPLACE FUNCTION f_get_dname
(
   eno IN NUMBER
)
RETURN VARCHAR2
IS
 dn dept.dname%TYPE;
BEGIN
   SELECT dname INTO dn
   FROM dept
```

```
                    WHERE deptno = (SELECT deptno FROM emp
                                        WHERE empno = eno);
        RETURN dn;
    END;
    /
```

From the highlighted code, you can observe that you are returning a value of the type VARCHAR2 back to the application (or environment).

```
    Private Sub btnUDFDemo_Click(ByVal sender As
        System.Object, ByVal e As System.EventArgs) Handles
        btnUDFDemo.Click
        'create connection to db
        Dim cn As New OracleConnection("Data Source=xe; _
                            User Id=scott;Password=tiger")
        Try
            'create command object
            Dim cmd As New OracleCommand
            With cmd
                'specify that you are working with
                'stored procedure
                .CommandType = CommandType.StoredProcedure
                'provide the name of stored procedure
                .CommandText = "f_get_dname"
                'provide parameter details
                cmd.Parameters.Add("dname",
                        OracleDbType.Varchar2, 20, Nothing,
                        ParameterDirection.ReturnValue)
                cmd.Parameters.Add("eno", OracleDbType.Decimal,
                        Nothing, 7369, ParameterDirection.Input)

                'proceed with execution
                .Connection = cn
                .Connection.Open()
                .ExecuteNonQuery()
                Dim Result As String = _
                        cmd.Parameters("dname").Value.ToString
                .Connection.Close()
                .Dispose()
                MessageBox.Show("Succesfully executed with
                                        result: " & Result)
            End With

        Catch ex As Exception
            'display if any error occurs
```

```
        MessageBox.Show("Error: " & ex.Message)
        'close the connection if it is still open
        If cn.State = ConnectionState.Open Then
          cn.Close()
        End If
      End Try
   End Sub
```

The most important issue to remember from the above code is the `Direction` set to `ReturnValue` (as seen in the highlighted section). This is mainly necessary when you are working with PL/SQL user-defined functions. Every PL/SQL user-defined function will certainly return a value back to the application and it must be handled only by specifying `ParameterDirection` as `ReturnValue`.

PL/SQL Packages, Tables, and REF CURSOR

We have already covered ODP.NET with PL/SQL in several areas including server-side programming like stored procedures, user-defined functions, etc. Now, let us work with PL/SQL packages, PL/SQL tables, and REF CURSOR.

Executing Routines in a PL/SQL Package

Before trying to access a PL/SQL package using ODP.NET, we need to create a PL/SQL package. To create a PL/SQL package, we need to create a **package definition** and a **package body**.

The following is a sample PL/SQL package created for demonstration:

```
CREATE OR REPLACE PACKAGE pck_emp_operations IS
  PROCEDURE IncreaseSalaries (v_IncSal NUMBER);
  FUNCTION getSalaryGrade(v_empno NUMBER) RETURN
                                          NUMBER;
END pck_emp_operations;
/

CREATE OR REPLACE PACKAGE BODY pck_emp_operations IS
  PROCEDURE IncreaseSalaries (v_IncSal NUMBER) IS
  BEGIN
     UPDATE emp SET sal = sal + v_IncSal;
  END;

  FUNCTION getSalaryGrade(v_empno NUMBER)
                       RETURN NUMBER IS
```

```
      v_grade NUMBER;
  BEGIN
    SELECT grade INTO v_grade
    FROM salgrade
    WHERE (SELECT sal FROM emp WHERE empno=v_empno)
    BETWEEN losal AND hisal;
    RETURN v_grade;
  END;

  END pck_emp_operations;
  /
```

From the above code, you can observe that a package named `pck_emp_operations` is created with two subroutines `IncreaseSalaries` and `getSalaryGrade`. The `IncreaseSalaries` subroutine simply accepts a parameter and increments the salaries of all employees. It is defined as follows:

```
PROCEDURE IncreaseSalaries (v_IncSal NUMBER) IS
BEGIN
  UPDATE emp SET sal = sal + v_IncSal;
END;
```

The `getSalaryGrade` subroutine accepts an employee number as parameter and returns the employee's salary grade. It is defined as follows:

```
FUNCTION getSalaryGrade(v_empno NUMBER) RETURN NUMBER IS
  v_grade NUMBER;
  BEGIN
    SELECT grade INTO v_grade
    FROM salgrade
    WHERE (SELECT sal FROM emp WHERE empno=v_empno)
    BETWEEN losal AND hisal;
    RETURN v_grade;
  END;
```

Executing a Procedure in a PL/SQL Package

The following is the `IncreaseSalaries` procedure available in `pck_emp_operations`:

```
PROCEDURE IncreaseSalaries (v_IncSal NUMBER) IS
  BEGIN
    UPDATE emp SET sal = sal + v_IncSal;
  END;
```

The following is the code that tries to execute the above procedure:

```
Private Sub btnExecuteSP_Click(ByVal sender As
   System.Object, ByVal e As System.EventArgs) Handles
   btnExecuteSP.Click
      'create connection to db
      Dim cn As New OracleConnection("Data Source=xe; _
                          User Id=scott;Password=tiger")
      Try
        'create command object
        Dim cmd As New OracleCommand
        With cmd
           'specify that you are working with stored
           'procedure
           .CommandType = CommandType.StoredProcedure
           'provide the name of routine
           .CommandText =
               "pck_emp_operations.IncreaseSalaries"
           'provide parameter details
           Dim p_amt As New OracleParameter
           p_amt.ParameterName = "v_IncSal"
           p_amt.OracleDbType = OracleDbType.Int32
           p_amt.Direction = ParameterDirection.Input
           p_amt.Value = 500
           .Parameters.Add(p_amt)
           'proceed with execution
           .Connection = cn
           .Connection.Open()
           .ExecuteNonQuery()
           .Connection.Close()
           .Dispose()
        End With
        MessageBox.Show("Succesfully executed")
      Catch ex As Exception
        'display if any error occurs
        MessageBox.Show("Error: " & ex.Message)
        'close the connection if it is still open
        If cn.State = ConnectionState.Open Then
           cn.Close()
        End If
      End Try
End Sub
```

To execute a routine in a PL/SQL package, the `CommandType` of `OracleCommand` object must be specified with `StoredProcedure` as following:

```
.CommandType = CommandType.StoredProcedure
```

Now, we need to provide the details of the routine (procedure or function) available as part of the PL/SQL package to execute. It is done as follows:

```
.CommandText = "pck_emp_operations.IncreaseSalaries"
```

As the routine accepts a parameter (v_IncSal), we provide the parameter details as follows:

```
Dim p_amt As New OracleParameter
p_amt.ParameterName = "v_IncSal"
p_amt.OracleDbType = OracleDbType.Int32
p_amt.Direction = ParameterDirection.Input
p_amt.Value = 500
.Parameters.Add(p_amt)
```

Finally, we execute the `OracleCommand` using the following statement:

```
.ExecuteNonQuery()
```

Executing a User-Defined Function in a PL/SQL Package

The following is the `getSalaryGrade` function available in `pck_emp_operations`:

```
FUNCTION getSalaryGrade(v_empno NUMBER) RETURN NUMBER IS
  v_grade NUMBER;
   BEGIN
    SELECT grade INTO v_grade
    FROM salgrade
    WHERE (SELECT sal FROM emp WHERE empno=v_empno)
    BETWEEN losal AND hisal;
    RETURN v_grade;
   END;
```

The following is the code which tries to execute the above function:

```
Private Sub btnExecuteUDF_Click(ByVal sender As
  System.Object, ByVal e As System.EventArgs) Handles
  btnExecuteUDF.Click
    'create connection to db
    Dim cn As New OracleConnection("Data Source=xe; _
                     User Id=scott;Password=tiger")
    Try
      'create command object
      Dim cmd As New OracleCommand
      With cmd
```

```
                'specify that you are working with
                'stored procedure
                .CommandType = CommandType.StoredProcedure
                'provide the name of routine
                .CommandText =
                    "pck_emp_operations.getSalaryGrade"
                'provide parameter details
                .Parameters.Add("v_grade", OracleDbType.Int16,
                        Nothing, Nothing,
                        ParameterDirection.ReturnValue)
                .Parameters.Add("v_empno", OracleDbType.Decimal,
                        Nothing, 7839,
                        ParameterDirection.Input)

                'proceed with execution
                .Connection = cn
                .Connection.Open()
                .ExecuteNonQuery()
                Dim Result As String = _
                    .Parameters("v_grade").Value.ToString
                .Connection.Close()
                .Dispose()
                MessageBox.Show("Succesfully executed with
                                result: " & Result)
            End With

        Catch ex As Exception
            'display if any error occurs
            MessageBox.Show("Error: " & ex.Message)
            'close the connection if it is still open
            If cn.State = ConnectionState.Open Then
                cn.Close()
            End If
        End Try
    End Sub
```

The following statement indicates that a stored routine is being executed:

```
.CommandType = CommandType.StoredProcedure
```

The following statement specifies the name of the routine to be executed (along with the package name):

```
.CommandText = "pck_emp_operations.getSalaryGrade"
```

As the routine `getSalaryGrade` accepts one parameter and returns one value, the following statements add two parameters (one for the input parameter and the other for the return value) to `OracleCommand`:

```
.Parameters.Add("v_grade", OracleDbType.Int16,
   Nothing, Nothing, ParameterDirection.ReturnValue)
.Parameters.Add("v_empno", OracleDbType.Decimal,
   Nothing, 7839, ParameterDirection.Input)
```

Once the `OracleCommand` is executed, the value is retrieved using the following statement:

```
Dim Result As String = _
.Parameters("v_grade").Value.ToString
```

Finally, the output is displayed using the following statement:

```
MessageBox.Show("Succesfully executed with result: "
                                        & Result)
```

Passing Arrays to and Receiving Arrays from Oracle Database

There are several methods to send information to Oracle database. We can send information using parameters, XML, Associative Arrays, Ref Cursors, etc. If you would like to send a single value to Oracle database, it is very easy by using parameters. If you would like to send several (an unknown number of) values to Oracle, the issue becomes a bit complicated. We may have to use PL/SQL packages along with certain Oracle constructs to handle our application requirements.

In this section, we will cover using associative arrays in ODP.NET to send arrays of information to and receive arrays from Oracle database.

Sending an Array to Oracle Database

The following package demonstrates the use of the PL/SQL table type to receive an array from an application outside the Oracle database:

```
CREATE OR REPLACE PACKAGE pck_emp_tabledemo IS
   TYPE t_num_array IS TABLE OF NUMBER INDEX BY
                                    BINARY_INTEGER;
   PROCEDURE IncreaseSalaries(v_EmpArray t_num_array,
                           v_IncSal number);
END pck_emp_tabledemo;
/
```

```
CREATE OR REPLACE PACKAGE BODY pck_emp_tabledemo IS
   PROCEDURE IncreaseSalaries(v_EmpArray t_num_array,
                              v_IncSal number) IS
   BEGIN
     FOR i IN 1..v_EmpArray.LAST
     LOOP
     UPDATE emp SET sal = sal + v_IncSal
     WHERE empno = v_EmpArray(i);
     END LOOP;
   END;
END pck_emp_tabledemo;
/
```

In this package, you can observe that a PL/SQL table type is declared as follows:

```
TYPE t_num_array IS TABLE OF NUMBER INDEX BY
                             BINARY_INTEGER;
```

It is simply a user-defined data type that can hold a set of numbers. The routine available as part of the package accepts a parameter, which is of the same data type, as follows:

```
PROCEDURE IncreaseSalaries(v_EmpArray t_num_array,
                           v_IncSal number);
```

The following code sends an array of values to the procedure available in the PL/SQL package:

```
Private Sub btnPassArrayToSP_Click(ByVal sender As
   System.Object, ByVal e As System.EventArgs) Handles
   btnPassArrayToSP.Click
     'create connection to db
     Dim cn As New OracleConnection("Data Source=xe; _
                     User Id=scott;Password=tiger")
   Try
      'create command object
      Dim cmd As New OracleCommand
      With cmd
        'specify that you are working with stored
        'procedure
        .CommandType = CommandType.StoredProcedure
        'provide the name of stored procedure
        .CommandText =
           "pck_emp_tabledemo.IncreaseSalaries"
        'provide parameter details
```

```
Dim p_empno As OracleParameter =
.Parameters.Add("v_EmpArray",
OracleDbType.Int32, ParameterDirection.Input)
p_empno.CollectionType =
OracleCollectionType.PLSQLAssociativeArray
p_empno.Value = New Int32() {7788, 7876, 7934}
.Parameters.Add("v_IncSal", OracleDbType.Decimal,
            Nothing, 500, ParameterDirection.Input)
'proceed with execution
.Connection = cn
.Connection.Open()
.ExecuteNonQuery()
.Connection.Close()
.Dispose()
MessageBox.Show("Succesfully executed")
End With

Catch ex As Exception
  'display if any error occurs
  MessageBox.Show("Error: " & ex.Message)
  'close the connection if it is still open
  If cn.State = ConnectionState.Open Then
    cn.Close()
  End If
End Try
End Sub
```

Let us go step by step as follows:

```
Dim p_empno As OracleParameter = _
    .Parameters.Add("v_EmpArray", OracleDbType.Int32,
    ParameterDirection.Input)
```

The above defines a new OracleParameter named v_EmpArray.

```
p_empno.CollectionType =
  OracleCollectionType.PLSQLAssociativeArray
```

The parameter p_empno is specified as a CollectionType and that too of the type PLSQLAssociativeArray. When the OracleParameter is defined with this type, then it is capable of holding multiple values.

```
p_empno.Value = New Int32() {7788, 7876, 7934}
```

As p_empno can hold multiple values, the above statement assigns a set of values in the form of an array.

Receiving an Array from Oracle Database

The following package demonstrates the use of the PL/SQL table type to send an array of values from Oracle database to external applications:

```
CREATE OR REPLACE PACKAGE pck_emp_tabledemo IS
   TYPE t_num_array IS TABLE OF NUMBER INDEX BY
      BINARY_INTEGER;
   PROCEDURE GetEmployeesOfDept(v_Deptno NUMBER,
                      v_EmpArray OUT t_num_array);
END pck_emp_tabledemo;
/

CREATE OR REPLACE PACKAGE BODY pck_emp_tabledemo IS
   PROCEDURE GetEmployeesOfDept(v_Deptno NUMBER,
      v_EmpArray OUT t_num_array) IS
      i NUMBER(3) := 1;
   BEGIN
    FOR e IN (SELECT empno FROM emp WHERE
                            deptno = v_Deptno)
     LOOP
       v_EmpArray(i) := e.empno;
       i := i + 1;
     END LOOP;
   END;
END pck_emp_tabledemo;
```

The above highlighted code is where we define output parameters to send the arrays back to the application. If you are familiar with BULK COLLECT, you can rewrite the package body as follows (just to minimize code and make it very efficient):

```
CREATE OR REPLACE PACKAGE BODY pck_emp_tabledemo IS
   PROCEDURE GetEmployeesOfDept(v_Deptno NUMBER,
      v_EmpArray OUT t_num_array) IS
   BEGIN
   SELECT empno BULK COLLECT INTO v_EmpArray
   FROM emp WHERE deptno = v_Deptno;
   END;
END pck_emp_tabledemo;
/
```

The following code receives an array of values from the procedure available in the PL/SQL package:

```
Private Sub btnReceiveAryFromSP_Click(ByVal sender As
   System.Object, ByVal e As System.EventArgs) Handles
   btnReceiveAryFromSP.Click
     'create connection to db
```

```vb
Dim cn As New OracleConnection("Data Source=xe; _
                        User Id=scott;Password=tiger")
Try
  'create command object
  Dim cmd As New OracleCommand
  With cmd
    'specify that you are working with
    'stored procedure
    .CommandType = CommandType.StoredProcedure
    'provide the name of stored procedure
    .CommandText =
        "pck_emp_tabledemo.GetEmployeesOfDept"
    'provide parameter details
    .Parameters.Add("v_Deptno", OracleDbType.Int32,
                    10, ParameterDirection.Input)
    Dim p_empno As OracleParameter = _
      .Parameters.Add("v_EmpArray",
      OracleDbType.Int32, ParameterDirection.Output)
    p_empno.CollectionType = _
      OracleCollectionType.PLSQLAssociativeArray
    p_empno.Size = 10
    'proceed with execution
    .Connection = cn
    .Connection.Open()
    .ExecuteNonQuery()
    'get the result out
    Dim Empno() As _
        Oracle.DataAccess.Types.OracleDecimal =
                                p_empno.Value
    .Connection.Close()
    .Dispose()
    Dim strEmpno As String = String.Empty
    For Each en As
    Oracle.DataAccess.Types.OracleDecimal In Empno
      strEmpno &= en.ToString & ","
    Next
    MessageBox.Show("Succesfully executed with
                        result: " & strEmpno)
  End With

Catch ex As Exception
  'display if any error occurs
  MessageBox.Show("Error: " & ex.Message)
```

```
    'close the connection if it is still open
    If cn.State = ConnectionState.Open Then
      cn.Close()
    End If
  End Try

End Sub
```

Let us go step by step:

```
Dim p_empno As OracleParameter = _
  .Parameters.Add("v_EmpArray", OracleDbType.Int32,
  ParameterDirection.Output)
p_empno.CollectionType =
  OracleCollectionType.PLSQLAssociativeArray
p_empno.Size = 10
```

The above defines an `OracleParameter` named `p_empno` as `PLSQLAssociativeArray`. You must note that it is defined as an `Output` parameter. We are also required to specify the number of values (`Size`) expected in that parameter.

Once the `OracleCommand` gets executed, we retrieve the whole set of values into an array as follows:

```
Dim Empno() As Oracle.DataAccess.Types.OracleDecimal = _
                                    p_empno.Value
```

Finally, we concatenate all those values to form a single string value and display the string back to the user using the following statements:

```
For Each en As Oracle.DataAccess.Types.OracleDecimal
                                    In Empno
strEmpno &= en.ToString & ","
Next
MessageBox.Show("Succesfully executed with result: "
                                    & strEmpno)
```

Another important point to note is that the number of values you are about to receive must be already known to you for specifying the `Size`. If the value is higher than the number of values being received from database, it doesn't really give us any problem. But, if the value is lower, it certainly raises an error.

You can observe that specifying `Size` in advance is bit problematic and really not practical in every scenario. In such situations, you are encouraged to opt for the usage of REF CURSOR.

Working with REF CURSOR Using ODP.NET

A REF CURSOR is simply a pointer or reference to the result set available at the server. Before we can use REF CURSOR, it is required to open it using a SELECT statement. REF CURSOR is very helpful to .NET to retrieve server-side result sets efficiently. Unlike associative arrays with PL/SQL tables, we need not specify the number of values or rows being returned.

Pulling from REF CURSOR Using OracleDataReader

Let us start with creating a REF CURSOR within a PL/SQL package and then try to access it using a .NET application. Following is the sample PL/SQL package developed for this demonstration:

```
CREATE OR REPLACE PACKAGE pck_emp_Curdemo IS
  TYPE t_cursor IS REF CURSOR;
  PROCEDURE GetList(cur_emp OUT t_cursor);
END pck_emp_Curdemo;
/

CREATE OR REPLACE PACKAGE BODY pck_emp_Curdemo IS
  PROCEDURE GetList(cur_emp OUT t_cursor) IS
  BEGIN
  OPEN cur_emp FOR
  SELECT empno,ename,sal,deptno
  FROM emp;
  END;
END pck_emp_Curdemo;
/
```

In the above package, a separate user-defined datatype t_cursor (which is of type REF CURSOR) is declared as follows:

```
TYPE t_cursor IS REF CURSOR;
```

If you don't want to declare a special type for REF CURSOR, you can modify the above code as follows, which deals with SYS_REFCURSOR:

```
CREATE OR REPLACE PACKAGE pck_emp_Curdemo IS
  PROCEDURE GetList(cur_emp OUT SYS_REFCURSOR);
END pck_emp_Curdemo;
/

CREATE OR REPLACE PACKAGE BODY pck_emp_Curdemo IS
  PROCEDURE GetList(cur_emp OUT SYS_REFCURSOR) IS
  BEGIN
  OPEN cur_emp FOR
```

```
    SELECT empno,ename,sal,deptno
    FROM emp;
    END;
END pck_emp_Curdemo;
/
```

In any case, the procedure `GetList` simply returns the output of a `SELECT` statement executed by the `OPEN` statement of PL/SQL to the calling application using the output parameter `cur_emp`.

The following code displays all employees by pulling data from `REF CURSOR` using `OracleDataReader`:

```
Private Sub btnGetEmployees_Click(ByVal sender As
  System.Object, ByVal e As System.EventArgs) Handles
  btnGetEmployees.Click
    'create connection to db
    Dim cn As New OracleConnection("Data Source=xe; _
                      User Id=scott;Password=tiger")
    Try
      'create command object
      Dim cmd As New OracleCommand
      With cmd
        'specify that you are working with
        'stored procedure
        .CommandType = CommandType.StoredProcedure
        'provide the name of stored procedure
        .CommandText = "pck_emp_Curdemo.GetList"
        'provide parameter details
        .Parameters.Add("cur_emp",
                  OracleDbType.RefCursor,
                  ParameterDirection.Output)
        'proceed with execution
        .Connection = cn
        .Connection.Open()
        'get the DataReader object from command object
        Dim rdr As OracleDataReader =
      cmd.ExecuteReader(CommandBehavior.CloseConnection)
        'check if it has any rows
        If rdr.HasRows Then
          With Me.DataGridView1
            'remove existing rows from grid
            .Rows.Clear()
            'get the number of columns
            Dim ColumnCount As Integer = rdr.FieldCount
            'add grid header row
            For i As Integer = 0 To ColumnCount - 1
```

```
                    .Columns.Add(rdr.GetName(i),
                                    rdr.GetName(i))
            Next
            .AutoSizeColumnsMode =
            DataGridViewAutoSizeColumnsMode.ColumnHeader
            'loop through every row
            While rdr.Read
               'get all row values into an array
               Dim objCells(ColumnCount - 1) As Object
               rdr.GetValues(objCells)
               'add array as a row to grid
               .Rows.Add(objCells)
            End While
         End With
         Else
            'display message if no rows found
            MessageBox.Show("Not found")
            Me.DataGridView1.Rows.Clear()
         End If
         'clear up the resources
         rdr.Close()
         .Connection.Close()
         .Dispose()
         MessageBox.Show("Succesfully executed")
      End With
   Catch ex As Exception
      'display if any error occurs
      MessageBox.Show("Error: " & ex.Message)
      'close the connection if it is still open
      If cn.State = ConnectionState.Open Then
         cn.Close()
      End If
   End Try
End Sub
```

The only new statement from this code is the `OracleParameter` defined with the type `OracleDbType.RefCursor` (which is also defined as an `Output` parameter) as follows:

```
.Parameters.Add("cur_emp", OracleDbType.RefCursor,
                       ParameterDirection.Output)
```

This definition, at run time, would automatically hook up with the REF CURSOR being returned from the procedure `GetList` available as part of the PL/SQL Package. To receive information from the REF CURSOR, we used an `OracleDataReader` as follows:

```
Dim rdr As OracleDataReader = _
   cmd.ExecuteReader(CommandBehavior.CloseConnection)
```

Once the reader is ready, we filled up the grid with rows and columns.

Filling a Dataset from REF CURSOR

In the previous section, we used OracleDataReader to pull the information from REF CURSOR. In this section, we will use OracleDataAdapter to do the same and fill a DataSet. We will be still using the same PL/SQL package listed in the previous section.

The following code makes use of OracleDataAdapter to fill a DataSet by pulling the information out of REF CURSOR:

```
Private Sub btnGetEmployeesDS_Click(ByVal sender As
   System.Object, ByVal e As System.EventArgs) Handles
   btnGetEmployeesDS.Click
     Me.DataGridView1.Rows.Clear()
     'create connection to db
     Dim cn As New OracleConnection("Data Source=xe; _
                       User Id=scott;Password=tiger")
     Try
       'create command object
       Dim cmd As New OracleCommand
       With cmd
         'specify that you are working with
         'stored procedure
         .CommandType = CommandType.StoredProcedure
         'provide the name of stored procedure
         .CommandText = "pck_emp_Curdemo.GetList"
         'provide parameter details
         .Parameters.Add("cur_emp",
                   OracleDbType.RefCursor,
                   ParameterDirection.Output)
         'proceed with execution
         .Connection = cn
       End With
       Dim ds As New DataSet
       Dim da As New OracleDataAdapter(cmd)
       da.Fill(ds, "emp")
       da.Dispose()
       Me.DataGridView1.DataSource = ds.Tables("emp")
       MessageBox.Show("Succesfully executed")
     Catch ex As Exception
       'display if any error occurs
       MessageBox.Show("Error: " & ex.Message)
       'close the connection if it is still open
       If cn.State = ConnectionState.Open Then
```

```
            cn.Close()
        End If
    End Try
End Sub
```

Even in this program, there is nothing new again except that `OracleParameter` is defined of type `OracleDbType.RefCursor` as follows:

```
.CommandType = CommandType.StoredProcedure
.CommandText = "pck_emp_Curdemo.GetList"
.Parameters.Add("cur_emp", OracleDbType.RefCursor, ParameterDirection.
Output)
```

Once the parameters are set, the dataset is filled using the following set of statements:

```
Dim ds As New DataSet
Dim da As New OracleDataAdapter(cmd)
da.Fill(ds, "emp")
da.Dispose()
```

Finally, we display the information back to the user by showing the grid as follows:

```
Me.DataGridView1.DataSource = ds.Tables("emp")
MessageBox.Show("Succesfully executed")
```

Working with Multiple Active Result Sets (MARS)

Now that we have seen REF CURSOR and how to access it from .NET, it is time to work with multiple Ref Cursors simultaneously. A routine in a PL/SQL package can even return more than one REF CURSOR. Following is a sample PL/SQL package, which does this:

```
CREATE OR REPLACE PACKAGE pck_emp IS
   PROCEDURE get_all(p_emp OUT SYS_REFCURSOR,
                     p_dept OUT SYS_REFCURSOR);
END pck_emp;
/

CREATE OR REPLACE PACKAGE BODY pck_emp IS
   PROCEDURE get_all(p_emp OUT SYS_REFCURSOR,
                     p_dept OUT SYS_REFCURSOR) IS
   BEGIN
   OPEN p_emp FOR SELECT empno,ename,sal,deptno FROM emp;
   OPEN p_dept FOR SELECT deptno,dname,loc FROM dept;
   END;
END pck_emp;
/
```

From this PL/SQL package, you can observe that the `get_all` routine is returning two Ref Cursors back to the calling program or our .NET application. It is declared as follows:

```
PROCEDURE get_all(p_emp OUT SYS_REFCURSOR,
                        p_dept OUT SYS_REFCURSOR);
```

As two Ref Cursors are used, we need to work with two OPEN statements as follows:

```
OPEN p_emp FOR SELECT empno,ename,sal,deptno FROM emp;
OPEN p_dept FOR SELECT deptno,dname,loc FROM dept;
```

The following code reads both of those Ref Cursors using `OracleDataReader` and displays the result in two different grids:

```
Private Sub btnGetDataset_Click(ByVal sender As
    System.Object, ByVal e As System.EventArgs) Handles
    btnGetDataset.Click
    Me.DataGridView1.Rows.Clear()
    Me.DataGridView2.Rows.Clear()
    'create connection to db
    Dim cn As New OracleConnection("Data Source=xe; _
                        User Id=scott;Password=tiger")
    Try
      'create command object
      Dim cmd As New OracleCommand
      With cmd
        'specify that you are working with stored
        'procedure
        .CommandType = CommandType.StoredProcedure
        'provide the name of stored procedure
        .CommandText = "pck_emp.Get_All"
        'provide parameter details
        .Parameters.Add("p_emp", OracleDbType.RefCursor,
                            ParameterDirection.Output)
        .Parameters.Add("p_dept",OracleDbType.RefCursor,
                            ParameterDirection.Output)
        'proceed with execution
        .Connection = cn
        .Connection.Open()
        'execute the query
        .ExecuteNonQuery()
        'get the DataReader objects from
        'parameter objects
        Dim rdr_emp As OracleDataReader = _
            CType(.Parameters("p_emp").Value,
            Oracle.DataAccess.Types.OracleRefCursor)
            .GetDataReader
```

```vb
Dim rdr_dept As OracleDataReader = _
    CType(.Parameters("p_dept").Value,
    Oracle.DataAccess.Types.OracleRefCursor)
    .GetDataReader
'check if rdr_emp has any rows
If rdr_emp.HasRows Then
  With Me.DataGridView1
    'remove existing rows from grid
    .Rows.Clear()
    'get the number of columns
    Dim ColumnCount As Integer = _
                    rdr_emp.FieldCount
    'add grid header row
    For i As Integer = 0 To ColumnCount - 1
      .Columns.Add(rdr_emp.GetName(i),
                        rdr_emp.GetName(i))
    Next
    .AutoSizeColumnsMode =
    DataGridViewAutoSizeColumnsMode.ColumnHeader
    'loop through every row
    While rdr_emp.Read
      'get all row values into an array
      Dim objCells(ColumnCount - 1) As Object
      rdr_emp.GetValues(objCells)
      'add array as a row to grid
      .Rows.Add(objCells)
    End While
  End With
End If

'check if rdr_dept has any rows
If rdr_dept.HasRows Then
  With Me.DataGridView2
    'remove existing rows from grid
    .Rows.Clear()
    'get the number of columns
    Dim ColumnCount As Integer = _
                    rdr_dept.FieldCount
    'add grid header row
    For i As Integer = 0 To ColumnCount - 1
      .Columns.Add(rdr_dept.GetName(i),
                        rdr_emp.GetName(i))
    Next
    .AutoSizeColumnsMode =
    DataGridViewAutoSizeColumnsMode.ColumnHeader
    'loop through every row
    While rdr_dept.Read
```

```
                  'get all row values into an array
                  Dim objCells(ColumnCount - 1) As Object
                  rdr_dept.GetValues(objCells)
                  'add array as a row to grid
                  .Rows.Add(objCells)
               End While
            End With
         End If
         'clear up the resources
         rdr_emp.Close()
         'clear up the resources
         rdr_dept.Close()

         .Connection.Close()
         .Dispose()
         MessageBox.Show("Succesfully executed")
      End With

   Catch ex As Exception
      'display if any error occurs
      MessageBox.Show("Error: " & ex.Message)
      'close the connection if it is still open
      If cn.State = ConnectionState.Open Then
         cn.Close()
      End If
   End Try
End Sub
```

From the highlighted code, you can observe that two `OracleParameter` objects (which are of type `REF CURSOR`) are defined. They are as follows:

```
.Parameters.Add("p_emp", OracleDbType.RefCursor,
                     ParameterDirection.Output)
.Parameters.Add("p_dept", OracleDbType.RefCursor,
                     ParameterDirection.Output)
```

After that, we executed the routine in the PL/SQL package with `ExecuteNonQuery`. This is very important to note. We are not using `ExecuteReader` anymore, when dealing with multiple result sets. Instead, we are using the `GetDataReader` method of `OracleRefCursor` (which creates `OracleDataReader` objects) to pull information from the output parameters. The first statement that uses it is as follows:

```
Dim rdr_emp As OracleDataReader = _
   CType(.Parameters("p_emp").Value, _
   Oracle.DataAccess.Types.OracleRefCursor).GetDataReader
```

This returns the result set of of the first REF CURSOR in the form of an OracleDataReader. Immediately after that, we used another similar statement to retrieve the next result set as follows:

```
Dim rdr_dept As OracleDataReader = _
    CType(.Parameters("p_dept").Value, _
    Oracle.DataAccess.Types.OracleRefCursor).GetDataReader
```

Once both the readers were ready, we filled up the grids and finally closed the readers using the following statements:

```
rdr_emp.Close()
rdr_dept.Close()
```

Summary

In this chapter, we mainly concentrated on working with PL/SQL blocks, stored procedures, PL/SQL packages, PL/SQL tables, and Ref Cursors. While dealing with stored procedures, we also covered passing and retrieving parameter values with different types of parameters (IN, OUT, IN OUT). We have also seen techniques for sending arrays to and receiving arrays from Oracle database using packages and finally concluded with working on Multiple Active Result Sets (MARS).

6
Dealing with Large Objects (LOBs)

Oracle database offers the capability of storing and retrieving images, music, video, and any other binary information in the form of large objects. The large objects are typically of type BFILE, BLOB, and CLOB (or NCLOB).

BFILE is generally used when you have files residing in the file system of the Oracle database server, outside the database. A BFILE value is simply a pointer to an existing file in the host operating system and does not store the file itself within the database. However, BLOB (Binary Large Object) gives the capability to store the binary file or binary information typically of huge size directly within the database without having any relation with the file system of Oracle server. CLOB (Character Large Object) is very similar to BLOB, except that it is optimized to store huge text information efficiently. And finally, NCLOB is very similar to CLOB and enhanced towards storing multi-byte national character set (synonymous with UNICODE).

In simple words, BFILE data is stored externally on the database server and BLOB, CLOB, and NCLOB data is stored internally within the database. Now, we shall examine how ODP.NET handles each of these objects.

Working with BFILEs

As explained previously, BFILE-related files are always stored external to the database. Within the database, we only store the pointers of those files, without affecting the database size. As the files always stay outside the database, they are always automatically made read-only for security purposes. Before working with BFILE type, we need to set up the environment to deal with sample BFILE data.

Setting Up the Environment to Work with BFILEs

The first step to prepare for the sample data is to create a folder named `EmpPhotos` on your favorite drive (in my case, it is `C:\EmpPhotos`). Make sure that you create that at the Oracle database server (or a drive accessible at the database server) and not at our application/client system.

Once you have created the folder (which maintains BFILE related files), copy a few image files manually into that folder (in my case, I copied `WinVista.jpg` and `Win2003.jpg` into that folder).

Now, you need to create a logical directory object within Oracle database, which points to the folder you created above. You need to have special privileges to create or administer directory objects in Oracle. If you have access to `system` user, you can proceed as follows; else you need to contact your DBA to help you:

```
sql>CONNECT system/manager;
sql>GRANT CREATE ANY DIRECTORY TO scott;
sql>GRANT DROP ANY DIRECTORY TO scott;
sql>CONNECT scott/tiger;
sql>CREATE OR REPLACE DIRECTORY EMPPHOTOSDIR
                    AS 'c:\EmpPhotos';
```

The highlighted code above creates a logical directory object pointing to your required folder.

Now, create a table that can hold the pointers to the BFILEs as follows:

```
sql>CREATE TABLE EmpPhotos
   (
      empno NUMBER(4) PRIMARY KEY,
      photo BFILE
   );
```

The above table simply holds employee numbers and pointers to the files existing at the server.

Following is the sample form designed to work with the BFILE demonstration:

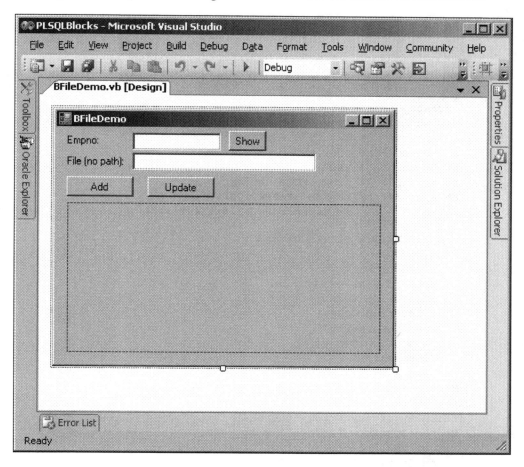

Adding a New Row Containing BFILE

To work with BFILEs, you need not learn anything new. It is just the same INSERT or UPDATE statement you will use, while inserting or updating rows containing BFILE information.

The following code adds an entry into the table created according to our BFILE setup:

```
Private Sub btnAdd_Click(ByVal sender As System.Object, _
    ByVal e As System.EventArgs) Handles btnAdd.Click
    'create connection to db
    Dim cn As New OracleConnection("Data Source=xe; _
                      User Id=scott;Password=tiger")
    Try
        'create command object
        Dim sb As New System.Text.StringBuilder
        sb.Append(" INSERT INTO EmpPhotos")
        sb.Append(" (empno, photo)")
        sb.Append(" VALUES")
        sb.Append(" (" & Me.txtEmpno.Text & ", ")
        sb.Append(" BFILENAME('EMPPHOTOSDIR', '" &
                      Me.txtPhotoPath.Text & "'))")

        Dim cmd As New OracleCommand
        With cmd
            .CommandText = sb.ToString
            'proceed with execution
            .Connection = cn
            .Connection.Open()
            .ExecuteNonQuery()
            .Connection.Close()
            .Dispose()
        End With
        MessageBox.Show("Succesfully Uploaded")
    Catch ex As Exception
        'display if any error occurs
        MessageBox.Show("Error: " & ex.Message)
        'close the connection if it is still open
        If cn.State = ConnectionState.Open Then
            cn.Close()
        End If
    End Try
End Sub
```

From the above highlighted code, you can observe that an Oracle built-in function BFILENAME is used. It simply accepts the logical Oracle directory name and the file name; the rest is automatically taken care of by Oracle!

 While executing the application, you must only provide the file name without any path of the file at the database server (it is identified by the logical directory object).

If everything gets executed fine, you should get output similar to the following:

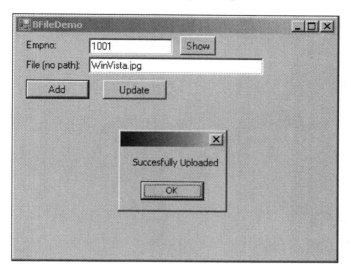

Updating an Existing BFILE Row

The code for updating an existing BFILE is very similar to that for inserting except that we need to replace the INSERT statement with an appropriate UPDATE statement.

The following code updates an existing entry in the table containing BFILE information.

```
Private Sub btnUpdate_Click(ByVal sender As
   System.Object, ByVal e As System.EventArgs) Handles
   btnUpdate.Click
     'create connection to db
     Dim cn As New OracleConnection("Data Source=xe; _
                   User Id=scott;Password=tiger")
     Try
       'create command object
       Dim sb As New System.Text.StringBuilder
       sb.Append(" UPDATE EmpPhotos SET")
       sb.Append("    photo=")
       sb.Append("    BFILENAME('EMPPHOTOSDIR', '" &
                   Me.txtPhotoPath.Text & "')")
       sb.Append(" WHERE empno=" & Me.txtEmpno.Text)

       Dim cmd As New OracleCommand
       With cmd
         .CommandText = sb.ToString
         'proceed with execution
```

```
        .Connection = cn
        .Connection.Open()
        .ExecuteNonQuery()
        .Connection.Close()
        .Dispose()
      End With
      MessageBox.Show("Succesfully Uploaded")
    Catch ex As Exception
      'display if any error occurs
      MessageBox.Show("Error: " & ex.Message)
      'close the connection if it is still open
      If cn.State = ConnectionState.Open Then
        cn.Close()
      End If
    End Try
  End Sub
```

You can observe from the highlighted code that we replaced the entire INSERT statement with an UPDATE statement.

Retrieving BFILE Information from a Database

Now that we have seen how to update BFILE information to the database, it is time to retrieve BFILE information from the table. When we try to retrieve BFILE information from the database, it doesn't retrieve a pointer or link to that file. Instead, it directly returns you the file (using the BFILE pointer) stored in the file system of Oracle database server!

The following code retrieves the BFILE information from the database:

```
Private Sub btnShow_Click(ByVal sender As System.Object, _
    ByVal e As System.EventArgs) Handles btnShow.Click
    'create connection to db
    Dim cn As New OracleConnection("Data Source=xe; _
                    User Id=scott;Password=tiger")
    Try
      'create command object
      Dim sb As New System.Text.StringBuilder
      sb.Append(" SELECT photo FROM EmpPhotos")
      sb.Append(" WHERE empno = " & Me.txtEmpno.Text)

      Dim cmd As New OracleCommand(sb.ToString, cn)
      With cmd
        .Connection.Open()
        Dim rdr As OracleDataReader = .ExecuteReader
        If rdr.Read Then
          Me.PictureBox1.Image =
```

```
            Image.FromStream(New IO.MemoryStream
            (rdr.GetOracleBFile(rdr.GetOrdinal
            ("photo")).Value))
        End If
        .Connection.Close()
        .Dispose()
    End With
Catch ex As Exception
    'display if any error occurs
    MessageBox.Show("Error: " & ex.Message)
    'close the connection if it is still open
    If cn.State = ConnectionState.Open Then
        cn.Close()
    End If
End Try
End Sub
```

In the above code, `OracleDataReader` is used for convenience. You can also use `OracleDataAdapter` and populate the same into data tables or data sets. The most important method is `GetOracleBFile`. It is the method that returns the BFILE information back to the application. As we would like to transform that file into an image, we are temporarily reading the whole BFILE information into a temporary `MemoryStream` and later we get it displayed on the form using the `static` method `Image.FromStream`.

You should receive output similar to the following if everything gets successfully executed:

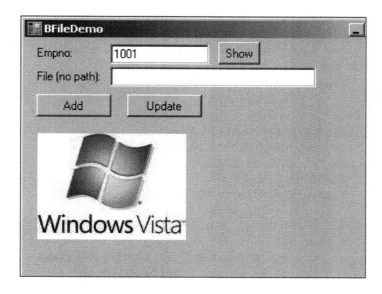

Retrieving Properties of a BFILE

You can even retrieve some extra information about a BFILE, when you are using `OracleBFile`. You can retrieve and test for certain properties like whether the file exists at the server, whether it is readable, filename, size, etc.

The following code retrieves the BFILE along with extra information from the database:

```
Private Sub btnShowPhoto_Click(ByVal sender As
   System.Object, ByVal e As System.EventArgs) Handles
   btnShowPhoto.Click
     'create connection to db
     Dim cn As New OracleConnection("Data Source=xe; _
                       User Id=scott;Password=tiger")
     Try
       'create command object
       Dim sb As New System.Text.StringBuilder
       sb.Append(" SELECT photo FROM EmpPhotos")
       sb.Append(" WHERE empno = " & Me.txtEmpno.Text)

       Dim cmd As New OracleCommand(sb.ToString, cn)
       With cmd
         .Connection.Open()
         Dim rdr As OracleDataReader = .ExecuteReader
         If Not rdr.Read Then
           MessageBox.Show("No employee exists")
         Else
           Dim bfile As _
             Oracle.DataAccess.Types.OracleBFile =
             rdr.GetOracleBFile(rdr.GetOrdinal("photo"))
           If Not bfile.FileExists Then
           MessageBox.Show("Photo File does not exist
                                        at server")
         Else
           If Not bfile.CanRead Then
             MessageBox.Show("You do not have
                      permission to view the photo")
           Else
             If bfile.IsEmpty Or bfile.IsNull Then
               MessageBox.Show("Photo not assigned
                                to the employee")
             Else
               Dim dir As String = bfile.DirectoryName
               Dim fn As String = bfile.FileName
```

```
            Dim size As Long = bfile.Length
            Me.PictureBox1.Image =
            Image.FromStream(New IO.MemoryStream
                                (bfile.Value))
            Dim bfiledetails As New _
                      System.Text.StringBuilder
            bfiledetails.Append("Directory:" & dir
                        & ControlChars.NewLine)
            bfiledetails.Append("File Name:" & fn
                        & ControlChars.NewLine)
            bfiledetails.Append("Size:" & size
                        & ControlChars.NewLine)
            MessageBox.Show(bfiledetails.ToString)
          End If 'is null or is empty
        End If 'can read
      End If 'is file exists
    End If 'rdr
    .Connection.Close()
    rdr.Dispose()
    .Dispose()

  End With
  Catch ex As Exception
    'display if any error occurs
    MessageBox.Show("Error: " & ex.Message)
    'close the connection if it is still open
    If cn.State = ConnectionState.Open Then
      cn.Close()
    End If
  End Try
End Sub
```

The highlighted code shows you how to retrieve several properties of a BFILE object. The following table summarizes the properties used in this code:

Property	Description
FileExists	Indicates whether or not the file exists at the server
CanRead	Indicates whether or not the file can be read
IsEmpty, IsNull	Indicates whether the file is empty or not
DirectoryName	Gives the directory (folder) name of the file
FileName	The name of the file
Length	The size of the file in bytes

Working with CLOBs

CLOB (Character Large Object) gives us the capability to store huge character information (or huge strings) directly within the database without having any relation with the file system at Oracle server.

 Before trying to design databases with CLOB functionality, you may have to consider the issues of storage and performance.

Inserting Huge Text Information into Oracle Database

As CLOBs get stored internally within the Oracle database, we need not create any directories or work with file systems any more. To demonstrate the functionality of CLOBs, a table is planned as follows:

```
CREATE TABLE EmpRemarks
(
 empno NUMBER(4) PRIMARY KEY,
 remarks CLOB
)
```

You can observe from the above highlighted line that a column remarks of type CLOB is created. Here is the code that stores huge text into that CLOB column:

```
Private Sub btnAdd_Click(ByVal sender As System.Object,
ByVal e As System.EventArgs) Handles btnAdd.Click
    'create connection to db
    Dim cn As New OracleConnection("Data Source=xe; _
                      User Id=scott;Password=tiger")
    Try
       'create command object
       Dim sb As New System.Text.StringBuilder
       sb.Append(" INSERT INTO EmpRemarks")
       sb.Append(" (empno, remarks)")
       sb.Append(" VALUES")
       sb.Append(" (:1,:2)")

       Dim cmd As New OracleCommand
       With cmd
         .CommandText = sb.ToString
         'define parameters
         Dim p_empno As New OracleParameter(":1", _
                             OracleDbType.Int16)
```

```
        p_empno.Value = Me.txtEmpno.Text
        Dim p_remarks As New OracleParameter(":2", _
                                OracleDbType.Clob)
        p_remarks.Size = Me.txtRemarks.Text.Length
        p_remarks.Value = Me.txtRemarks.Text
        .Parameters.Add(p_empno)
        .Parameters.Add(p_remarks)
        'proceed with execution
        .Connection = cn
        .Connection.Open()
        .ExecuteNonQuery()
        .Connection.Close()
      End With
      MessageBox.Show("Succesfully added")
    Catch ex As Exception
      'display if any error occurs
      MessageBox.Show("Error: " & ex.Message)
      'close the connection if it is still open
      If cn.State = ConnectionState.Open Then
        cn.Close()
      End If
    End Try
  End Sub
```

The highlighted section creates an OracleParameter which is of the type
OracleDbType.Clob as shown. Once the parameter is defined, we specify the size of
text being inserted and assign the text directly. Following is the sample screen for the
above code:

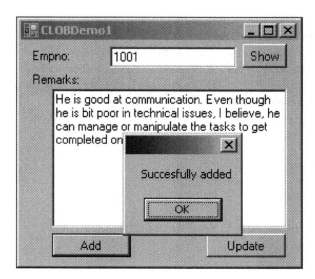

Updating CLOB Information Using OracleClob

Updating CLOB information is very similar to inserting it. However, I would like to introduce the OracleClob class to deal with CLOB. You can make use of this class for both inserting and updating CLOBs.

The following code uses the OracleClob class to update a row having a CLOB column:

```
Private Sub btnUpdate_Click(ByVal sender As
   System.Object, ByVal e As System.EventArgs) Handles
   btnUpdate.Click
      'create connection to db
      Dim cn As New OracleConnection("Data Source=xe; _
                       User Id=scott;Password=tiger")
      Try
         'create command object
         Dim sb As New System.Text.StringBuilder
         sb.Append(" UPDATE EmpRemarks SET")
         sb.Append(" remarks = :1")
         sb.Append(" WHERE empno = :2")

         Dim cmd As New OracleCommand
         With cmd
            .CommandText = sb.ToString
            'open the connection first
            .Connection = cn
            .Connection.Open()
            'define parameters
            Dim objClob As New _
            Oracle.DataAccess.Types.OracleClob(cn)
            objClob.Write(Me.txtRemarks.Text.ToCharArray,
                       0, Me.txtRemarks.Text.Length)
            .Parameters.Add(New OracleParameter(":1",
                                            objClob))
            .Parameters.Add(New OracleParameter(":2",
                                      Me.txtEmpno.Text))
            'proceed with execution
            .ExecuteNonQuery()
            .Connection.Close()
         End With
         MessageBox.Show("Succesfully updated")
      Catch ex As Exception
```

```
            'display if any error occurs
            MessageBox.Show("Error: " & ex.Message)
            'close the connection if it is still open
            If cn.State = ConnectionState.Open Then
               cn.Close()
            End If
         End Try
      End Sub
```

Let us go step by step.

```
   Dim objClob As New Oracle.DataAccess.Types.OracleClob(cn)
```

The above statement declares an `objClob` object of the type `OracleClob` (available in `Oracle.DataAccess.Types`).

```
   objClob.Write(Me.txtRemarks.Text.ToCharArray, 0,
                       Me.txtRemarks.Text.Length)
```

Using the `Write` method of `OracleClob`, the above statement dumps the entire information of text into the CLOB object (`objClob`).

```
   .Parameters.Add(New OracleParameter(":1", objClob))
```

Once the CLOB is filled with information, the above statement adds it as a parameter to the `OracleCommand`.

Retrieving CLOB Information from Oracle Database

Now that we understand how to insert or update CLOB information in a database, it is time to retrieve CLOB information from the table. The following code retrieves the CLOB information (huge text) from Oracle database:

```
Private Sub btnShow_Click(ByVal sender As System.Object,
   ByVal e As System.EventArgs) Handles btnShow.Click
      Me.txtRemarks.Text = ""
      'create connection to db
      Dim cn As New OracleConnection("Data Source=xe; _
                       User Id=scott;Password=tiger")
      Try
         'create command object
         Dim sb As New System.Text.StringBuilder
         sb.Append(" SELECT remarks FROM EmpRemarks")
```

```
            sb.Append(" WHERE empno = " & Me.txtEmpno.Text)

            Dim cmd As New OracleCommand(sb.ToString, cn)
            With cmd
                .Connection.Open()
                Dim rdr As OracleDataReader = .ExecuteReader
                If rdr.Read Then
                    Me.txtRemarks.Text =
                            rdr.GetOracleClob(rdr.GetOrdinal
                                        ("remarks")).Value

                End If
                .Connection.Close()
            End With
        Catch ex As Exception
            'display if any error occurs
            MessageBox.Show("Error: " & ex.Message)
            'close the connection if it is still open
            If cn.State = ConnectionState.Open Then
                cn.Close()
            End If
        End Try
    End Sub
```

In the above code, `OracleDataReader` is used for convenience. You can also use `OracleDataAdapter` and populate the same into data tables or data sets. The most important method from the highlighted code above is `GetOracleCLOB`. It is the method that returns the CLOB information back to the application.

Reading a Text File and Uploading as CLOB

Now, let us read a text file and upload that information as CLOB into Oracle database. Before going for the code, let us have a look at the screen design:

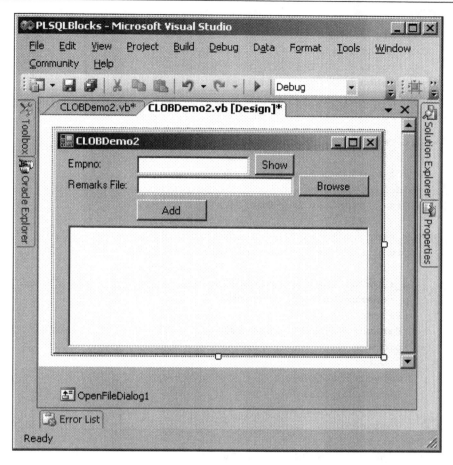

The following code uploads a text file into a CLOB column in a table:

```vb
Private Sub btnAdd_Click(ByVal sender As System.Object, _
  ByVal e As System.EventArgs) Handles btnAdd.Click

    If Me.txtRemarksFileName.Text.Trim.Length = 0 Then
      MessageBox.Show("No file chosen")
      Exit Sub
    End If

    'reading  the file
    Dim contents As String = _
    File.ReadAllText(Me.txtRemarksFileName.Text)
    'create connection to db
    Dim cn As New OracleConnection("Data Source=xe; _
                    User Id=scott;Password=tiger")
```

```vbnet
    Try
        'create command object
        Dim sb As New System.Text.StringBuilder
        sb.Append(" INSERT INTO EmpRemarks")
        sb.Append(" (empno, remarks)")
        sb.Append(" VALUES")
        sb.Append(" (:1, :2)")

        Dim cmd As New OracleCommand
        With cmd
            .CommandText = sb.ToString
            'define parameters
            Dim p_empno As New OracleParameter(":1",
                            OracleDbType.Int16)
            p_empno.Value = Me.txtEmpno.Text
            Dim p_remarks As New OracleParameter(":2",
                            OracleDbType.Clob)
            p_remarks.Size = contents.Length
            p_remarks.Value = contents
            .Parameters.Add(p_empno)
            .Parameters.Add(p_remarks)
            'proceed with execution
            .Connection = cn
            .Connection.Open()
            .ExecuteNonQuery()
            .Connection.Close()
            .Dispose()
        End With
        MessageBox.Show("Succesfully added")
    Catch ex As Exception
        'display if any error occurs
        MessageBox.Show("Error: " & ex.Message)
        'close the connection if it is still open
        If cn.State = ConnectionState.Open Then
            cn.Close()
        End If
    End Try
End Sub
```

Let us go step by step:

```vbnet
Dim contents As String = _
    File.ReadAllText(Me.txtRemarksFileName.Text)
```

This statement reads the entire information available in a file using `File.ReadAllText` and assigns it as a string to the variable `contents`.

```
sb.Append(" INSERT INTO EmpRemarks")
sb.Append(" (empno, remarks)")
sb.Append(" VALUES")
sb.Append(" (:1,:2)")
```

The above `INSERT` statement tries to insert a row that includes CLOB information. You can observe that we are using two bind variables for providing the values. The first is simply an employee number. The second is the CLOB, which is specified as follows:

```
Dim p_remarks As New OracleParameter(":2",
                        OracleDbType.Clob)
p_remarks.Size = contents.Length
p_remarks.Value = contents
```

The above parameter makes use of the `contents` variable, which contains the entire file content (which is read previously). The rest is the same as provided in previous sections.

How about NCLOB?

To deal with NCLOB, just replace `OracleDbType.Clob` with `OracleDbType.NClob` or work directly with `OracleNClob`.

Working with BLOBs

BLOB (Binary Large Object) gives us the capability to store binary files or binary information typically of huge size directly within the database (without having any relation with file system at the Oracle server).

Before trying to design databases with BLOB functionality, you may have to consider the issues of storage and performance.

Setting Up the Environment to Work with BLOBs

As BLOBs get stored internally within the Oracle database, we need not create any directories or work with file systems. To demonstrate the functionality of BLOBs, we plan to use two tables. The first table is mainly to store images directly within the database. It is defined as follows:

```
CREATE TABLE EmpImages
(
    empno NUMBER(4) PRIMARY KEY,
    image BLOB
)
```

The second table is mainly to store other binary information (in this case, we would like to store the resume of each employee in the form of a Microsoft Word document). It is defined as follows:

```
CREATE TABLE EmpDocs
(
    empno NUMBER(4) PRIMARY KEY,
    doc BLOB
)
```

In the highlighted code (from both CREATE statements), we define two columns with data type BLOB.

 From the point of view of the Oracle database, it doesn't know the difference between an image or a document or a music file. All it knows is simply a binary file.

The following is an illustration of a sample form designed to work with
BLOB images:

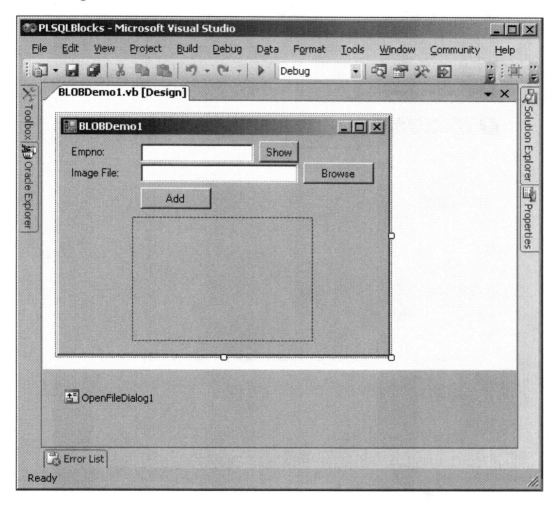

The following is an illustration of a sample form designed to work with
BLOB documents:

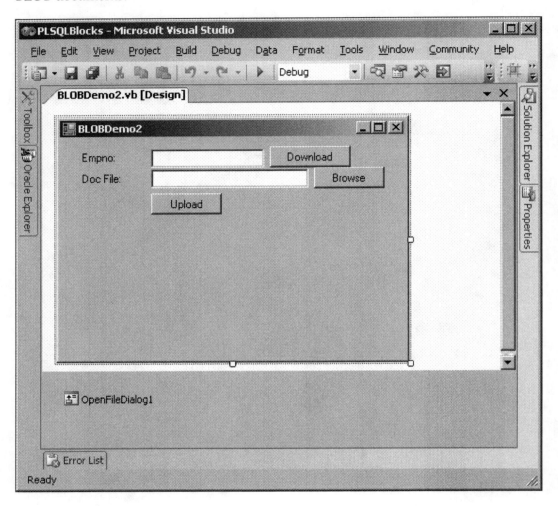

Uploading Images to Oracle Database Using BLOB

It is very simple to upload BLOB information into Oracle database. All we need to do
is read the entire file (in the form of bytes) and use OracleParameter together with
OracleCommand to upload it.

The following code uploads an image into the `EmpImages` table:

```
Private Sub btnAdd_Click(ByVal sender As System.Object,
ByVal e As System.EventArgs) Handles btnAdd.Click
  If Me.txtImageFile.Text.Trim.Length = 0 Then
    MessageBox.Show("No file chosen")
    Exit Sub
  End If

  'Now, read the entire file into a string
  Dim contents() As Byte = _
          File.ReadAllBytes(Me.txtImageFile.Text)

  'create connection to db
  Dim cn As New OracleConnection("Data Source=xe; _
                    User Id=scott;Password=tiger")
  Try
    'create command object
    Dim sb As New System.Text.StringBuilder
    sb.Append(" INSERT INTO EmpImages")
    sb.Append(" (empno, image)")
    sb.Append(" VALUES")
    sb.Append(" (:1,:2)")

    Dim cmd As New OracleCommand
    With cmd
      .CommandText = sb.ToString
      'define parameters
      Dim p_empno As New OracleParameter(":1",_
                      OracleDbType.Int16)
      p_empno.Value = Me.txtEmpno.Text
      Dim p_img As New OracleParameter(":2", _
                      OracleDbType.Blob)
      p_img.Size = contents.Length
      p_img.Value = contents
      .Parameters.Add(p_empno)
      .Parameters.Add(p_img)
      'proceed with execution
      .Connection = cn
      .Connection.Open()
      .ExecuteNonQuery()
      .Connection.Close()
      .Dispose()
    End With
```

```
      MessageBox.Show("Succesfully added")
    Catch ex As Exception
      'display if any error occurs
      MessageBox.Show("Error: " & ex.Message)
      'close the connection if it is still open
      If cn.State = ConnectionState.Open Then
        cn.Close()
      End If
    End Try
  End Sub
```

Using the `ReadAllBytes()` method is the fastest way to read the entire information from a file in the form of bytes. Once the file is read in the form of bytes, we need to set up an `OracleParameter` of the type `OracleDbType.Blob` and provide other properties as follows:

```
Dim p_img As New OracleParameter(":2", OracleDbType.Blob)
p_img.Size = contents.Length
p_img.Value = contents
```

Finally, the BLOB parameter must be added to the `OracleCommand` object. Once you execute it, a message box confirming that the file has been successfully added will be displayed.

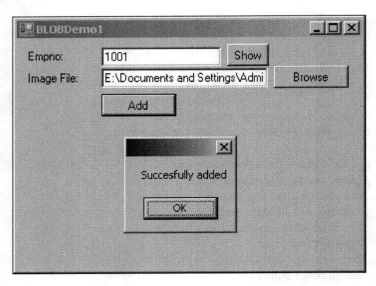

Retrieving Images from Oracle Database Using BLOB

Now that we have seen how to insert BLOB information in to the database, it is time to retrieve BLOB information from the table. The following code retrieves BLOB information (images) from Oracle database:

```
Private Sub btnShow_Click(ByVal sender As System.Object, _
   ByVal e As System.EventArgs) Handles btnShow.Click
     'create connection to db
     Dim cn As New OracleConnection("Data Source=xe; _
                User Id=scott;Password=tiger")
     Try
       'create command object
       Dim sb As New System.Text.StringBuilder
       sb.Append(" SELECT image FROM EmpImages")
       sb.Append(" WHERE empno = " & Me.txtEmpno.Text)

       Dim cmd As New OracleCommand(sb.ToString, cn)
       With cmd
         .Connection.Open()
         Dim rdr As OracleDataReader = .ExecuteReader
         If rdr.Read Then
           Me.PictureBox1.Image = Image.FromStream
                (New MemoryStream(rdr.GetOracleBlob
                  (rdr.GetOrdinal("image")).Value))
         End If
         .Connection.Close()
         .Dispose()
       End With
     Catch ex As Exception
       'display if any error occurs
       MessageBox.Show("Error: " & ex.Message)
       'close the connection if it is still open
       If cn.State = ConnectionState.Open Then
         cn.Close()
       End If
     End Try
End Sub
```

Earlier, we used GetOracleCLOB to work with CLOBs. In the above highlighted code, we are using GetOracleBLOB, which returns the BLOB information back to the application. As we need to transform that file as an image, we begin by reading the whole BLOB information into a temporary MemoryStream and later we get it displayed on the form using the static method Image.FromStream.

You should receive output similar to the following if everything gets successfully executed:

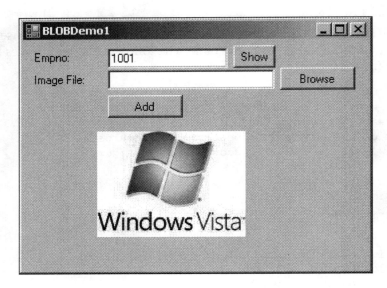

Uploading Documents to and Retrieving Documents from Oracle Database

Until now, we have worked with images. Now, we shall concentrate on inserting documents into and retrieving documents from Oracle database.

Even though the coding in this section is mainly concentrated on Microsoft Word Documents, it works fine for any other binary files like Excel documents, music files (MP3, Wav, etc.), video files (AVI, RM, etc.) by changing the filename and extension.

The following code uploads a Microsoft Word document into the Oracle database (it is very similar to the code provided in previous sections):

```
Private Sub btnUpload_Click(ByVal sender As
  System.Object, ByVal e As System.EventArgs) Handles
  btnUpload.Click
    If Me.txtDocFile.Text.Trim.Length = 0 Then
      MessageBox.Show("No file chosen")
      Exit Sub
    End If

    'Now, read the entire file into a string
```

```vb
    Dim contents() As Byte = _
            File.ReadAllBytes(Me.txtDocFile.Text)

  'create connection to db
  Dim cn As New OracleConnection("Data Source=xe; _
                    User Id=scott;Password=tiger")
  Try
    'create command object
    Dim sb As New System.Text.StringBuilder
    sb.Append(" INSERT INTO EmpDocs")
    sb.Append(" (empno, doc)")
    sb.Append(" VALUES")
    sb.Append(" (:1,:2)")

    Dim cmd As New OracleCommand
    With cmd
      .CommandText = sb.ToString
      'define parameters
      Dim p_empno As New OracleParameter(":1", _
                          OracleDbType.Int16)
      p_empno.Value = Me.txtEmpno.Text
      Dim p_doc As New OracleParameter(":2", _
                          OracleDbType.Blob)
      p_doc.Size = contents.Length
      p_doc.Value = contents
      .Parameters.Add(p_empno)
      .Parameters.Add(p_doc)
      'proceed with execution
      .Connection = cn
      .Connection.Open()
      .ExecuteNonQuery()
      .Connection.Close()
      .Dispose()
    End With
    MessageBox.Show("File Succesfully uploaded")
  Catch ex As Exception
    'display if any error occurs
    MessageBox.Show("Error: " & ex.Message)
    'close the connection if it is still open
    If cn.State = ConnectionState.Open Then
      cn.Close()
    End If
  End Try
End Sub
```

The following statement reads an entire file in the form of bytes:

```
Dim contents() As Byte = _
        File.ReadAllBytes(Me.txtDocFile.Text)
```

Once the file is read, we need to create an `OracleParameter` and assign those bytes to it as follows:

```
Dim p_doc As New OracleParameter(":2", OracleDbType.Blob)
p_doc.Size = contents.Length
p_doc.Value = contents
```

Finally, add the `OracleParameter` to `OracleCommand` using the following statement:

```
.Parameters.Add(p_doc)
```

Now that we have seen how to upload a Microsoft Word document, we need to focus on retrieving a Microsoft Word document already uploaded.

The following code retrieves a Word document or binary information stored in the Oracle database:

```
Private Sub btnDownload_Click(ByVal sender As
   System.Object, ByVal e As System.EventArgs) Handles
   btnDownload.Click
    'create connection to db
    Dim cn As New OracleConnection("Data Source=xe; _
                    User Id=scott;Password=tiger")
    Try
      'create command object
      Dim sb As New System.Text.StringBuilder
      sb.Append(" SELECT doc FROM EmpDocs")
      sb.Append(" WHERE empno = " & Me.txtEmpno.Text)

      Dim cmd As New OracleCommand(sb.ToString, cn)
      With cmd
        .Connection.Open()
        Dim rdr As OracleDataReader = .ExecuteReader
        Dim buf() As Byte
        If rdr.Read Then
          buf =
          rdr.GetOracleBlob(rdr.GetOrdinal("doc")).Value
          Dim DesktopPath As String = _
                  Environment.GetFolderPath
                  (Environment.SpecialFolder.Desktop)
```

```
                File.WriteAllBytes(DesktopPath & "\temp.doc",
                                                          buf)
          End If
          .Connection.Close()
          .Dispose()
          MessageBox.Show("File Succesfully downloaded
                                           to desktop")
        End With
      Catch ex As Exception
        'display if any error occurs
        MessageBox.Show("Error: " & ex.Message)
        'close the connection if it is still open
        If cn.State = ConnectionState.Open Then
          cn.Close()
        End If
      End Try
    End Sub
```

From the highlighted code, you can observe that a byte array is declared to hold the entire binary information being retrieved from database. Further on, we have the following statement:

```
buf = rdr.GetOracleBlob(rdr.GetOrdinal("doc")).Value
```

Just as in the previous section, the GetOracleBlob method is used to retrieve binary information (in this case, it is going to be a Microsoft Word document) from the database and assign it to a byte array. To retrieve the path of the local desktop (to which to save the file) into the variable DesktopPath, we can use the Environment object as follows:

```
Dim DesktopPath As String = _
                Environment.GetFolderPath
                (Environment.SpecialFolder.Desktop)
```

Once the path is available, we simply copy all the bytes into a new file named temp. doc on the desktop using the following statement:

```
File.WriteAllBytes(DesktopPath & "\temp.doc", buf)
```

Once the download is complete, we should be able to see a confirmation message as shown below.

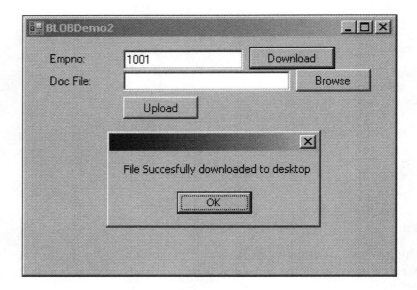

Summary

In this chapter, we concentrated on working with BFILE, CLOB, and BLOB using ODP.NET. Using different types of LOBs (Large Objects) in Oracle, we have seen how to upload and download images, documents, and textual information to and from Oracle database server.

7
XML and XML DB Development with ODP.NET

XML (eXtensible Markup Language) is a standard for representing structured data in a readable text format. The data in XML is surrounded with user-defined open and close tags (similar to those of HTML). The beauty of XML is that it can be used for information exchange by any number of applications, irrespective of any platform.

XML is very useful when the data is semi-structured. That is, it has a regular structure, but that structure varies enough that mapping it to a relational database results in either a large number of columns with null values or a large number of tables. This makes the database design inefficient. To face the challenges of storing semi-structured data (XML), database vendors started supporting XML as part of the database itself.

Any database used for managing XML must be able to contain XML documents within the same database. Oracle database offers the capability of storing XML data natively. Apart from simply storing XML, we can also benefit from other features like indexing, parsing, navigating, searching (querying) XML data using other XML technologies like XPath, XQuery, etc. All these features are available as a part of Oracle XML DB, an add-on feature of Oracle database.

Oracle XML DB is a new feature of Oracle database 9i and 10g that provides high-performance, native XML storage and retrieval technology together with full support for XML Schema, which defines the structure of an XML document.

 Oracle XML DB is not included as part of Oracle 10g Express Edition (Oracle 10g XE) installation.

A Fast Track on XML with Oracle

Before directly jumping into ODP.NET and trying to access XML data, let us have a fast-track introduction (only for dummies) to XML in Oracle and how to work with it. If you are already familiar with XML in Oracle, you can skip this section.

Let us start with generating an XML document based on a SELECT statement. The following command automatically generates an XML document based on the output of the internal SELECT statement:

```
SELECT
DBMS_XMLGEN.GETXML('SELECT empno, ename, sal,
                              deptno FROM emp')
FROM DUAL;
```

You can observe that we are simply generating an XML document and not really storing or retrieving native XML data.

To store and retrieve native XML data, we need to create a table with a column of type XMLType; XMLType is a special data type (object type) in Oracle, which is mainly optimized to work with XML data. It gives more flexibility (towards searching, modifying, validating, etc.) to work with XML data compared to a VARCHAR2 field.

 To understand completely about XMLType, you should have some basic knowledge on Object Types (or Object Oriented topics) available in Oracle, which is beyond the scope this book.

The following demonstration table will be used through out this chapter:

```
CREATE TABLE Employee
(
empno VARCHAR2(10) PRIMARY KEY,
ename VARCHAR2(20),
Address XMLType
);
```

The highlighted column (Address) declared is of type XMLType, which can be used to store native XML information. It is important to understand that XMLType is an *object type*. Unlike standard data types, to work with object types in Oracle, we need to create an object by using the constructor (which will have the same name as the type name) of that object type. Let us go through an example first.

The following INSERT command can add a row to the table created above:

```
INSERT INTO Employee VALUES
(
'1001',
```

```
'Jag',
XMLType('
        <Address>
            <Street>13-20-26, Nallam vari thota</Street>
            <City>Bhimavaram</City>
            <Zip>534201</Zip>
            <State>AP</State>
        </Address>')
        );
```

You can observe a new keyword XMLType, which is nothing but the constructor of object type XMLType. It is mainly used to convert raw information to native XML and natively store XML information into the table. To retrieve the rows from the table along with XML data, we can use a SELECT statement as follows:

```
SELECT a.empno, a.ename, a.Address.getStringVal()
FROM    Employee a;
```

The above code simply gives all values along with the exact XML information we inserted previously. getStringVal is a method available as part of the object type XMLType. Every object type can have several methods and XMLType is a pre-defined object type that has several methods designed to work with XML data in a flexible manner.

Sometimes, we may want to display the XML information in the form of logical columns not in the form of XML anymore. The following SELECT statement does this:

```
SELECT
a.empno,
a.ename,
a.Address.extract('//Address/Street/text()')
                            .getStringVal() as Street,
a.Address.extract('//Address/City/text()')
                            .getStringVal() as City,
a.Address.extract('//Address/Zip/text()')
                            .getStringVal() as Zip,
a.Address.extract('//Address/State/text()')
                            .getStringVal() as State
FROM    Employee a;
```

In the above SELECT statement, XPath expressions are used to extract XML information and display it as separate columns. You can observe that extract is another method available as part of the XMLType object. You can also work with XQuery for greater flexibility of searching or querying XML data.

Let us try to update a piece of data available in XML. The following command modifies the Zip of a particular employee:

```
UPDATE Employee a
SET a.Address = updateXML(a.Address,
                    '//Address/Zip/text()','534202')
   WHERE    a.empno = '1001'
   AND EXISTSNODE(a.Address, '//Address/Zip') = 1;
```

updateXML and EXISTSNODE are two of the several built-in functions available in Oracle to deal with XML data. EXISTSNODE can be used to test whether an XML construct has a particular node or not. updateXML is mainly used to modify the information available as part of an XML construct. Similar to updateXML, we also have deleteXML to remove information from XML constructs. It is demonstrated as follows:

```
UPDATE Employee a
SET a.Address = deleteXML(a.Address, '//Address/Zip')
   WHERE    a.empno = '1001'
   AND EXISTSNODE(a.Address, '//Address/Zip') = 1;
```

When we are able to modify and remove XML information from an XMLType column, we should also be able to insert new information as part of XML. The following command demonstrates this:

```
UPDATE Employee a
SET a.Address = INSERTXMLBEFORE(a.Address,
                    '/Address/State',
                    XMLType('<Zip>534201</Zip>'))
WHERE a.empno = '1001'
```

To remove the entire XML content from the XMLType column of a particular row, you can simply update the column with null as follows:

```
UPDATE Employee a
SET a.Address = null
   WHERE a.empno = '1001'
```

And finally, to provide a complete XML construct to an already existing row, we can use the following command:

```
UPDATE Employee a
SET a.Address = XMLType('
        <Address>
            <Street>13-20-26, Nallam vari thota</Street>
            <City>Bhimavaram</City>
            <Zip>534201</Zip>
            <State>AP</State>
        </Address>')
WHERE a.empno = '1001'
```

Generating XML from Existing Rows in Tables

Oracle database stores information into tables in the form of rows. In fact, Oracle is primarily an RDBMS and later got enhanced with other features like Object Types, Java, XML, .NET, etc. Most production databases still use Oracle to store RDBMS information. Sometimes, it would be necessary to expose the existing RDBMS information (rows of tables) in the form of XML, so that heterogeneous applications can share information easily and flexibly.

Generate XML Using ADO.NET DataSet

There are several methods to generate XML from an existing set of rows. As the internal framework of ADO.NET is completely based on XML, it is very easy to generate XML from a `DataSet`.

The following code shows you XML generated by an ADO.NET-related `DataSet`:

```
Private Sub btnShowDS_Click(ByVal sender As
  System.Object, ByVal e As System.EventArgs) Handles
  btnShowDS.Click
    'create connection to db
    Dim cn As New OracleConnection("Data Source=orcl; _
                      User Id=scott;Password=tiger")
    Try
      'create command object
      Dim cmd As New OracleCommand(Me.txtSQL.Text, cn)
      'create adapter object
      Dim da As New OracleDataAdapter(cmd)
      'create dataset
      Dim ds As New DataSet("Result")
      'fill dataset
      da.Fill(ds, "Rows")
      'clear resources
      da.Dispose()
      cmd.Dispose()
      'display the information
      Me.txtXML.Text = ds.GetXml
    Catch ex As Exception
      'display if any error occurs
      MessageBox.Show("Error: " & ex.Message)
      'close the connection if it is still open
      If cn.State = ConnectionState.Open Then
```

```
        cn.Close()
      End If
    End Try
End Sub
```

The only new statement from the above code is the highlighted one. That single line automatically generates the entire XML for the result set fetched from the database. The following is sample output:

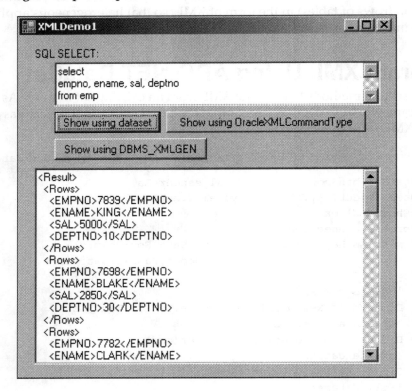

Generate XML Using ExecuteXMLReader

`OracleCommand` offers a method `ExecuteXMLReader` to exclusively generate XML, based on the data it receives. It is very similar to `ExecuteReader`, which was covered previously. The only difference between the two of them is that `ExecuteXMLReader` returns an object of type `XmlReader`. Let us go through the following code first:

```
Private Sub btnShowOraXML_Click(ByVal sender As
  System.Object, ByVal e As System.EventArgs) Handles
  btnShowOraXML.Click
    'create connection to db
```

```
Dim cn As New OracleConnection("Data Source=orcl; _
                    User Id=scott;Password=tiger")
Try
   'create command object and set properties
   Dim cmd As New OracleCommand(Me.txtSQL.Text, cn)
   cmd.XmlCommandType = OracleXmlCommandType.Query
   cmd.XmlQueryProperties.RootTag = "Result"
   cmd.XmlQueryProperties.RowTag = "Rows"
   'open connection and execute the command
   cmd.Connection.Open()
   Dim dr As Xml.XmlReader = cmd.ExecuteXmlReader
   'load the XML into a document
   Dim doc As New Xml.XmlDocument
   doc.Load(dr)
   'release resources
   cmd.Connection.Close()
   cmd.Dispose()
   'display the information
   Me.txtXML.Text = doc.OuterXml
Catch ex As Exception
   'display if any error occurs
   MessageBox.Show("Error: " & ex.Message)
   'close the connection if it is still open
   If cn.State = ConnectionState.Open Then
      cn.Close()
   End If
End Try
End Sub
```

From the above highlighted code, you can understand that we are modifying some of the properties of the OracleCommand object before executing it with ExecuteXMLReader. The following are the statements that are new in the above program:

```
cmd.XmlCommandType = OracleXmlCommandType.Query
cmd.XmlQueryProperties.RootTag = "Result"
cmd.XmlQueryProperties.RowTag = "Rows"
```

The first line specifies that the type of command is query. The second line specifies that the root tag of the XML document being generated must be Result. The third line specifies that each set of elements of a row must be embedded in the Rows tag. The following statement executes the query and returns the result in the form of XML or an XmlReader object.

```
Dim dr As Xml.XmlReader = cmd.ExecuteXmlReader
```

To read the entire information from the `XmlReader` object, we used `XmlDocument` as follows:

```
Dim doc As New Xml.XmlDocument
doc.Load(dr)
```

`Load` is a method of `XmlDocument` that can take an `XmlReader` as argument and populate the `XmlDocument`.

Finally, to retrieve the XML from the `XmlDocument`, we can simply work with the property `OuterXml` as follows.

```
Me.txtXML.Text = doc.OuterXml
```

Generate XML Using DBMS_XMLGEN

This is the simplest of all of the methods available. DBMS_XMLGEN is a built-in PL/SQL package, which is mainly used to generate XML documents based on the SELECT query passed to it.

 You need to have Oracle XML DB installed on your database to work with DBMS_XMLGEN package.

The following code uses DBMS_XMLGEN to generate XML:

```
Private Sub btnShowUsingXMLGEN_Click(ByVal sender As
  System.Object, ByVal e As System.EventArgs) Handles
  btnShowUsingXMLGEN.Click
    Dim cn As New OracleConnection("Data Source=orcl; _
                     User Id=scott;Password=tiger")
    Try
      'create command object
      Dim sql As New System.Text.StringBuilder
      sql.Append(" SELECT ")
      sql.Append(" DBMS_XMLGEN.GETXML('" &
                     Me.txtSQL.Text & "')")
      sql.Append(" FROM dual")
      Dim cmd As New OracleCommand(sql.ToString, cn)
      cmd.Connection.Open()
      'display the information
      Me.txtXML.Text = cmd.ExecuteScalar
      'release resources
      cmd.Connection.Close()
      cmd.Dispose()
    Catch ex As Exception
```

```
    'display if any error occurs
    MessageBox.Show("Error: " & ex.Message)
    'close the connection if it is still open
    If cn.State = ConnectionState.Open Then
      cn.Close()
    End If
  End Try
```

There is nothing new from the above code except the SELECT statement, which uses the DBMS_XMLGEN package. The DBMS_XMLGEN package contains a member GETXML, which can accept a SELECT query as parameter. The GETXML first executes the SELECT query passed to it and it automatically converts the output of the SELECT statement to XML and returns this in the form of a string.

Converting Rows to HTML Using XML and XSLT

Anyone who designs web pages using any tool/designer would certainly know what CSS is. We use HTML in combination with CSS to design and present web pages in a more efficient manner. Basically a stylesheet presents a set of styles, which would affect certain tag(s) in a web document. By modifying the underlying stylesheets, sometimes the look and feel of an entire website gets changed dramatically.

As HTML is made up of standard pre-defined tags, we can simply design and apply stylesheets for the necessary tags using CSS, and a browser can understand all those details very easily. But any XML document is generally designed using user-defined tags (elements); a browser may not understand all those new tags (elements). Just as we use CSS to present HTML document in a well-formatted and understandable manner, we use XSL to present (transform) an XML document into any format we require.

XSL stands for **eXtensible Stylesheet Language**. It is a language used to design and apply stylesheets especially for XML documents. Originally the research started to provide stylesheet technology to XML using XSL, but finally ended up with three divisions of XSL. So, XSL now consists of three parts, namely XSLT, XPath, and XSL-FO. **XSLT** is a language for transforming XML documents (even today, some programmers call XSLT XSL). **XPath** is a language to filter, search, or sort information available in XML documents. **XSL-FO** is a language for formatting XML documents. In this article we mainly focus on XSLT, which stands for XSL Transformations.

As of now, we can already generate XML based on a SELECT statement. Now, let us try transforming the XML (which is generated) to HTML using XSLT together with ODP.NET!

The following XSLT script is used for transformation (`ReportStyle.xsl`):

```
<?xml version="1.0" encoding="ISO-8859-1" ?>
<xsl:stylesheet version="1.0"
  xmlns:xsl="http://www.w3.org/1999/XSL/Transform">
<xsl:template match="/">
<html>
  <body>
    <table width="50%" cellspacing="0" cellpadding="0"
     style="font-family:verdana;font-size:X-Small"
     border="1">
      <tr bgcolor="#336699">
        <th align="left">
          <font color="White">Name</font>
        </th>
        <th align="right">
          <font color="White">Salary</font>
        </th>
      </tr>
      <xsl:for-each select="EMPLOYEES/EMPLOYEE">
        <tr>
          <td align="left">
            <xsl:value-of select="ENAME" />
          </td>
          <td align="right">
            <xsl:value-of select="SAL" />
          </td>
        </tr>
      </xsl:for-each>
    </table>
  </body>
</html>
</xsl:template>
</xsl:stylesheet>
```

Initially, when the above XSLT is applied to an XML document, the following gets executed:

```
<html>
  <body>
    <table width="50%" cellspacing="0" cellpadding="0"
     style="font-family:verdana;font-size:X-Small"
     border="1">
      <tr bgcolor="#336699">
        <th align="left">
          <font color="White">Name</font>
        </th>
```

```
            <th align="right">
              <font color="White">Salary</font>
            </th>
          </tr>
```

After that, for each EMPLOYEES/EMPLOYEE element found in the XML document, it adds a new row to the table with the respective employee details as shown in the following example:

```
<tr>
  <td align="left">Jag
  </td>
  <td align="right">3400
  </td>
</tr>
```

Once the whole XML document is parsed, the following code gets executed (which closes the HTML document):

```
      </table>
    </body>
  </html>
```

The following code applies the transformation to the XML generated from a SELECT statement.

```
Private Sub btnShow_Click(ByVal sender As System.Object,
    ByVal e As System.EventArgs) Handles btnShow.Click
      'create connection to db
      Dim cn As New OracleConnection("Data Source=orcl; _
                        User Id=scott;Password=tiger")
      Try
        'get XSLT content from XSL file
        Dim XSL As String = _
      System.IO.File.ReadAllText("..\..\ReportStyle.xsl")
        'create command object and set properties
        Dim cmd As New OracleCommand("SELECT ename, _
                                sal FROM emp", cn)
        With cmd
          .XmlCommandType = OracleXmlCommandType.Query
          .XmlQueryProperties.RootTag = "EMPLOYEES"
          .XmlQueryProperties.RowTag = "EMPLOYEE"
          .XmlQueryProperties.Xslt = XSL
        End With
        'open connection and execute the command
        cmd.Connection.Open()
        Dim dr As Xml.XmlReader = cmd.ExecuteXmlReader
        'load the XML into a document
```

```
      Dim doc As New Xml.XmlDocument
      doc.Load(dr)
      'release resources
      cmd.Connection.Close()
      cmd.Dispose()
      'display the web report
      Me.WebBrowser1.DocumentText = doc.OuterXml
    Catch ex As Exception
      'display if any error occurs
      MessageBox.Show("Error: " & ex.Message)
      'close the connection if it is still open
      If cn.State = ConnectionState.Open Then
        cn.Close()
      End If
    End Try
  End Sub
```

From this code, you can observe that we are reading and loading the entire XSL file into a variable. After that, we create an `OracleCommand` object with a `SELECT` statement. The properties of the object are specified in such a way that it returns the result of query in the form of XML. While it is converting the rows to XML, it takes our XSLT into consideration (as we assigned the XSLT to the `Xslt` property) and applies the transformation immediately to the resultant XML (resulting in HTML). Once this transformation is done, the result is read through `XmlReader`. The transformation is loaded into an `XmlDocument` and finally presented in on a `WebBrowser` control. The following is sample output of our transformation:

Manipulating Rows in a Table Using XML

There are several methods to manipulate rows. We have already seen the concept of manipulating rows in previous chapters. Now, let us try to manipulate traditional RDBMS rows using XML! In simple words, we will try to insert or update existing rows in a table using XML!

 Inserting/updating rows using XML is quite different from inserting/updating XML into rows.

Inserting Rows into Oracle Using XML

Let us now insert traditional rows into the emp table using XML. The following code inserts a new row into an emp table, by only using XML:

```
Private Sub btnAddRow_Click(ByVal sender As
   System.Object, ByVal e As System.EventArgs) Handles
   btnAddRow.Click
   If Me.txtXML.Text.Trim.Length = 0 Then
     MessageBox.Show("No XML generated")
     Exit Sub
   End If

   'create connection to db
   Dim cn As New OracleConnection("Data Source=orcl; _
                     User Id=scott;Password=tiger")
   Try
     'create command object
     Dim cmd As New OracleCommand()
     With cmd
       .Connection = cn
       .Connection.Open()
       .XmlCommandType = OracleXmlCommandType.Insert
       .CommandText = Me.txtXML.Text
       .XmlSaveProperties.RowTag = "EMPLOYEE"
       .XmlSaveProperties.Table = "emp"
       .XmlSaveProperties.UpdateColumnsList = New
       String() {"EMPNO", "ENAME", "SAL", "DEPTNO"}
     Dim result As Integer = .ExecuteNonQuery
       .Connection.Close()
       .Dispose()
     MessageBox.Show("Succesfully added " & result & "
                                       rows")
```

```
            End With
        Catch ex As Exception
            'display if any error occurs
            MessageBox.Show("Error: " & ex.Message)
            'close the connection if it is still open
            If cn.State = ConnectionState.Open Then
                cn.Close()
            End If
        End Try
    End Sub
```

Let us go step by step:

```
.XmlCommandType = OracleXmlCommandType.Insert
```

The above statement specifies that we are trying to insert to a row using XML.

```
.CommandText = Me.txtXML.Text
```

The XML document (containing data to insert) is being assigned to the `CommandText` property. Further down, we have the following:

```
.XmlSaveProperties.RowTag = "EMPLOYEE"
.XmlSaveProperties.Table = "emp"
```

The first line specifies that the row should be identified with the tag EMPLOYEE. The second line specifies the table to insert.

```
.XmlSaveProperties.UpdateColumnsList = New String() _
            {"EMPNO", "ENAME", "SAL", "DEPTNO"}
```

The above line specifies the names of the columns or tags to insert and finally the following line executes the command:

```
Dim result As Integer = .ExecuteNonQuery
```

To frame XML manually (based on user-provided information), we are using a separate routine as follows:

```
Private Sub btnGenerateXML_Click(ByVal sender As
    System.Object, ByVal e As System.EventArgs) Handles
    btnGenerateXML.Click
    Dim sb As New System.Text.StringBuilder
    sb.Append("<?xml version = '1.0'?>" &
                            ControlChars.NewLine)
    sb.Append("<EMPLOYEES>" & ControlChars.NewLine)
    sb.Append("<EMPLOYEE>" & ControlChars.NewLine)
```

```
      sb.Append("<EMPNO>" & Me.txtEmpno.Text & "</EMPNO>" &
                                 ControlChars.NewLine)
      sb.Append("<ENAME>" & Me.txtName.Text & "</ENAME>" &
                                 ControlChars.NewLine)
      sb.Append("<SAL>" & Me.txtSal.Text & "</SAL>" &
                                 ControlChars.NewLine)
      sb.Append("<DEPTNO>" & Me.txtDeptno.Text &
                      "</DEPTNO>" & ControlChars.NewLine)
      sb.Append("</EMPLOYEE>" & ControlChars.NewLine)
      sb.Append("</EMPLOYEES>" & ControlChars.NewLine)
      Me.txtXML.Text = sb.ToString
   End Sub
```

The above routine simply generates an XML construct by concatenating the row information provided by the user (in text fields). You can also observe that the root tag is defined as EMPLOYEES and the row tag is defined as EMPLOYEE. The columns available as part of the XML construct should match exactly with the UpdateColumnList. The following is sample output for the above:

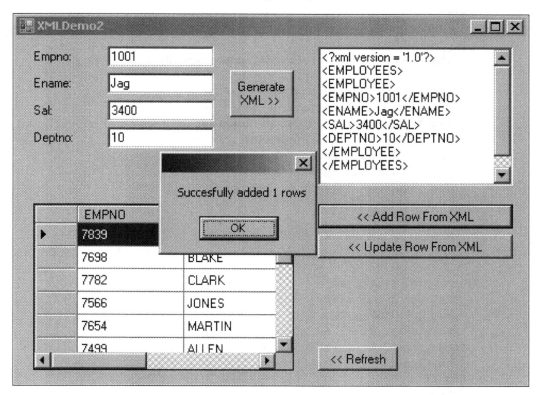

Updating Rows into Oracle Using XML

Now that we have seen how to insert rows using XML, let us deal with updating rows using XML. The following code updates an existing row in an emp table using XML:

```
Private Sub btnUpdateRow_Click(ByVal sender As
   System.Object, ByVal e As System.EventArgs) Handles
   btnUpdateRow.Click
      If Me.txtXML.Text.Trim.Length = 0 Then
         MessageBox.Show("No XML generated")
         Exit Sub
      End If

      'create connection to db
      Dim cn As New OracleConnection("Data Source=orcl; _
                        User Id=scott;Password=tiger")
      Try
        'create command object
        Dim cmd As New OracleCommand()
        With cmd
          .Connection = cn
          .Connection.Open()
          .XmlCommandType = OracleXmlCommandType.Update
          .CommandText = Me.txtXML.Text
          .XmlSaveProperties.RowTag = "EMPLOYEE"
          .XmlSaveProperties.Table = "emp"
          .XmlSaveProperties.UpdateColumnsList =
                  New String() {"ENAME", "SAL", "DEPTNO"}
          .XmlSaveProperties.KeyColumnsList =
                  New String() {"EMPNO"}
          Dim result As Integer = .ExecuteNonQuery
          .Connection.Close()
          .Dispose()
          MessageBox.Show("Succesfully updated " & result
                                             & " rows")

        End With
      Catch ex As Exception
        'display if any error occurs
        MessageBox.Show("Error: " & ex.Message)
        'close the connection if it is still open
        If cn.State = ConnectionState.Open Then
          cn.Close()
        End If
      End Try
End Sub
```

The code opposite is very similar to the previously given "insert" code except that we are providing different values to XmlCommandType, UpdateColumnsList, and KeyColumnsList. As we are trying to update existing rows, we are using OracleXmlCommandType.Update. The names of all the columns that need to be updated must be provided for UpdateColumnsList. The names of the columns that are used for conditions must be provided for KeyColumnsList.

Working with Native XML in Oracle Database

Oracle database supports native XML storage (information will be directly stored in the form of XML) very efficiently with the help of the data type XMLType. For the sake of this demonstration, a table is created with a column of type XMLType as follows:

```
CREATE TABLE Employee
(
empno VARCHAR2(4),
ename VARCHAR2(20),
address XMLType
)
/
```

You can understand from the above command that a column address of type XMLType is created.

Inserting XML Data into XMLType Using Traditional INSERT

Oracle supports the traditional INSERT statement to work with XMLType directly. Let us see how to insert a row using the INSERT statement together with ODP.NET code:

```
Private Sub btnAdd_Click(ByVal sender As System.Object,
ByVal e As System.EventArgs) Handles btnAdd.Click
  Dim SQL As New System.Text.StringBuilder
  SQL.Append("INSERT INTO Employee VALUES ")
  SQL.Append("(")
  SQL.Append(" '1001', ")
  SQL.Append(" 'Jag', ")
  SQL.Append(" XMLType('")
  SQL.Append("    <Address>")
  SQL.Append("    <Street>13-20-26, Gunupudi,
                        Nallamvari thota</Street>")
  SQL.Append("    <City>Bhimavaram</City>")
```

```
SQL.Append("    <Zip>534201</Zip>")
SQL.Append("    <State>AP</State>")
SQL.Append("    </Address>')")
SQL.Append(")")
'create connection to db
Dim cn As New OracleConnection("Data Source=xe; _
                   User Id=scott;Password=tiger")
Try
   'create command object
   Dim cmd As New OracleCommand(SQL.ToString, cn)
   cn.Open()
   Dim result As Integer = cmd.ExecuteNonQuery
   MessageBox.Show("Succesfully added " & result &
                                     " rows")
   cn.Close()
   cmd.Dispose()
Catch ex As Exception
   'display if any error occurs
   MessageBox.Show("Error: " & ex.Message)
   'close the connection if it is still open
   If cn.State = ConnectionState.Open Then
      cn.Close()
   End If
End Try
End Sub
```

There is nothing special about the previous code except that we are embedding XML information as part of the INSERT statement itself. The INSERT statement is as follows:

```
SQL.Append("INSERT INTO Employee VALUES ")
SQL.Append("(")
SQL.Append(" '1001', ")
SQL.Append(" 'Jag', ")
SQL.Append(" XMLType('")
SQL.Append(" <Address>")
SQL.Append(" <Street>13-20-26, Gunupudi,
                         Nallamvari thota</Street>")
SQL.Append(" <City>Bhimavaram</City>")
SQL.Append(" <Zip>534201</Zip>")
SQL.Append(" <State>AP</State>")
SQL.Append(" </Address>')")
SQL.Append(")")
```

The INSERT statement inserts three columns of which the last column is of the type XMLType (which is object type). As explained previously, the object type data must be created using a constructor and we used the same XMLType to create an instance of XML data.

Updating XML Data in XMLType Using Traditional UPDATE

Oracle supports the traditional UPDATE statement to work with XMLType directly.
Here, we will update XML in an existing row using the UPDATE statement together
with ODP.NET as follows:

```
Private Sub btnUpdate_Click(ByVal sender As
    System.Object, ByVal e As System.EventArgs) Handles
  btnUpdate.Click
    Dim SQL As New System.Text.StringBuilder
    SQL.Append("UPDATE Employee a ")
    SQL.Append("SET a.Ename='Winner', ")
    SQL.Append("a.Address = XMLType('")
    SQL.Append(" <Address>")
    SQL.Append(" <Street>13-20-26</Street>")
    SQL.Append(" <City>Bvrm</City>")
    SQL.Append(" <Zip>534201</Zip>")
    SQL.Append(" <State>AP</State>")
    SQL.Append(" </Address>') ")
    SQL.Append("WHERE  a.empno = '1001'")

    'create connection to db
    Dim cn As New OracleConnection("Data Source=xe; _
                    User Id=scott;Password=tiger")
    Try
      'create command object
      Dim cmd As New OracleCommand(SQL.ToString, cn)
      cn.Open()
      Dim result As Integer = cmd.ExecuteNonQuery
      MessageBox.Show("Succesfully updated " & result &
                                    " rows")
      cn.Close()
      cmd.Dispose()
    Catch ex As Exception
      'display if any error occurs
      MessageBox.Show("Error: " & ex.Message)
      'close the connection if it is still open
      If cn.State = ConnectionState.Open Then
        cn.Close()
      End If
    End Try
  End Sub
```

The following code generates the UPDATE statement used to update existing XML in a row.

```
SQL.Append("UPDATE Employee a ")
SQL.Append("SET a.Ename='Winner', ")
SQL.Append("a.Address = XMLType('")
SQL.Append(" <Address>")
SQL.Append(" <Street>13-20-26</Street>")
SQL.Append(" <City>Bvrm</City>")
SQL.Append(" <Zip>534201</Zip>")
SQL.Append(" <State>AP</State>")
SQL.Append(" </Address>') ")
SQL.Append("WHERE  a.empno = '1001'")
```

You can again observe that the constructor XMLType is being used to create an instance (or object) of XMLType object type.

Inserting XML Data Using OracleXmlType

Apart from directly embedding XML as part of SQL commands, we can create and use our own object of type OracleXMLType for greater flexibility. OracleXMLType is available as part of ODP.NET and it automatically communicates with the underlying columns of type XMLType.

The following code inserts XML data into a table using OracleXMLType:

```
Private Sub btnAdd2_Click(ByVal sender As
  System.Object, ByVal e As System.EventArgs) Handles
  btnAdd2.Click
    'create connection to db
    Dim cn As New OracleConnection("Data Source=xe; _
                    User Id=scott;Password=tiger")
    Try
      Dim SQL As New System.Text.StringBuilder
      SQL.Append("INSERT INTO Employee VALUES ")
      SQL.Append(" (")
      SQL.Append(" :empno, ")
      SQL.Append(" :ename, ")
      SQL.Append(" :address")
      SQL.Append(")")

      Dim XML As New System.Text.StringBuilder
      XML.Append(" <Address>")
      XML.Append(" <Street>10-37-2,
```

```
                        Beside A.P. State warehouse,
                        Indra Nagar</Street>")
       XML.Append(" <City>Tenali</City>")
       XML.Append(" <Zip>522202</Zip>")
       XML.Append(" <State>AP</State>")
       XML.Append(" </Address>")

       'create command object
       Dim cmd As New OracleCommand(SQL.ToString, cn)
       cn.Open()
       cmd.Parameters.Add(":empno", "1002")
       cmd.Parameters.Add(":ename", "Sunitha")
       Dim o_Address As New _
          Oracle.DataAccess.Types.OracleXmlType(cn,
          XML.ToString)
       cmd.Parameters.Add(":address", o_Address)
       Dim result As Integer = cmd.ExecuteNonQuery
       MessageBox.Show("Succesfully added " & result
                                         & " rows")

       cn.Close()
       cmd.Dispose()
   Catch ex As Exception
      'display if any error occurs
      MessageBox.Show("Error: " & ex.Message)
      'close the connection if it is still open
      If cn.State = ConnectionState.Open Then
         cn.Close()
      End If
   End Try
End Sub
```

The only new concept from the above code is the highlighted one. We created an object o_Address of type `OracleXmlType`, by passing `OracleConnection` and an XML construct (which needs to be inserted). ODP.NET automatically takes care of the rest!

Retrieving and Updating XML Data Using OracleXmlType

Once you know how to insert information, it is very easy to update information as well. To make it a bit challenging, let us update the information available in a particular node (rather than the entire XML).

The following code updates only the text of the `city` tag available as a part of the whole XML data in the row:

```vbnet
Private Sub btnUpdate2_Click(ByVal sender As
    System.Object, ByVal e As System.EventArgs) Handles
    btnUpdate2.Click
    'create connection to db
    Dim cn As New OracleConnection("Data Source=xe; _
                        User Id=scott;Password=tiger")
    Try

        'retrieve the entire XML information to modify
        Dim SQL As String
        SQL = "SELECT * FROM employee "
        SQL &= "WHERE empno=1001 "
        Dim cmd As New OracleCommand(SQL, cn)
        cmd.Connection.Open()
        Dim dr As OracleDataReader = cmd.ExecuteReader
        If Not dr.HasRows Then
            MessageBox.Show("No rows found")
            cmd.Connection.Close()
            cmd.Dispose()
            Exit Sub
        End If
        dr.Read()
        Dim empno As String = dr("empno")
        Dim ename As String = dr("ename")
        Dim xtAddress As
            Oracle.DataAccess.Types.OracleXmlType =
            dr.GetOracleXmlType(dr.GetOrdinal("Address"))
        dr.Dispose()

        'modify the city in XML and update to database
        xtAddress.Update("//Address/City/text()", "",
                                            "BVRM")

        SQL = "UPDATE Employee SET "
        SQL &= " address = :address "
        SQL &= " WHERE empno = :empno "
        cmd = New OracleCommand(SQL, cn)
        cmd.Parameters.Add(":address", xtAddress)
        cmd.Parameters.Add(":empno", "1001")
        Dim result As Integer = cmd.ExecuteNonQuery
        cmd.Connection.Close()
        cmd.Dispose()
```

```
        MessageBox.Show("Succesfully updated " & result &
                                                " rows")
      Catch ex As Exception
        'display if any error occurs
        MessageBox.Show("Error: " & ex.Message)
        'close the connection if it is still open
        If cn.State = ConnectionState.Open Then
          cn.Close()
        End If
      End Try
    End Sub
```

The following statement retrieves the XML information available in XMLType column into an object xtAddress of type OracleXmlType:

```
Dim xtAddress As Oracle.DataAccess.Types.OracleXmlType _
        = dr.GetOracleXmlType(dr.GetOrdinal("Address"))
```

We can update the information available in OracleXmlType using the Update method as follows:

```
xtAddress.Update("//Address/City/text()", "", "BVRM")
```

You can observe from the above statement that XPath is being used to identify particular tag and replace the text with user-specified information. Once the modifications are complete, we update back to database using an UPDATE statement together with bind variables as shown below:

```
SQL = "UPDATE Employee SET "
SQL &= " address = :address "
SQL &= " WHERE empno = :empno "
cmd = New OracleCommand(SQL, cn)
cmd.Parameters.Add(":address", xtAddress)
cmd.Parameters.Add(":empno", "1001")
```

Extracting Individual Node Information of an XMLType Value

Retrieving XML information can be easily done using OracleDataReader or OracleDataAdapter. But, there are several ways to extract each node or a group of nodes of information. Most of this searching or querying XML data can be accomplished using the System.Xml namespace (along with its sub-namespaces). But OracleXmlType supports extracting to the level of nodes as well.

The following code sample gives you the text available in some nodes of a particular XML construct stored as part of an XMLType column:

```
Private Sub btnRead_Click(ByVal sender As
System.Object, ByVal e As System.EventArgs) Handles
btnRead.Click
  'create connection to db
  Dim cn As New OracleConnection("Data Source=xe; _
                    User Id=scott;Password=tiger")
  Try
    Dim SQL As String
    SQL = "SELECT * FROM employee "
    SQL &= "WHERE empno=1001 "
    Dim cmd As New OracleCommand(SQL, cn)
    cmd.Connection.Open()
    Dim dr As OracleDataReader = cmd.ExecuteReader
    If Not dr.HasRows Then
      MessageBox.Show("No rows found")
      cmd.Connection.Close()
      cmd.Dispose()
      Exit Sub
    End If
    dr.Read()
    Dim empno As String = dr("empno")
    Dim ename As String = dr("ename")
    Dim xtAddress As _
      Oracle.DataAccess.Types.OracleXmlType = _
      dr.GetOracleXmlType(dr.GetOrdinal("Address"))
    Dim Street As String = _
      xtAddress.Extract("//Address/Street/text()",
                                        "").Value
    Dim City As String = _
      xtAddress.Extract("//Address/City/text()",
                                        "").Value
    Dim Zip As String = _
      xtAddress.Extract("//Address/Zip/text()",
                                        "").Value
    Dim State As String = _
      xtAddress.Extract("//Address/State/text()",
                                        "").Value
    dr.Dispose()
    cmd.Connection.Close()
    cmd.Dispose()
```

```
        MessageBox.Show(String.Format("{0},{1},{2},
            {3},{4},{5}", empno, ename, Street, City,
            Zip, State))
    Catch ex As Exception
      'display if any error occurs
      MessageBox.Show("Error: " & ex.Message)
      'close the connection if it is still open
      If cn.State = ConnectionState.Open Then
        cn.Close()
      End If
    End Try
  End Sub
```

The XML information from XMLType column Address is being retrieved into an object xtAddress of type OracleXmlType as follows:

```
Dim xtAddress As Oracle.DataAccess.Types.OracleXmlType _
    = dr.GetOracleXmlType(dr.GetOrdinal("Address"))
```

Once the information is available in xtAddress, we can retrieve the text information of a particular tag by using XPath expression as follows:

```
Dim Street As String = _
        xtAddress.Extract("//Address/Street/text()",
                                    "").Value
```

In the above case, it simply finds the Street tag of the Address tag and returns the text available in it. Similarly, after retrieving other tags' information into respective variables, we display it to the user as follows:

```
MessageBox.Show(String.Format("{0},{1},{2},
        {3},{4},{5}", empno, ename, Street, City,
        Zip, State))
```

Summary

In this chapter, we started with an introduction to XML and XML DB, worked through a few examples manipulating XML, generated XML from the database using various methods and finally used ODP.NET to deal with inserting, updating, retrieving, and extracting XML information from Oracle 10g database.

8

Application Development Using ODP.NET

We have covered almost all the important ODP.NET classes in previous chapters. In this chapter, we will make use of those ODP.NET classes (together with few more) and develop simple real-time applications with various .NET technologies.

We will mainly focus on ODP.NET together with the following:

- Notifying applications of database changes
- Asynchronous and multi-thread development
- Web application development using ASP.NET 2.0
- ASP.NET 2.0 Web reporting
- Object-Oriented Development
- Developing Web Services
- Smart Device (Pocket PC) application development

Notifying Applications of Database Changes

All database-related applications generally interact with databases and manipulate them based on the requirements. But, some applications need to have notifications from the database itself. These applications need to be notified automatically, when a change occurs at database level. This can be easily achieved using the `OracleDependency` class in ODP.NET (available with version 10.2 or above).

Before working with database change notifications, the respective database user must be provided with CHANGE NOTIFICATION privilege. For example:

GRANT CHANGE NOTIFICATION TO SCOTT

Catching Notifications

Let us start our discussion with providing only one notification to the application. For this demonstration, a Windows form is designed with two buttons, a multi-lined textbox, and a `DataGridView` as follows:

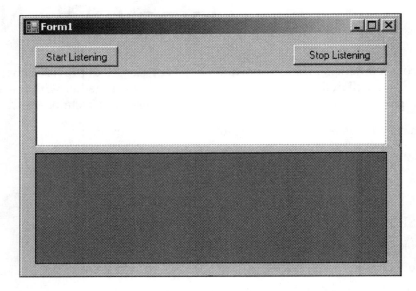

The entire code for the above is as follows:

```
Imports Oracle.DataAccess.Client

Public Class Form1

    Private cn As OracleConnection
    Private cmd As OracleCommand

    Private Sub btnStart_Click(ByVal sender As
    System.Object, ByVal e As System.EventArgs) Handles
    btnStart.Click
        'create connection to db
        cn = New OracleConnection("Data Source=xe; _
```

```
                         User Id=scott;Password=tiger")
   Try
      'create command object
      cmd = New OracleCommand
      With cmd
         'provide the sql to monitor
         .CommandText = "SELECT empno, ename FROM emp
                                     WHERE empno=7369"
         .Connection = cn
         .Connection.Open()
         'add the dependency & monitoring
         Dim dp As New OracleDependency(cmd)
         AddHandler dp.OnChange, AddressOf OnNotification
         Me.txtNotifications.Text = "Started listening..."
                                     & ControlChars.NewLine
         .ExecuteNonQuery()
      End With
   Catch ex As Exception
      'display if any error occurs
      MessageBox.Show("Error: " & ex.Message)
      'close the connection if it is still open
      If cn.State = ConnectionState.Open Then
         cn.Close()
      End If
   End Try
End Sub

Private Sub OnNotification(ByVal src As System.Object,
            ByVal args As OracleNotificationEventArgs)
   Dim ResName As String = _
                  args.Details.Rows(0)("ResourceName")
   Me.txtNotifications.Text &= ResName &
                               ControlChars.NewLine
   Me.DataGridView1.DataSource = args.Details
End Sub

Private Sub btnStop_Click(ByVal sender As
System.Object, ByVal e As System.EventArgs) Handles
btnStop.Click
   Try
      cmd.Connection.Close()
      cmd.Dispose()
   Catch ex As Exception
      If cn.State = ConnectionState.Open Then
```

```
            cn.Close()
        End If
    End Try
    Me.txtNotifications.Text &= "Stopped Listening..."
                            & ControlChars.NewLine
End Sub

Private Sub Form1_Load(ByVal sender As System.Object,
ByVal e As System.EventArgs) Handles MyBase.Load
    Control.CheckForIllegalCrossThreadCalls = False
End Sub

End Class
```

The code for the **Start** button simply opens a connection to the database and starts listening for any changes that happen to employee 7369. The code for the **Stop** button closes the connection to stop listening. Finally, the notifications (changes) are notified through the OnNotification() method.

From the highlighted code, you can observe that an OracleDependency object is created to continuously monitor the OracleCommand object (which focuses on employee 7369). If there is any change to the selected row of OracleCommand, it automatically fires OnNotification, which retrieves the details of the notification using OracleNotificationEventArgs.

The notification process always occurs on a new thread (different from the main thread) and tries to access controls on the main thread, which may not be permitted. To make it possible, we have to make sure that CheckForIllegalCrossThreadCalls is false.

The following are the steps to test the above code:

1. Run the application pressing *F5*.
2. Click on the **Start Listening** button.
3. Switch to SQL*Plus and update the employee information of employee number 7369 and commit it.
4. Switch back to the application and you should be able to see the notification.

 It is preferable to work with multi-threading (covered later) while working with database change notifications.

Catching Multiple Notifications

The previous code works with only a single notification (or catches only one notification). To get notified multiple times, we need to modify the code as follows:

```
Private Sub btnStart_Click(ByVal sender As
System.Object, ByVal e As System.EventArgs) Handles
btnStart.Click
  'create connection to db
  cn = New OracleConnection("Data Source=xe; _
              User Id=scott;Password=tiger")
  Try
    'create command object
    cmd = New OracleCommand
    With cmd
      'provide the sql to monitor
      .CommandText = "SELECT empno, ename FROM
                        emp WHERE empno=7369"
      .Connection = cn
      .Connection.Open()
      'add the dependency & monitoring
      Dim dp As New OracleDependency(cmd)
      AddHandler dp.OnChange, AddressOf OnNotification
      Me.txtNotifications.Text = "Started listening..."
                        & ControlChars.NewLine
      .Notification.IsNotifiedOnce = False
      .ExecuteNonQuery()
    End With
  Catch ex As Exception
    'display if any error occurs
    MessageBox.Show("Error: " & ex.Message)
    'close the connection if it is still open
    If cn.State = ConnectionState.Open Then
      cn.Close()
    End If
  End Try
End Sub
```

The single highlighted line in the code switches single notification to multiple continuous notifications. When we have multiple notifications, the output looks like the following:

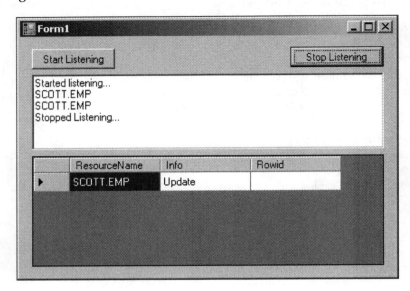

Identifying Rows Modified During Notifications

In both of the previous examples, we worked only on a single row. This section deals with multiple rows. Following is the complete modified code to achieve this:

```
Imports Oracle.DataAccess.Client

Public Class Form3

    Private cn As OracleConnection
    Private cmd As OracleCommand

    Private Sub btnStart_Click(ByVal sender As
    System.Object, ByVal e As System.EventArgs) Handles
    btnStart.Click
        'create connection to db
        cn = New OracleConnection("Data Source=xe; _
                        User Id=scott;Password=tiger")
        Try
            'create command object
            cmd = New OracleCommand
```

```vb
    With cmd
      'provide the sql to monitor
      .CommandText = "SELECT empno, ename FROM emp "
      .AddRowid = True
      .Connection = cn
      .Connection.Open()
      'add the dependency & monitoring
      Dim dp As New OracleDependency(cmd)
      AddHandler dp.OnChange, AddressOf OnNotification
      Me.txtNotifications.Text = "Started listening..."
                              & ControlChars.NewLine
      .Notification.IsNotifiedOnce = False
      .ExecuteNonQuery()
    End With
  Catch ex As Exception
    'display if any error occurs
    MessageBox.Show("Error: " & ex.Message)
    'close the connection if it is still open
    If cn.State = ConnectionState.Open Then
      cn.Close()
    End If
  End Try
End Sub

Private Sub OnNotification(ByVal src As System.Object,
ByVal args As OracleNotificationEventArgs)
  Dim ResName As String = _
                args.Details.Rows(0)("ResourceName")
  Dim RowID As String = args.Details.Rows(0)("RowID")
  Dim sql As String = "SELECT ename FROM emp WHERE
                          ROWID='" & RowID & "'"
  Dim cmd As OracleCommand = cn.CreateCommand
  cmd.CommandText = sql
  Dim rdr As OracleDataReader = cmd.ExecuteReader
  Dim ename As String = String.Empty
  If rdr.Read Then EName = rdr(0)
  Me.txtNotifications.Text &= ResName & ", Employee:"
                        & EName & ControlChars.NewLine
  Me.DataGridView1.DataSource = args.Details
End Sub

Private Sub btnStop_Click(ByVal sender As
System.Object, ByVal e As System.EventArgs) Handles
btnStop.Click
  Try
    cmd.Connection.Close()
    cmd.Dispose()
```

```
    Catch ex As Exception
      If cn.State = ConnectionState.Open Then
        cn.Close()
      End If
    End Try
    Me.txtNotifications.Text &= "Stopped Listening..." &
                                ControlChars.NewLine
  End Sub


  Private Sub Form1_Load(ByVal sender As System.Object,
  ByVal e As System.EventArgs) Handles MyBase.Load
      Control.CheckForIllegalCrossThreadCalls = False
  End Sub


End Class
```

Once the **Start** button is clicked, a new connection is opened up and starts listening (for changes) on all the rows of the emp table. As we would like to deal with multiple notifications, the following line is included:

```
.Notification.IsNotifiedOnce = False
```

Another important line to concentrate on from the highlighted code is the following:

```
.AddRowid = True
```

The above line makes sure that ROWID of the row that got modified in database is also carried back to the application along with the notification. Once the ROWID is available to the application (during notification), we simply retrieve the details of that specific row and present them on screen. This is achieved using the following code:

```
Dim RowID As String = args.Details.Rows(0)("RowID")
    Dim sql As String = "SELECT ename FROM emp _
                WHERE ROWID='" & RowID & "'"
    Dim cmd As OracleCommand = cn.CreateCommand
    cmd.CommandText = sql
    Dim rdr As OracleDataReader = cmd.ExecuteReader
    Dim ename As String = String.Empty
    If rdr.Read Then EName = rdr(0)
    Me.txtNotifications.Text &= ResName & ", Employee:"
                    & EName & ControlChars.NewLine
```

The output should look similar to the following screen:

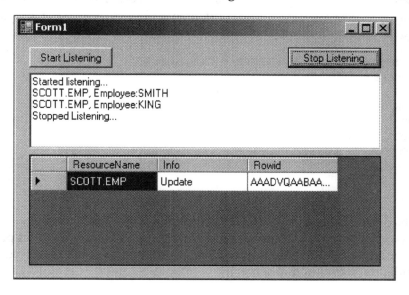

Developing Long-Running Applications

When we develop Windows-based desktop applications using .NET, we generally work with existing or third-party user-interface controls (like textbox, drop-down list, etc.). As long as those applications work with small tasks, we may not face any problems during execution.

If the applications work with long-running tasks like CPU-intensive processes, waiting for the network/database to be connected, executing a long-running stored procedure etc., the user interface becomes unresponsive till the process completes. This is an embarrassing situation to the end user who could even terminate (kill) the application abnormally. As long as we show the progress or messages and keep the user interface responsive, the user can be convinced that all is well.

To develop such applications dealing with long-running tasks, we may have to work with asynchronous programming together with multi-threading. Delving into the complete details of such techniques is beyond the scope of this book.

Just to introduce a practical example, we shall develop a user interface that calls a sample long-running stored procedure. The user interface becomes non-responsive when it is executed. After that, we will enhance it to work with asynchronous programming together with multi-threading to make it responsive to the user.

The Devil of Applications: "Not Responding"

Let us now try to develop an application that tries to execute a stored procedure given below:

```
CREATE OR REPLACE PROCEDURE p_Longtask AS
i NUMBER;
BEGIN
  FOR i IN 1..10000
LOOP
  UPDATE emp SET sal = sal;
  COMMIT;
END LOOP;
END;
/
```

You may have to modify the maximum limit of the loop based on the speed of the processor (without waiting too much or too little time). The above stored procedure would never harm the database information. It simply makes the server busy (not recommended on a production server)!

The following code tries to execute the above stored procedure:

```
Private Sub btnExecute_Click(ByVal sender As
System.Object, ByVal e As System.EventArgs) Handles
btnExecute.Click
  'create connection to db
  Me.lblMsg.Text = "creating connection object..."
  Dim cn As New OracleConnection("Data Source=xe; _
                  User Id=scott;Password=tiger")
  Try
    Me.lblMsg.Text = "creating command object..."
    'create command object
    Dim cmd As New OracleCommand
    With cmd
      'provide the sql to monitor
      .CommandText = "p_longtask"
      .CommandType = CommandType.StoredProcedure
      .Connection = cn
      Me.lblMsg.Text = "Opening connection to
                                    database.."
      .Connection.Open()
      Me.lblMsg.Text = "executing the
                              stored procedure..."
      .ExecuteNonQuery()
    End With
    Me.lblMsg.Text = ""
```

```
      MessageBox.Show("Succesfully executed")
    Catch ex As Exception
      'display if any error occurs
      MessageBox.Show("Error: " & ex.Message)
      'close the connection if it is still open
      If cn.State = ConnectionState.Open Then
        cn.Close()
      End If
    End Try
  End Sub
End Sub
```

The above code simply opens up a connection, creates an `OracleCommand` object and tries to execute the stored procedure named `p_longtask`. Once the execution of stored procedure gets completed, it pops up a message showing success.

The following output is received while executing the stored procedure. You can observe that the form became **Not Responding** on the title bar (and sometimes even a plain white window that doesn't repaint or refresh).

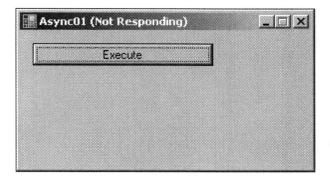

Asynchronous Task with Multi-Threading

Let us modify the previous form to make it responsive to the user along with notifying the stages of execution to the user. The following code is completely modified to achieve this:

```
Imports Oracle.DataAccess.Client
Imports System.Threading

Public Class Async02

  Private Sub btnExecute_Click(ByVal sender As
  System.Object, ByVal e As System.EventArgs) Handles
  btnExecute.Click
    StartExecuteTaskAsync()
```

```
    End Sub

#Region "Asynchronous handling"

    Dim thExecuteTaskAsync As Thread = Nothing
    Private Sub StartExecuteTaskAsync()
        'clear existing thread
        If Not thExecuteTaskAsync Is Nothing Then
            thExecuteTaskAsync.Abort()
            thExecuteTaskAsync.Join()
            thExecuteTaskAsync = Nothing
        End If
        'start a new thread to execute the
        'task asynchronously
        thExecuteTaskAsync =
                New Thread(AddressOf ExecuteTaskAsync)
        thExecuteTaskAsync.Start()
    End Sub

    Private Sub ExecuteTaskAsync()
        'create connection to db
        'access delegate to show status on GUI
        Invoke(ShowStatus, New Object() {"creating
                            connection object..."})
        Dim cn As New OracleConnection("Data Source=xe; _
                        User Id=scott;Password=tiger")
        Try
            'access delegate to show status on GUI
            Invoke(ShowStatus, New Object() {"creating
                                command object..."})

            'create command object
            Dim cmd As New OracleCommand
            With cmd
                'provide the sql to monitor
                .CommandText = "p_longtask"
                .CommandType = CommandType.StoredProcedure
                .Connection = cn
                'access delegate to show status on GUI
                Invoke(ShowStatus, New Object() {"Opening
                            connection to database.."})
                .Connection.Open()
                'access delegate to show status on GUI
                Invoke(ShowStatus, New Object() {"executing the
                                stored procedure..."})
                .ExecuteNonQuery()
            End With
```

```
      'access delegate to show status on GUI
      Invoke(ShowStatus, New Object() {"Done!"})
    Catch ex As Exception
      'display if any error occurs
      MessageBox.Show("Error: " & ex.Message)
      'close the connection if it is still open
      If cn.State = ConnectionState.Open Then
        cn.Close()
      End If
    End Try

  End Sub


  '=====================================================
  =========   ''DELEGATE declaration
  ''(generally used when the task needs to
                              communicate with GUI)
  '''''''''''''''''''''''''''''''''''''''''''''''''''''
  Private Delegate Sub delShowStatus(ByVal msg As
                                            String)
  Dim ShowStatus As New delShowStatus(AddressOf ShowMsg)
  Private Sub ShowMsg(ByVal msg As String)
    Me.lblMsg.Text = msg
  End Sub
  '=============================================
  ==============
  Private Sub Form1_FormClosing(ByVal sender As Object,
  ByVal e As System.Windows.Forms.FormClosingEventArgs)
  Handles Me.FormClosing
     'this is necessary if the form is trying to close,
     'even before the completion of task
     If Not thExecuteTaskAsync Is Nothing Then
                        thExecuteTaskAsync.Abort()
  End Sub

#End Region
End Class
```

Let us go through the code step by step.

When the button **Execute** is clicked, the following method gets executed:

```
StartExecuteTaskAsync()
```

A reference to a new thread will be maintained in `thExecuteTaskAsync`, which is declared as follows:

```
Dim thExecuteTaskAsync As Thread = Nothing
```

The `StartExecuteTaskAsync` method starts with checking the thread `thExecuteTaskAsync`. If the thread is already busy, we terminate it using the following snippet:

```
If Not thExecuteTaskAsync Is Nothing Then
   thExecuteTaskAsync.Abort()
   thExecuteTaskAsync.Join()
   thExecuteTaskAsync = Nothing
End If
```

After that, we start a new thread, different from the main thread, which executes the method `ExecuteTaskAsync` as follows:

```
thExecuteTaskAsync = New Thread(AddressOf
                               ExecuteTaskAsync)
thExecuteTaskAsync.Start()
```

The `ExecuteTaskAsync` method simply opens up a connection to the database and tries to execute the stored procedure using an `OracleCommand` object. It is not much different from the previous program except that it has few `Invoke` statements, which look like the following:

```
Invoke(ShowStatus, New Object() {"Opening connection
                                to database.."})
```

The above statement invokes `ShowStatus` synchronously. That means the messages are shown to user on an urgent basis! The delegate and the respective method `ShowMsg` are defined as follows:

```
Private Delegate Sub delShowStatus(ByVal msg As String)
   Dim ShowStatus As New delShowStatus(AddressOf ShowMsg)
   Private Sub ShowMsg(ByVal msg As String)
     Me.lblMsg.Text = msg
End Sub
```

While the thread is still in the process of execution (say, still executing the stored procedure) if the user closes the form, we need to abort the thread as well. This is implemented in the following snippet.

```
Private Sub Form1_FormClosing(ByVal sender As Object,
   ByVal e As System.Windows.Forms.FormClosingEventArgs)
   Handles Me.FormClosing
     'this is necessary if the form is trying to close,
     'even before the completion of task
     If Not thExecuteTaskAsync Is Nothing Then
                 thExecuteTaskAsync.Abort()
   End Sub
```

The following is the output we receive while executing the stored procedure (and while keeping the user interface responsive to the user).

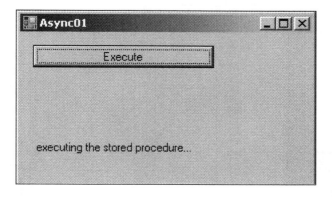

Developing Web Applications Using ASP.NET and ODP.NET

ASP.NET is the part of .NET Framework that is mainly meant for web-application development on IIS. Now, we shall look into a few of the widely used methods to develop ASP.NET applications together with ODP.NET.

Web Development Using Smart Data Binding

Data binding is the feature available in ASP.NET that is mainly used to populate the controls with database information and write back to the database when the user modifies this information. It helps the developer to be more productive without writing any, or writing much less, code.

Populating an ASP.NET DropDownList Control

Let us now develop a simple ASP.NET web application that contains a drop-down list bound to the department table of the user SCOTT. The following are the steps to achieve this:

1. Open Visual Studio 2005 environment.

2. Go to **File | New | Web site**.

3. Within the **New Web Site** dialog box, select **ASP.NET Web Site** as the template, select **Location** as **File System**, **Language** as **Visual Basic**, provide the folder as **WebDemo1**, as shown in the following figure, and click **OK**.

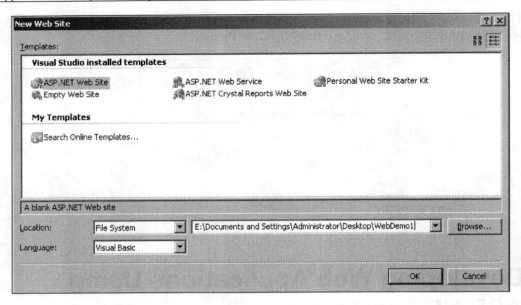

4. By default, you will be provided with **Source** mode. You can switch from **Source** to **Design** and vice-versa using the bottom tabs shown in the following figure:

5. Before proceeding further, you need to add a reference to ODP.NET. From the **Solution Explorer**, right-click on the project (`WebDemo1`) and choose **Add Reference...** as shown in the following figure:

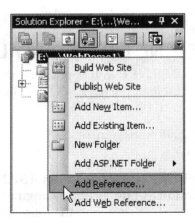

6. Within the **Add Reference** dialog box, select the **.NET** tab and scroll down to select **Oracle.DataAccess** and click on **OK**.

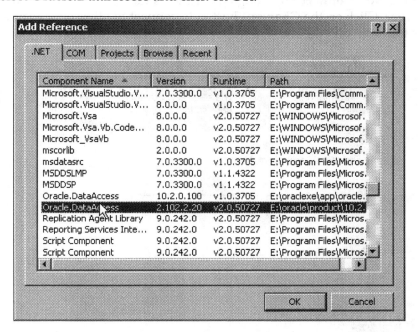

7. Switch to **Design** mode, drag and drop a drop-down list on to the form and name it `ddlDept`.

8. Similarly, drag and drop **SqlDataSource** (from the **Data** group of the toolbox) on to the form and name it `dsrcDept`. At this point, the form should look like the following:

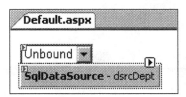

9. Using the smart tag of **SqlDataSource**, click on **Configure Data Source...** as seen in the following screenshot:

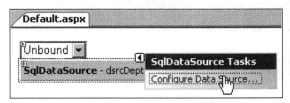

10. In the **Configure Data Source** dialog box, click on **New Connection**.

11. In the **Add Connection** dialog box, it shows the default connectivity to SQL Server. Click on the **Change...** button to connect to other data sources as follows:

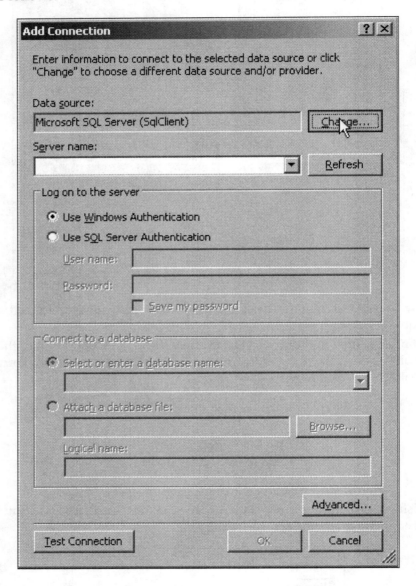

12. In the **Change Data Source** dialog box, select **Oracle Database** as data source and click on **OK** as follows:

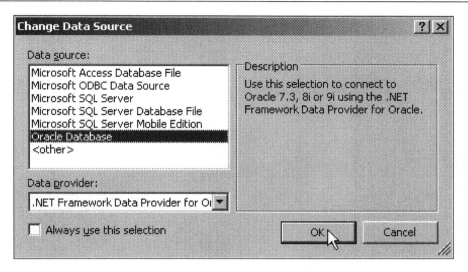

13. In the **Add Connection** dialog box, provide your Oracle service name together with user name and password (in this case **scott** and **tiger**) and test the connection. Make sure that the test succeeds as seen in the following screenshot:

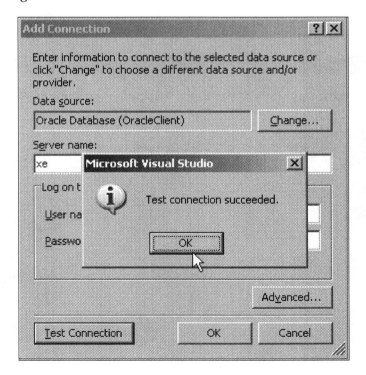

14. Once everything is tested successfully, make sure that **Save my password** is checked on and click **OK**. You will be taken back to the **Configure Data Source** dialog box as follows:

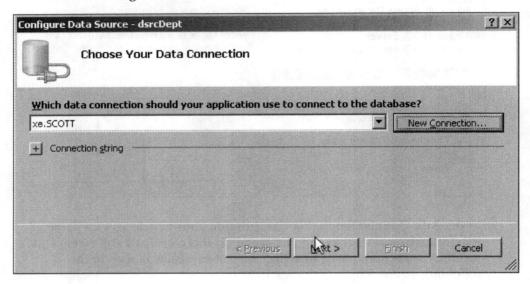

15. Once you click on **Next**, you will be asked to save the connection string with a name. Provide `OrConnectionString` as the name and click **Next**:

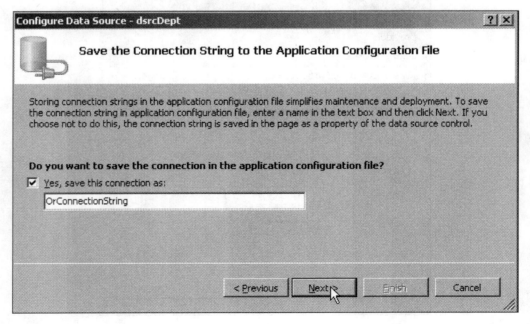

16. In the next screen, select **DEPT** as the table name and check **DEPTNO** and **DNAME** as columns and click **Next**.

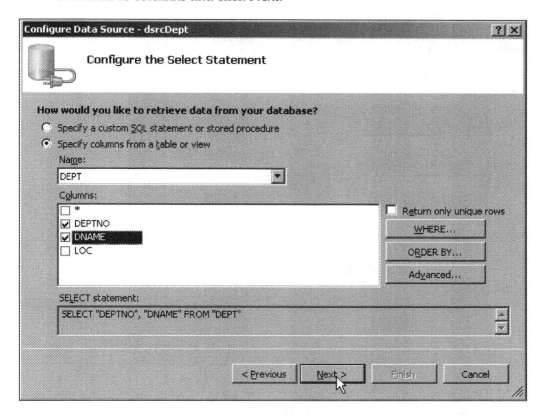

17. And finally click on **Finish**. This completes the configuration of the data source.

18. Now, we need to map the data source to the drop-down list. Click on the smart tag of drop-down list and click on **Choose Data Source...**:

19. In the **Data Source Configuration Wizard**, select data source as **dsrcDept**, data field to display as **DNAME**, and data field for value as **DEPTNO**, and click on **OK**.

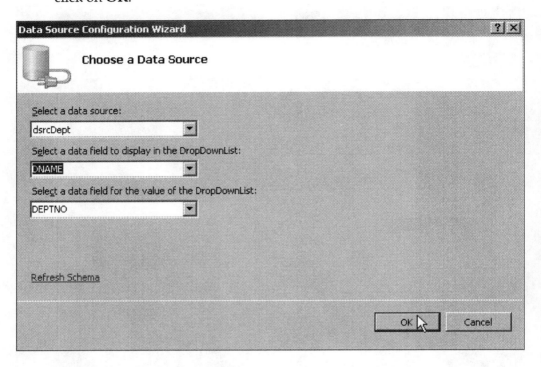

20. Once you execute the application by pressing *F5*, you will be prompted to modify Web.config as seen in the following screenshot. Just click on **OK** to enable debugging and proceed.

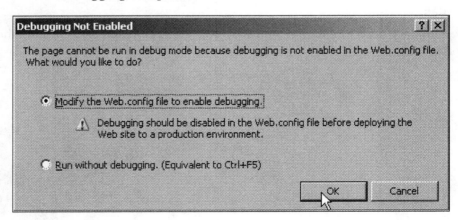

21. The output of the application looks similar to the following:

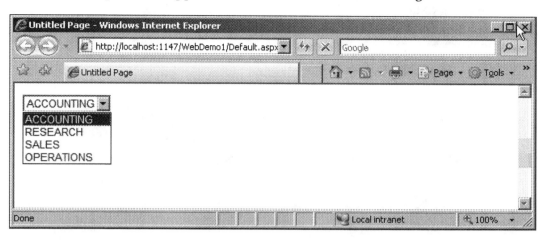

Linking an ASP.NET GridView Control with a DropDownList Control

As we have already started populating an ASP.NET drop-down list control, let us now extend the same with an ASP.NET GridView control. In this scenario, let us try to display all the employee information in the GridView based on the department selected in the drop-down list.

The following are the steps to achieve this:

1. Using the same form designed previously, drag and drop a **Gridview**.
2. Drag and drop one more **SqlDataSource** and name it as **dsrcEmp**.

3. Using the smart tag of **dsrcEmp**, configure the data source by selecting the existing data source **OrConnectionString** and click **Next**.

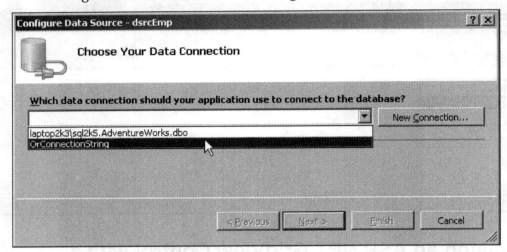

4. Select the table name as **EMP** and check on the columns **EMPNO, ENAME, SAL,** and **DEPTNO** as shown below:

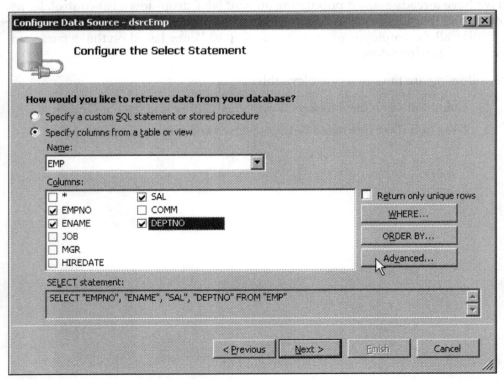

5. The SELECT statement created must be provided with a WHERE condition based on the DropDownList. Click on **Advanced...** and provide the details as follows:

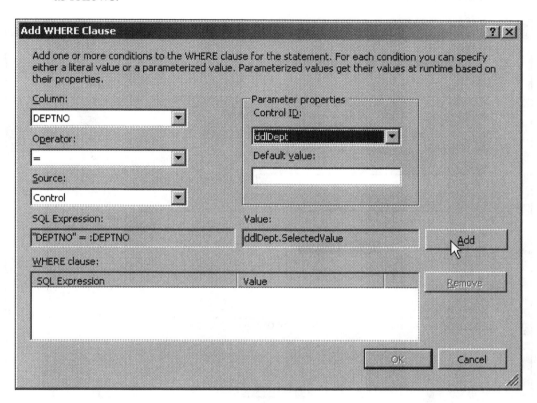

6. Once you provide the details of the **WHERE clause** as shown, click on **Add** and click on **OK**. At this point, the SELECT statement should look like the following:

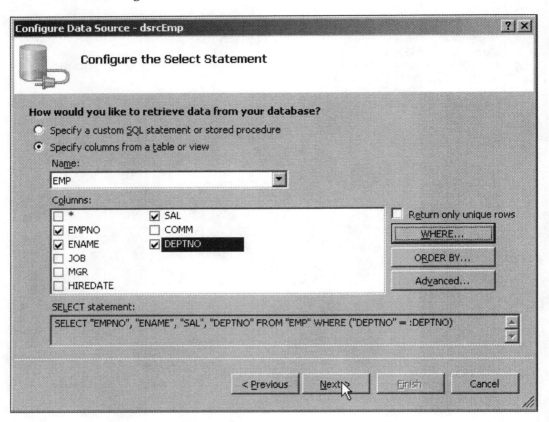

7. Click on **Next** and click on **Finish**.

8. From the smart tag of **DropDownList Tasks**, switch on the **Enable AutoPostBack** as follows:

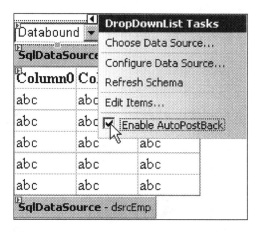

9. Using the smart tag of **GridView**, choose the data source as **dsrcEmp** as follows:

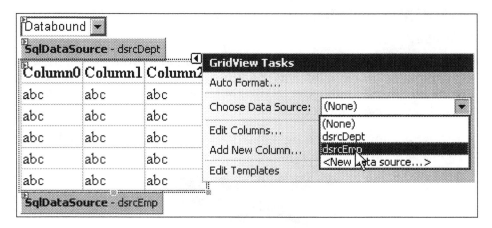

10. Once you press *F5*, you should have output like the following:

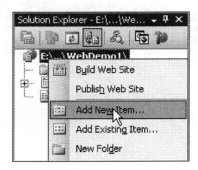

Add, Update, or Delete a Row Using GridView and FormView

In the previous forms, we simply retrieved the information from the database. Now, we shall manipulate database information using smart data binding. Let us add a new form Departments.aspx, which is meant for adding, updating, or deleting a department from Department table.

1. Using **Solution Explorer**, right-click on the project and go to **Add New Item...** as shown in the following screenshot:

2. In the **Add New Item** dialog box, select **Web Form** as template, provide the name as **Departments.aspx**, and click on **Add** as shown in the following screenshot:

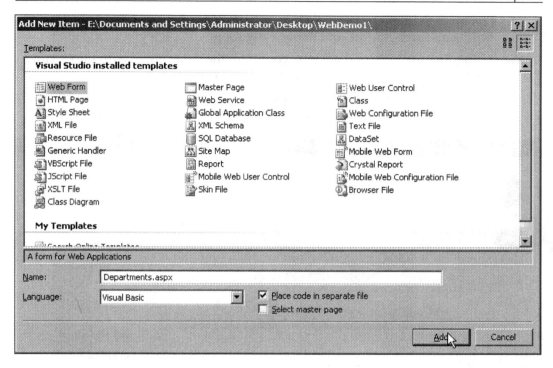

3. Using the **Solution Explorer**, right-click on **Departments.aspx** and click on **Set as Start Page** as shown in the following screenshot:

4. Switch to the **Design** view of **Departments.aspx**, drag and drop a **SqlDataSource** control, and name it **dsrcDept**.

5. Using the smart tag of **dsrcDept**, configure the data source with the existing connection **OrConnectionString** and click **Next**.

6. Select the table name as **DEPT**, check on **DEPTNO**, **DNAME**, and **LOC** for columns, and click on **Advanced...** as shown in the following screenshot:

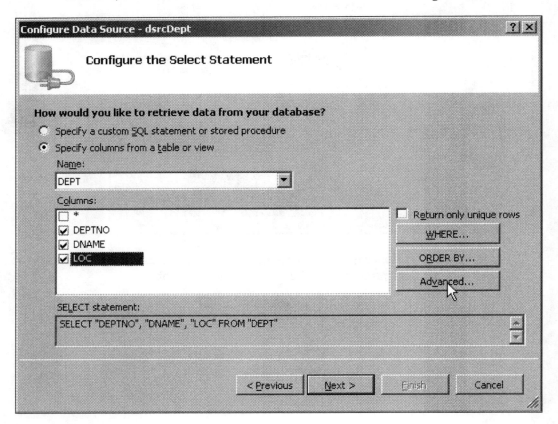

7. Within the **Advanced SQL Generation Options** dialog box, check on **Generate INSERT, UPDATE, and DELETE statements** and click **OK**.

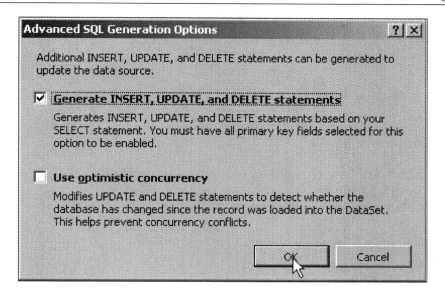

8. Click on **Next** and finally click on **Finish**.

9. Drag and drop a GridView from the toolbox on to the form, using the smart tag configure the data source, and select the options as shown below:

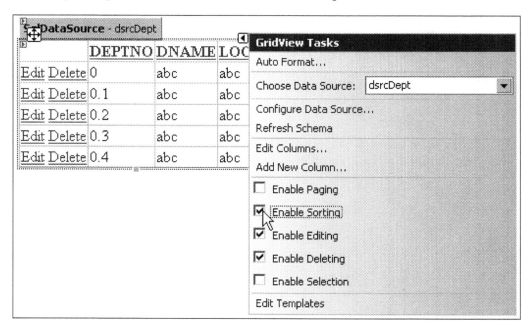

10. Using the properties of the GridView, provide **DEPTNO** as a value for the **DataKeyNames** property as shown below:

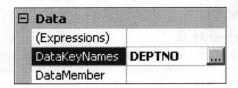

11. Drag a FormView control from the toolbox and drop it on to the form. Using its smart tag, configure its data source as **dsrcDept**. At this point, your form should look like the following:

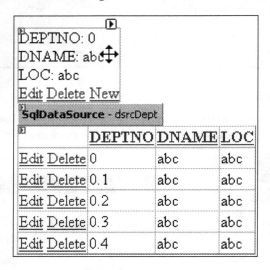

12. Again open up the smart tag of the FormView control and click on **Edit Templates**.

13. Select **InsertItemTemplate** as display mode:

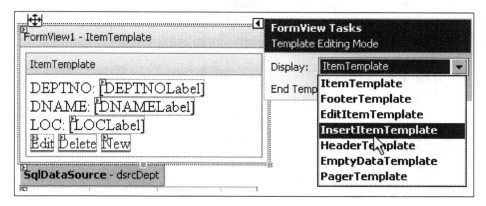

14. Within the template, select **Cancel** and press *Delete* to remove from the template.

15. Using the smart tag again, click on **End Template Editing** as shown below.

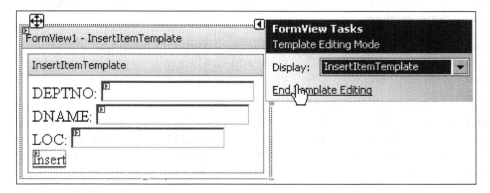

16. Using the properties of the FormView control change the **DefaultMode** to **Insert** as shown below:

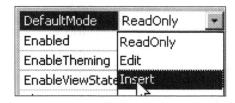

17. You can execute the form by pressing *F5* and play with all the **Insert**, **Edit**, and **Delete** options as shown in the following figure:

	DEPTNO	DNAME	LOC

DEPTNO:
DNAME:
LOC:
Insert

		DEPTNO	DNAME	LOC
Edit Delete		10	ACCOUNTING	NEW YORK
Update Cancel		20	RESEARCH	DALLAS
Edit Delete		30	SALES	CHICAGO
Edit Delete		40	OPERATIONS	BOSTON

Working with Web Controls Manually

In all of the previous examples, we didn't write one line of code! All the operations were achieved by simply configuring the data sources and controls together with mapping between them.

But, not every scenario would be solved using smart data binding. Let us now try to develop a new form with drop-down list and GridView controls, and develop code to bind those controls.

Add a new form to your project (set it as the start page) and drag and drop a drop-down list control (ddlDept) and a GridView control (gvEmp). Just for the sake of information, drag and drop a Label to provide the text **Select Department**. Make sure that the **AutoPostBack** property of the drop-down list control is modified to **true**. At this point, the form design should look like the following:

Select Department: Unbound ▼

Column0	Column1	Column2
abc	abc	abc
abc	abc	abc
abc	abc	abc
abc	abc	abc
abc	abc	abc

Modify your connection strings in `web.config` as follows (with your own values):

```
<connectionStrings>
  <add name="OrConnectionString"
    connectionString="Data Source=xe;Persist
    Security Info=True;
    User ID=scott;Password=tiger;Unicode=True"
    providerName="System.Data.OracleClient"/>
  <add name="OraConnStr"
    connectionString="Data Source=xe;
    User Id=scott;Password=tiger"
    providerName="System.Data.OracleClient"/>
</connectionStrings>
```

Modify your code in such a way that it looks like the following:

```
Protected Sub Page_Load(ByVal sender As Object,
ByVal e As System.EventArgs) Handles Me.Load
  If Not IsPostBack Then
    Me.ddlDept.DataSource = getResultSet("SELECT
                          deptno,dname FROM dept")
    Me.ddlDept.DataTextField = "dname"
    Me.ddlDept.DataValueField = "deptno"
    Me.ddlDept.DataBind()
    ddlDept_SelectedIndexChanged(Nothing, Nothing)
  End If
End Sub

Private Function getResultSet(ByVal strSQL As String)
                                        As DataTable
  Try
    Dim dt As New DataTable
    Dim da As New OracleDataAdapter(strSQL,
        New OracleConnection
        (ConfigurationManager.ConnectionStrings
        ("OraConnStr").ConnectionString.ToString))
    da.Fill(dt)
    da.Dispose()
    Return dt
  Catch ex As Exception
    Return Nothing
  End Try
End Function


Protected Sub ddlDept_SelectedIndexChanged(ByVal
```

```
sender As Object, ByVal e As System.EventArgs) Handles
ddlDept.SelectedIndexChanged
  Me.gvEmp.DataSource = getResultSet("SELECT
    empno,ename,sal,deptno FROM emp WHERE deptno = "
    & Me.ddlDept.SelectedItem.Value)
  Me.gvEmp.DataBind()
End Sub
```

In the above code, `getResultSet` is a method defined to accept a `SELECT` statement
as parameter and return the result set as a `DataTable` object. In the `Page_Load` event,
we populate the drop-down list using the following statements:

```
Me.ddlDept.DataSource = getResultSet("SELECT
                          deptno,dname FROM dept")
Me.ddlDept.DataTextField = "dname"
Me.ddlDept.DataValueField = "deptno"
Me.ddlDept.DataBind()
```

When the user selects a different item in the drop-down list, `ddlDept_`
`SelectedIndexChanged` gets fired and the GridView gets automatically populated
using the following statements:

```
Me.gvEmp.DataSource = getResultSet("SELECT
  empno,ename,sal,deptno FROM emp WHERE deptno = "
  & Me.ddlDept.SelectedItem.Value)
Me.gvEmp.DataBind()
```

Once you press *F5*, the output should look like the following screenshot:

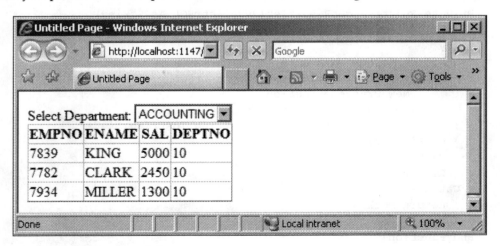

Developing Web Reports Using ASP.NET

We have several methods to design and develop reports using ASP.NET. In most scenarios, data web controls (like GridView, DataList, Repeater, etc.) are more than enough. But, there do exist other robust methods, which are dedicated only for reporting. One of these is .NET local or embedded reporting.

Let us start with a basic report. Even though we can work with a new solution, the previous solution is used to lessen the steps required. Before starting a report, we need to generate a strongly-typed dataset. Later, the report gets bound to this dataset.

Creating a Strongly-Typed Dataset Using Designer

The following are the steps to create a strongly-typed dataset:

1. Using the **Solution Explorer**, right-click on the project and go to **Add New Item**.

2. Select **Dataset** as template, provide the name as **Employee.xsd**, and click **Add**.

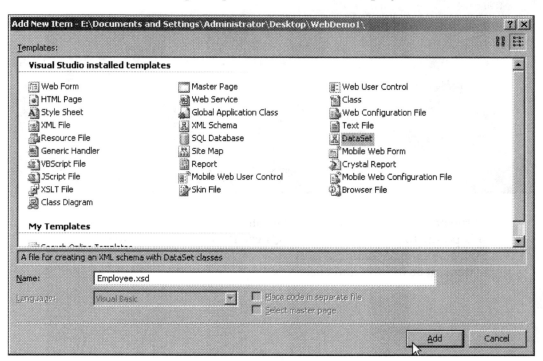

3. It will prompt you to place the dataset in a folder. Just press **Yes** and proceed.

4. The dataset gets created and the **TableAdapter Configuration Wizard** automatically starts. Create a **new connection** or select an existing connection to the database and click **Next**.

5. Select **Use SQL statements** as in the following screenshot and click **Next**.

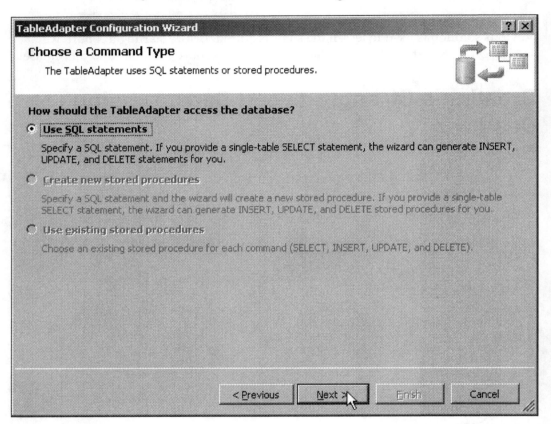

6. In the next screen, you will be prompted to enter an SQL statement. At this point, you can either use the **Query Builder...** button (to generate the SQL statement dynamically) or provide your own query. Provide the SQL statement as follows and click **Next**.

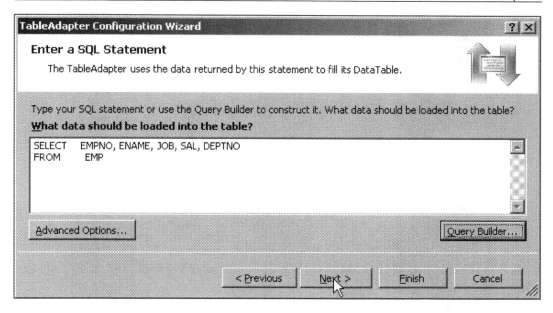

7. Select all the checkboxes in the next screen and click **Next** as shown below:

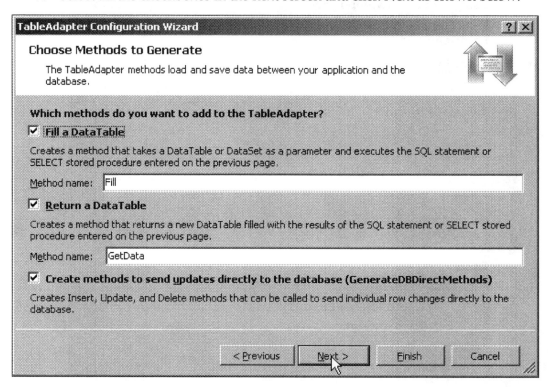

8. And finally click **Finish**. This causes the dataset to be automatically bound to the SELECT statement provided. At this point, the screen should look like the following:

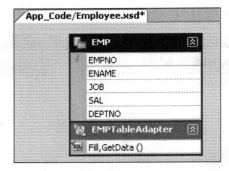

Designing and Binding a Report to the Dataset

Now that we have completed generating a strongly-typed dataset, it is time to start with a basic report design.

1. Using **Solution Explorer**, right-click on the project and go for **Add New Item**.
2. Within the **Add New Item** dialog box, select **Report** as template, provide **EmpReport.rdlc** as file name, and click on **Add**.

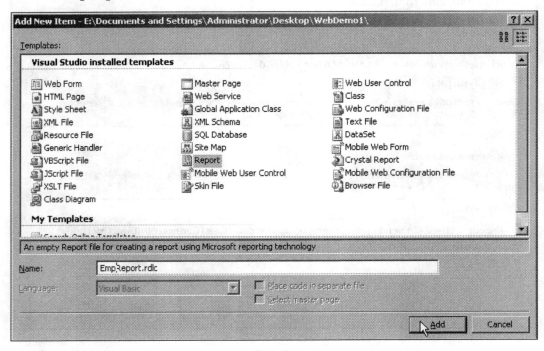

3. Once the report layout area is opened, you should also be able to see the **Web Data Sources** tool window (showing the dataset) as follows:

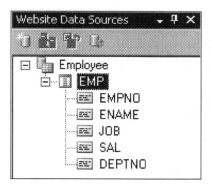

4. Select a **Table** from the toolbox and drop it on to the report layout.

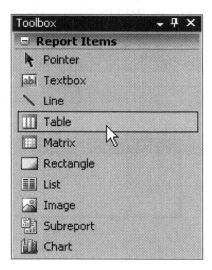

5. Drag and drop each of the fields from **Web Data Sources** into the **Detail** section of the table as follows:

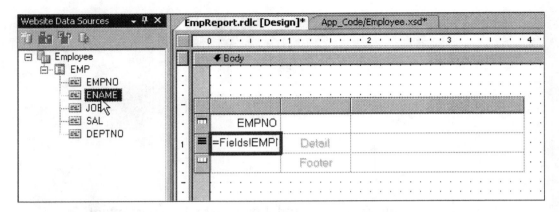

6. You can add columns to the right by right-clicking on the last column as follows:

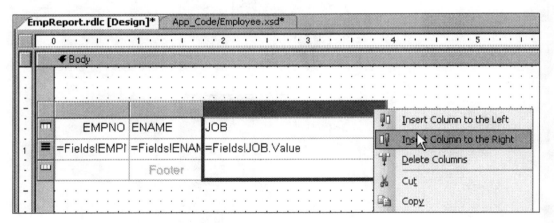

7. Once all the necessary columns are dropped into the table, select all the column headings (you can modify them according to your requirements) and make them bold as follows:

EMPNO	ENAME	JOB		SAL	DEPTNO
=Fields!EMPI	=Fields!ENAM	=Fields!JOB.Value	=Fields!SAL.Valu	=Fields!DEPTNO.	
		Footer			

8. At this point, the basic report design is completed. Now, we need to display the report as part of a web page. Add a new Web Form (make it a start page) **EmployeeReport.aspx** to the solution and switch to the **Design** mode.

9. Select a **ReportViewer** control from the **Toolbox** (as follows) and drop it on to the form.

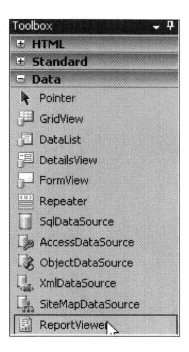

10. Using the smart tag of the **Report Viewer Tasks** control, select **EmpReport.rdlc**. This will automatically create a **ObjectDataSource** control.

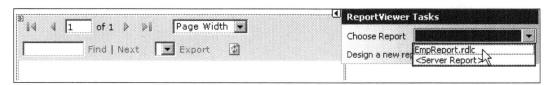

11. Once you execute the report using *F5*, the report should look like the following:

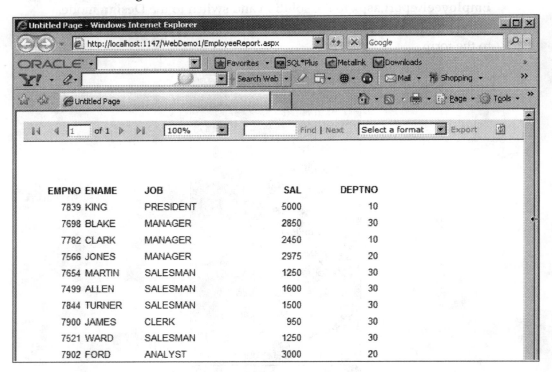

Grouping and Displaying Sub-Totals

Now, we shall expand the previous basic report to include grouping and displaying sub-totals. Let us group the list with respect to job and provide sub-totals for salaries. The following are the steps to achieve this:

1. Open the previous report, select a row in the table, right-click and select **Insert Group** as follows:

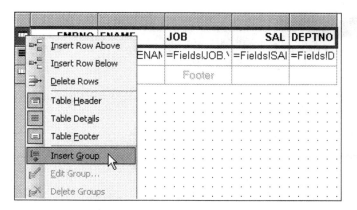

2. Select **Expression** as `=Fields!JOB.Value` as follows and click on **OK**.

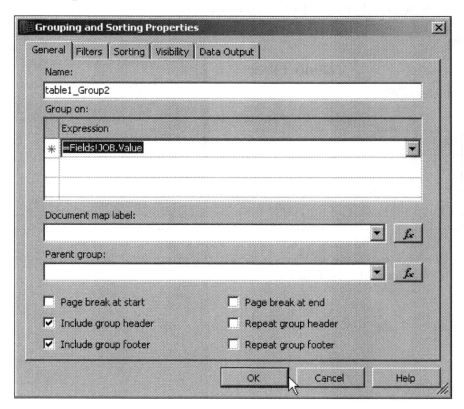

3. As we would like to display job in the first column, add a new first column manually to the table as follows:

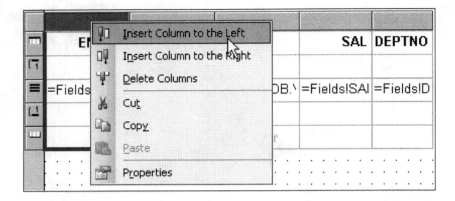

4. Drag the job-related cell (or field) into the group header cell of the first column and delete the **Job** column as follows:

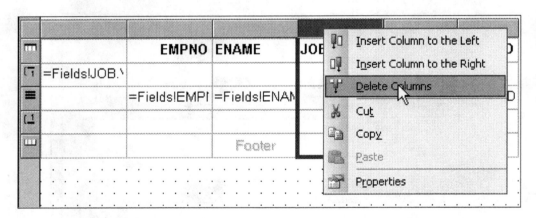

5. Press *F5* to execute and have a look at the grouping achieved. The report should look like the following:

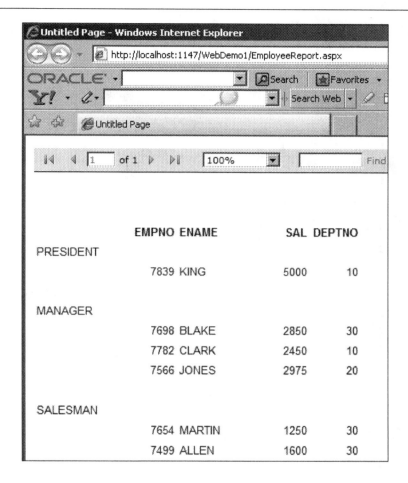

6. Switch back the **Design** mode and type `Total` in the Group footer of the **ENAME** column.

7. Drag and drop the **SAL** column from **Web Data Sources** into the Group footer of the **SAL** column.

	EMPNO	ENAME	SAL	DEPTNO
=Fields!JOB.				
	=Fields!EMP|	=Fields!ENAN	=Fields!SA|	=Fields!D
		Total	=Sum(Field	
		Footer		

8. You can play with different formats like italics, bold, etc., and finally press *F5* to execute the report.

9. The report should look like the following:

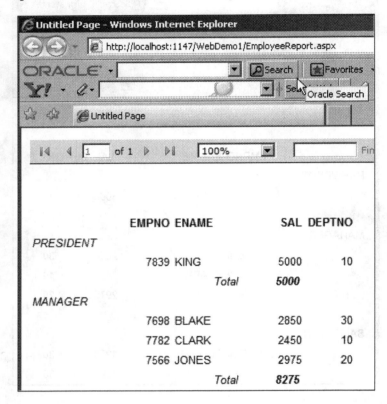

Embedding Charts (Graphs) in Reports

We shall further expand the previous report to embed charts (or graphs) as part of the same report. The following are the steps to achieve this:

1. Open the previous report, select **chart** from the **Toolbox** (as shown next), and drop it just to the right of the table in the report layout.

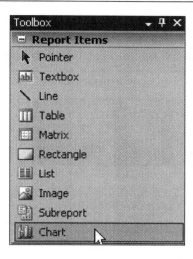

2. Drag **SAL** from **Web Data Sources** and drop it into the data fields. Similarly, drag **DEPTNO** from **Web Data Sources** and drop it into the category fields:

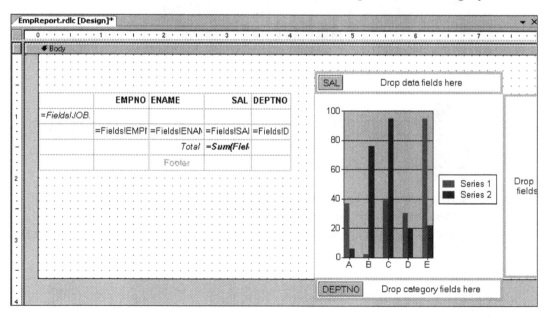

3. Right-click on the chart and go to its properties to modify the characteristics of the chart.

4. In the **General** tab, type **Department wise Salaries Title** as as follows:

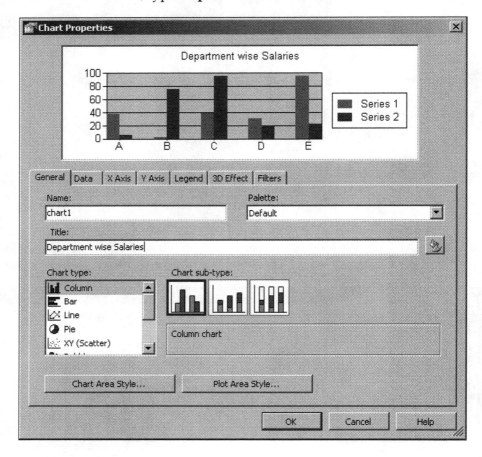

5. Similarly, provide titles for **X-Axis** and **Y-Axis** as Departments and Salaries respectively (using the respective tabs).

6. Remove the **Legend** just for clarity, switch on **3-D visual effect** and click **OK**.

7. Once you press *F5*, the report looks like the following:

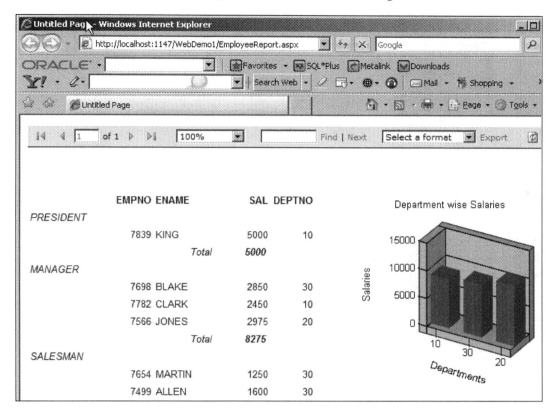

Object-Oriented Development Using ASP. NET and ODP.NET

In all of the previous sections, we simply programmed with traditional structured development. For better scalability, maintainability, and reusability, it is highly recommended to implement **OOP (Object-Oriented Programming)** in all of our applications.

ASP.NET has a plenty of support for OOP. And, the `ObjectDataSource` control is mainly meant for that. To make use of the full power of `ObjectDataSource`, we need to define some classes that map tables and database interactions and finally attach them to `ObjectDataSource`. Once the `ObjectDataSource` is configured, it can be used as a data source to other data web controls (like `GridView`, `DropDownList`, etc.).

In this scenario, two classes are added as follows:

- OraDBHelper to make the database interactions transparent to business logic.
- Emp, a business logic class that maps its properties to the columns of the Emp table and provides operations on that table. This class in turn uses OraDBHelper.

Once the Emp class is defined, we can use it for any number of ObjectDataSource controls spanned across any number of web forms. You may have to make sure that the connection strings are properly configured in web.config (as seen in *Working with Web Controls Manually*).

Developing a Simple Oracle Database Helper Class

An Oracle database helper is a class that is meant to interact with Oracle database. This makes the database interactions completely transparent to (or independent of) any of the business logic classes.

The following is a simple Oracle database helper class (OraDBHelper.vb) developed as part of this demonstration:

```vb
Imports Microsoft.VisualBasic
Imports Oracle.DataAccess.Client
Imports System.Data

Public Class OraDBHelper
   Public Shared Sub SQLExecute(ByVal strSQL As String)

     Dim cmd As OracleCommand = Nothing
     Try
       cmd = New OracleCommand(strSQL,
       New OracleConnection(ConnectionString))
       cmd.Connection.Open()
       cmd.ExecuteNonQuery()
       cmd.Connection.Close()
       cmd.Dispose()
     Catch ex As Exception
       If Not cmd Is Nothing Then
         If cmd.Connection.State = ConnectionState.Open
           Then
           cmd.Connection.Close()
         End If
       End If
```

```
      Throw New Exception(ex.Message)
    End Try
  End Sub

  Public Shared Function getResultSet(ByVal strSQL As
                                 String) As DataSet
    Try
      Dim ds As New DataSet
      Dim da As New OracleDataAdapter(strSQL,
          New OracleConnection(ConnectionString))
      da.Fill(ds)
      da.Dispose()
      Return ds
    Catch ex As Exception
      Throw New Exception(ex.Message)
    End Try
  End Function

  Private Shared ReadOnly Property ConnectionString() As
                                             String
    Get
      Return ConfigurationManager.ConnectionStrings
             ("OraConnStr").ConnectionString.ToString
    End Get
  End Property
End Class
```

This class contains two methods, namely `SQLExecute` and `GetResultSet`. Both of those methods are declared as `Shared` (static), which means they can be directly called or executed without creating any instance of the class `OraDBHelper`.

`SQLExecute` is used to execute any DML command (the DML command should be passed as parameter). The method is declared as follows:

```
Public Shared Sub SQLExecute(ByVal strSQL As String)
```

It simply opens a connection to the database and uses an `OracleCommand` to execute the DML command as shown below:

```
cmd = New OracleCommand(strSQL,
          New OracleConnection(ConnectionString))
cmd.Connection.Open()
cmd.ExecuteNonQuery()
cmd.Connection.Close()
cmd.Dispose()
```

GetResultSet is used to retrieve information from Oracle database. It accepts any SELECT command as parameter and returns a Dataset object. It is declared as follows:

```
Public Shared Function getResultSet(ByVal strSQL As
                                    String) As DataSet
```

It works with the OracleDataAdapter object to fill the DataSet object as shown below:

```
Dim ds As New DataSet
Dim da As New OracleDataAdapter(strSQL,
          New OracleConnection(ConnectionString))
da.Fill(ds)
da.Dispose()
Return ds
```

Finally, the connection string is retrieved from the web.config file using the following statement (part of the ConnectionString property):

```
ConfigurationManager.ConnectionStrings("OraConnStr").

                            ConnectionString.ToString
```

 The class is simply for demonstration. You can further improve it by providing support for automatic dataset updates, stored procedures, etc.

Developing a Simple Business Logic Class

A business logic class or component implements business rules for validation and processing besides providing information to the presentation layer (web form). In this scenario, we will develop a simple business logic class that maps to the Emp table. It in turn uses the Oracle database helper class discussed previously.

The following is a simple business logic class (Emp.vb) developed for demonstration:

```
Imports Microsoft.VisualBasic

Public Class Emp

    Private _empno As Integer
    Private _ename As String
    Private _sal As Double
    Private _deptno As Integer

#Region "Properties"
```

```vbnet
    Public Property Empno() As Integer
      Get
        Return _empno
      End Get
      Set(ByVal value As Integer)
        _empno = value
      End Set
    End Property

    Public Property Ename() As String
      Get
        Return _ename
      End Get
      Set(ByVal value As String)
        _ename = value
      End Set
    End Property

    Public Property Sal() As Double
      Get
        Return _sal
      End Get
      Set(ByVal value As Double)
        _sal = value
      End Set
    End Property

    Public Property Deptno() As Integer
      Get
        Return _deptno
      End Get
      Set(ByVal value As Integer)
        _deptno = value
      End Set
    End Property

#End Region

#Region "Operations"

  Public Function Insert(ByVal Emp As Emp) As String
    Dim sql As String
    sql = "INSERT INTO emp (empno,ename,sal,deptno) "
    sql &= "VALUES "
    sql &= "(" & Emp.Empno & ",'" & Emp.Ename & "',"
                    & Emp.Sal & "," & Emp.Deptno & ")"
```

```vbnet
    Try
       OraDBHelper.SQLExecute(sql)
       Return Nothing
    Catch ex As Exception
       Return ex.Message
    End Try
  End Function

  Public Function Update(ByVal Emp As Emp) As String
    Dim sql As String
    sql = "UPDATE emp SET "
    sql &= " ename='" & Emp.Ename & "', sal=" & Emp.Sal
                                  & ", deptno=" & Emp.Deptno
    sql &= " WHERE empno=" & Emp.Empno
    Try
       OraDBHelper.SQLExecute(sql)
       Return Nothing
    Catch ex As Exception
       Return ex.Message
    End Try
  End Function

  Public Function Delete(ByVal Emp As Emp) As String
    Dim sql As String
    sql = "DELETE FROM emp "
    sql &= " WHERE empno=" & Emp.Empno
    Try
       OraDBHelper.SQLExecute(sql)
       Return Nothing
    Catch ex As Exception
       Return ex.Message
    End Try
  End Function

  Public Function GetEmpList() As System.Data.DataSet
    Dim sql As String
    sql = "SELECT empno,ename,sal,deptno FROM emp"
    Return OraDBHelper.getResultSet(sql)
  End Function

#End Region

End Class
```

This class holds a row of employee information in the following fields:

```
Private _empno As Integer
Private _ename As String
Private _sal As Double
Private _deptno As Integer
```

All of the above fields (or private variables) are exposed with respective public properties as shown below:

```
Public Property Empno() As Integer
Public Property Ename() As String
Public Property Sal() As Double
Public Property Deptno() As Integer
```

To update or list employee information from the database, the above class is equipped with four methods declared as follows:

```
Public Function Insert(ByVal Emp As Emp) As String
Public Function Update(ByVal Emp As Emp) As String
Public Function Delete(ByVal Emp As Emp) As String
Public Function GetEmpList() As System.Data.DataSet
```

Each of those methods dynamically builds up its DML command and in turn works with the `OraDBHelper` class to interact with database. The `Insert`, `Update`, and `Delete` methods accept employee information as parameters of type `Emp` class itself.

Working with ObjectDataSource in an ASP.NET 2.0 Web Form

Now that we have developed database helper and business logic, it is time to develop a web form (or user interface) based on those classes. We will make use of the `ObjectDataSource` control available as part of ASP.NET 2.0 to interact with business logic.

The following are the steps to achieve this:

1. Add a new web form (`EmpUI.aspx`) to the solution and switch to design mode.

2. Drag and drop an **ObjectDataSource** control from the toolbox on to the web form and name it `odsrcEmp`.

3. Using the smart tag, click on **Configure Data Source**.

4. For **Choose your business object** in the **Configure Data Source** dialog box, select **Emp** as the business object, and click **Next**.

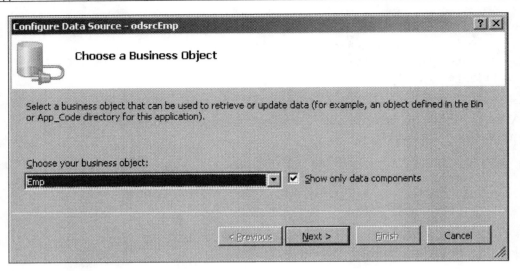

 If the object is not visible, uncheck **Show only data components** and try again.

5. Select **GetEmpList()** as the method of **SELECT**.

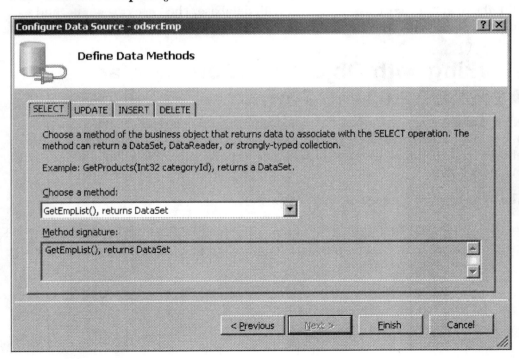

6. Select **Update(Emp Emp)** as the method of **UPDATE**.

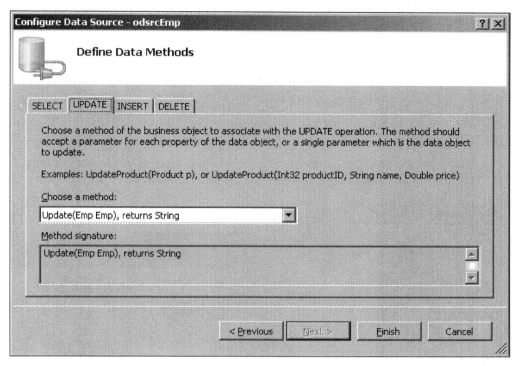

7. Similarly, select **Insert** as the method of **INSERT**, **Delete** as the method of **DELETE**, and click on **Finish**.

8. Drag and drop a **GridView** and configure the smart tag as follows:

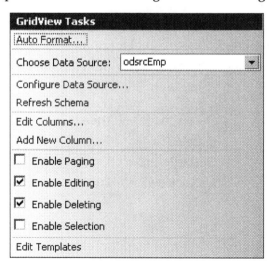

9. In the **Properties** window of the **GridView**, provide **empno** as a value for the property **DataKeyNames**:

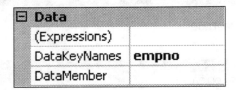

10. Drag and drop a **FormView** and configure the data source as **odsrcEmp**.

11. Using the **FormView** control, go to **Edit Templates** (of the smart tag) and choose **InsertItemTemplate**. Delete **Cancel**. It should look like the following:

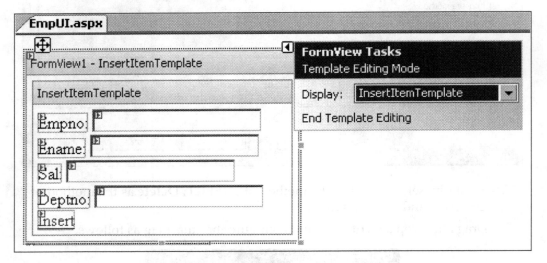

12. Click **End Template Editing** to get back to normal display.

13. Using the properties of the **FormView** control, change back the **DefaultMode** to **Insert** as follows:

DefaultMode	**Insert**
Enabled	True
EnableTheming	True
EnableViewState	True

14. Drag and drop a **label** and name it **lblMsg** (to display if any errors occur). At this point, the screen layout should look similar to the following:

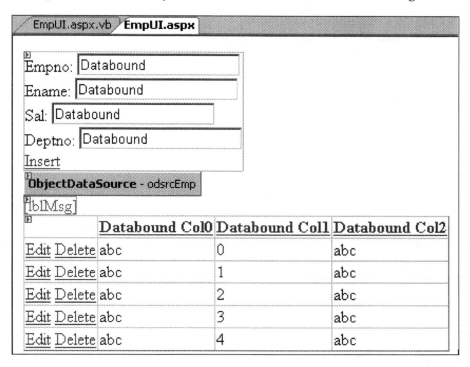

15. Modify your code to look similar to the following:

```
Partial Class EmpUI
  Inherits System.Web.UI.Page

  Protected Sub Page_Load(ByVal sender As Object,
  ByVal e As System.EventArgs) Handles Me.Load
    Me.lblMsg.Text = String.Empty
  End Sub

  Protected Sub odsrcEmp_Updated(ByVal sender As
  Object, ByVal e As System.Web.UI.WebControls.
  ObjectDataSourceStatusEventArgs) Handles
  odsrcEmp.Updated
    If Not e.ReturnValue = Nothing Then
      Me.lblMsg.Text &= e.ReturnValue
    End If
  End Sub
```

```
Protected Sub GridView1_RowUpdated(ByVal sender As
Object, ByVal e As System.Web.UI.WebControls.
GridViewUpdatedEventArgs) Handles
GridView1.RowUpdated
  If Not e.Exception Is Nothing Then
    Me.lblMsg.Text = e.Exception.Message
    e.ExceptionHandled = True
  End If
End Sub

End Class
```

In this code, during the `Page_Load` event, we clear the message area with the following statement:

```
Me.lblMsg.Text = String.Empty
```

The `odsrcEmp_Updated` is an event that gets fired when the **ObjectDataSource** control has finished executing the method related to the **UPDATE** operation (in this case, it is the `Update` method of the `Emp` class). Any error message during update gets displayed using the following construct:

```
If Not e.ReturnValue = Nothing Then
    Me.lblMsg.Text &= e.ReturnValue
End If
```

If the **GridVew** control receives any exception during the update, the message gets updated using the following construct available as part of the `GridView1_RowUpdated` event:

```
If Not e.Exception Is Nothing Then
    Me.lblMsg.Text = e.Exception.Message
    e.ExceptionHandled = True
End If
```

Once you press *F5*, the output should look similar to the following:

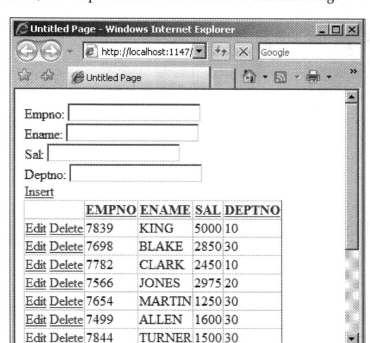

Developing Web Services Using ODP.NET

In this section, we will develop a simple .NET XML Web Service, which serves data from Oracle database to consuming applications. We will implement the Object-Oriented three-tier approach (as discussed previously) in this web service.

Creating the .NET XML Web Service

The following are the steps to create the Web Service:

1. Open your Visual Studio 2005 environment and go to **File** | **New** | **Web Site**.

2. In the **New Web Site** dialog box, select **ASP.NET Web Service** as the template, select **Location** as **HTTP** and provide the place as `http://localhost/OraService` as shown overleaf:

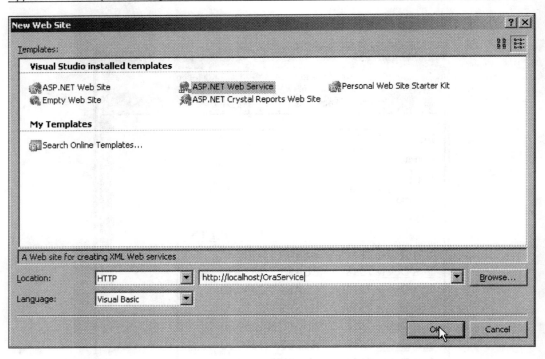

3. Add a reference to **Oracle.DataAccess** (as explained previously).

4. Add a new class file **OraDbLib.vb** and modify the code as follows:

```vb
Imports Oracle.DataAccess.Client
Imports Oracle.DataAccess.Types
Imports System.Xml
Imports System.Data

Public Class OraDbLib

  Dim _ConnStr As String
  Dim _DBConnError As String = ""

  Public Sub New()
    _ConnStr = ConfigurationManager.
                  ConnectionStrings("OraConnStr").
                   ConnectionString.ToString
  End Sub

  Public ReadOnly Property _
          ConnectionErrorDescription() As String
    Get
      Return _DBConnError
```

```vb
    End Get
  End Property

  Public Sub SQLExecute(ByVal sqlDML As String)
    Dim cn As New OracleConnection(_ConnStr)
    Try
      Dim SQL As String = sqlDML
      Dim cmd As New OracleCommand(SQL, cn)
      cmd.Connection.Open()
      cmd.ExecuteNonQuery()
      cmd.Connection.Close()
      cmd.Dispose()
    Catch ex As Exception
      Throw New Exception("Command cannot be executed.
          Received Error '" & ex.Message & "'
          when trying to execute the statement '"
          & sqlDML & "'")
    Finally
      If cn.State = ConnectionState.Open Then
        cn.Close()
      End If
    End Try
  End Sub

  Public Function getResultset(ByVal sqlSELECT As
                        String) As DataTable
    Dim cn As New OracleConnection(_ConnStr)
    Try
      Dim SQL As String = sqlSELECT
      Dim da As New OracleDataAdapter(SQL, cn)
      Dim dt As New DataTable
      da.Fill(dt)
      da.Dispose()
      Return dt
    Catch ex As Exception
      Throw New Exception("Command cannot be executed.
        Received Error '" & ex.Message & "' when
        trying to execute the statement '"
        & sqlSELECT & "'")
    Finally
      If cn.State = ConnectionState.Open Then
        cn.Close()
      End If
    End Try
  End Function
```

```
      Public Function getRowValue(ByVal sqlSELECT As
                                  String) As Object
        Dim cn As New OracleConnection(_ConnStr)
        Try
          Dim SQL As String = sqlSELECT
          Dim cmd As New OracleCommand(sqlSELECT, cn)
          cmd.Connection.Open()
          Dim value As Object = cmd.ExecuteScalar
          cmd.Connection.Close()
          cmd.Dispose()
          Return value
        Catch ex As Exception
          Throw New Exception("Command cannot be executed.
          Received Error '" & ex.Message & "' when trying
          to execute the statement '" & sqlSELECT & "'")
        Finally
          If cn.State = ConnectionState.Open Then
            cn.Close()
          End If
        End Try
      End Function

End Class
```

The class `OraDbLib` is very similar to the class `OraDBHelper` explained previously. Instead of working with `Shared` (static) methods (as in the `OraDBHelper` class), the above class defines normal methods, which are accessible only by creating an instance. `SQLExecute` and `getResultset` are already part of the `OraDBHelper` class and we have a new method added to this class called `getRowValue`, which is defined as follows:

```
Dim cn As New OracleConnection(_ConnStr)
Dim SQL As String = sqlSELECT
Dim cmd As New OracleCommand(sqlSELECT, cn)
cmd.Connection.Open()
Dim value As Object = cmd.ExecuteScalar
cmd.Connection.Close()
cmd.Dispose()
Return value
```

I removed the rest of the code for clarity. The above snippet simply connects to Oracle database, executes a SELECT statement, and returns only a single value or the value available in the first column of the first row.

Continuing from the previous steps, we need to proceed with the following:

5. Add a new class file **Emp.vb** and modify the code as follows:

```vb
Imports Microsoft.VisualBasic
Imports System.Data
Imports System.Xml.Serialization

Public Class Emp

    Private _empno As Integer
    Private _ename As String
    Private _sal As Double
    Private _deptno As Integer

    <XmlElement("Empno")> _
    Public Property Empno() As Integer
        Get
            Return _empno
        End Get
        Set(ByVal value As Integer)
            _empno = value
        End Set
    End Property

    <XmlElement("Ename")> _
    Public Property Ename() As String
        Get
            Return _ename
        End Get
        Set(ByVal value As String)
            _ename = value
        End Set
    End Property

    <XmlElement("Sal")> _
    Public Property Sal() As Double
        Get
            Return _sal
        End Get
        Set(ByVal value As Double)
            _sal = value
        End Set
    End Property

    <XmlElement("Deptno")> _
    Public Property Deptno() As Integer
        Get
```

```vb
      Return _deptno
    End Get
    Set(ByVal value As Integer)
      _deptno = value
    End Set
End Property

Public Function getList() As DataTable
  Dim SQL As String
  SQL = "SELECT Empno, Ename, Sal, Deptno "
  SQL &= "FROM    Emp"

  Try
    Dim oDB As New OraDbLib
    Dim dt As DataTable = oDB.getResultset(SQL)
    dt.TableName = "Emp"
    Return dt
  Catch ex As Exception
    Throw New Exception(ex.Message)
  End Try
End Function

Public Sub Find(ByVal empno As String)
  Dim SQL As String
  SQL = "SELECT Empno, Ename, Sal, Deptno "
  SQL &= "FROM    Emp"
  SQL &= "WHERE  empno = '" & empno & "'"

  Try
    Dim oDB As New OraDbLib()
    Dim dt As DataTable = oDB.getResultset(SQL)
    If dt.Rows.Count = 0 Then
      Throw New Exception("Employee not found")
    Else
      Me.Empno = dt.Rows(0)("empno")
      Me.Ename = dt.Rows(0)("ename")
      Me.Sal = dt.Rows(0)("sal")
      Me.Deptno = dt.Rows(0)("deptno")
    End If
  Catch ex As Exception
    Throw New Exception(ex.Message)
  End Try
End Sub

Public Sub Add(ByVal oEmp As Emp)
```

```vbnet
      Dim SQL As New System.Text.StringBuilder
      SQL.Append("INSERT INTO Emp(empno,ename,sal,deptno) VALUES ")
      SQL.Append("(")
      SQL.Append("     " & oEmp.Empno & ", ")
      SQL.Append("     '" & oEmp.Ename & "', ")
      SQL.Append("     " & oEmp.Sal & ", ")
      SQL.Append("     " & oEmp.Deptno & " ")
      SQL.Append(")")
      Try
        Dim oDB As New OraDbLib()
        oDB.SQLExecute(SQL.ToString)
      Catch ex As Exception
        Throw New Exception(ex.Message)
      End Try
    End Sub

    Public Sub Update(ByVal oEmp As Emp)
      Dim SQL As New System.Text.StringBuilder
      SQL.Append("UPDATE Emp ")
      SQL.Append("SET Ename='" & oEmp.Ename & "', ")
      SQL.Append(" Sal=" & oEmp.Sal & ", ")
      SQL.Append(" Deptno=" & oEmp.Deptno & " ")
      SQL.Append(" WHERE  empno = " & oEmp.Empno)
      Try
        Dim oDB As New OraDbLib()
        oDB.SQLExecute(Sql.ToString)
      Catch ex As Exception
        Throw New Exception(ex.Message)
      End Try
    End Sub

    Public Sub Delete(ByVal empno As String)
      Dim SQL As String
      SQL = "DELETE FROM Emp "
      SQL &= "WHERE empno = " & empno
      Try
        Dim oDB As New OraDbLib()
        oDB.SQLExecute(SQL)
      Catch ex As Exception
        Throw New Exception(ex.Message)
      End Try
    End Sub

End Class
```

This class has four properties declared with support for serialization as shown in the following:

```
<XmlElement("Empno")> _
Public Property Empno() As Integer

<XmlElement("Ename")> _
Public Property Ename() As String

<XmlElement("Sal")> _
Public Property Sal() As Double

<XmlElement("Deptno")> _
Public Property Deptno() As Integer
```

It is further declared with five methods as follows:

```
Public Function getList() As DataTable
Public Sub Find(ByVal empno As String)
Public Sub Add(ByVal oEmp As Emp)
Public Sub Update(ByVal oEmp As Emp)
Public Sub Delete(ByVal empno As String)
```

Each of those methods is specific to the respective operation with the database and all the operations are dealt with by an instance of the class `OraDbLib`.

To access a method (say `SQLExecute`) in the `OraDbLib` class, we simply need to create an instance out of it and directly access the method as shown below:

```
Dim oDB As New OraDbLib()
oDB.SQLExecute(Sql)
```

All of the methods in the above class interact with the database using an instance of the `OraDbLib` class.

Further continuing from the previous steps, we need to proceed with the following:

6. Modify the connection string section of **web.config** as follows:

```
<connectionStrings>
  <add name="OraConnStr" connectionString="Data
    Source=xe;User Id=scott;Password=tiger"
    providerName="System.Data.OracleClient"/>
</connectionStrings>
```

7. Make sure that **service.asmx** is set as start page and press F5 to execute and test the web service. If it prompts to modify **web.config for debugging,** press **OK**.

Consuming the Web Service from ASP.NET

Now, we will develop an ASP.NET web application that consumes the web service developed previously. The following are the steps:

1. Open Visual Studio 2005 environment.

2. Create a new website by going to **File | New | Web Site** and provide the information as shown in the following screenshot:

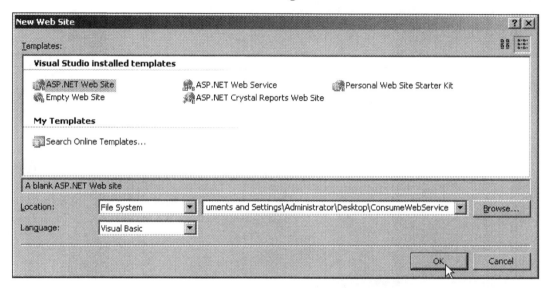

3. Using the **Solution Explorer**, right-click on the project and go to **Add Web Reference...** as follows:

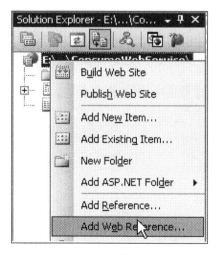

4. Browse the **Web services on the local machine** as shown below (if the web service is available on your local machine).

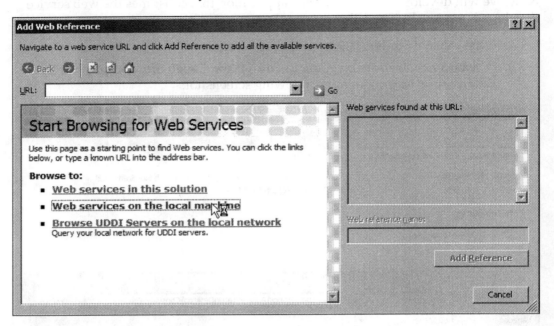

5. Select the web service created earlier:

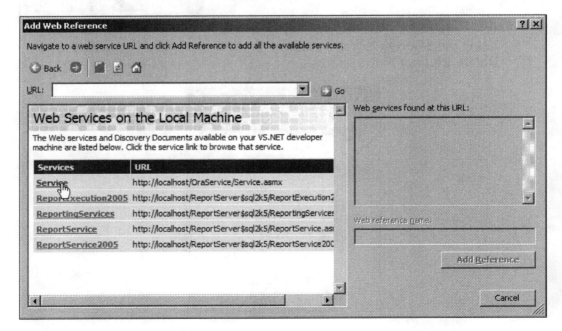

6. Provide the **Web reference name** as **EmpService** and click on **Add Reference**:

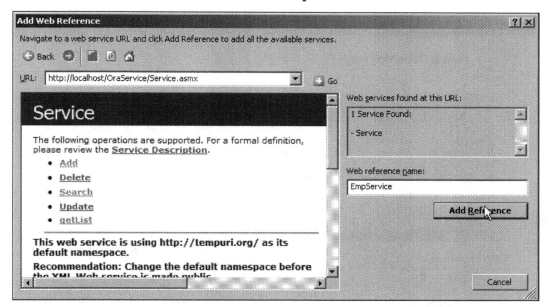

7. Drag a **GridView** control and an **ObjectDataSource** control on to the web form and configure the data source of **ObjectDataSource** (using the smart tag) as follows:

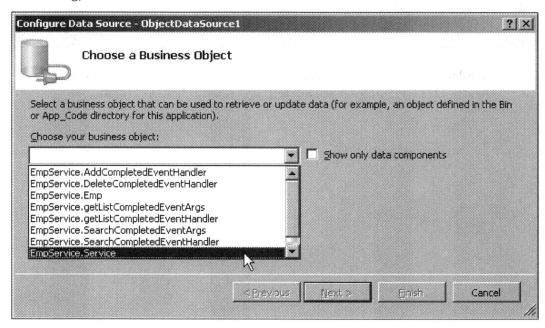

8. Click **Next** and provide the **SELECT** method as **getList()** as follows:

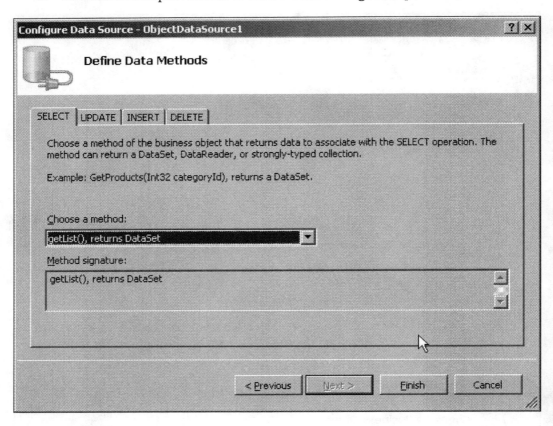

9. Similarly, provide the **UPDATE** method as **Update()**, **INSERT** method as **Add()**, **DELETE** method as **Delete()**, and finally click on **Finish**.

10. Using the smart tag of the GridView, configure its properties as follows:

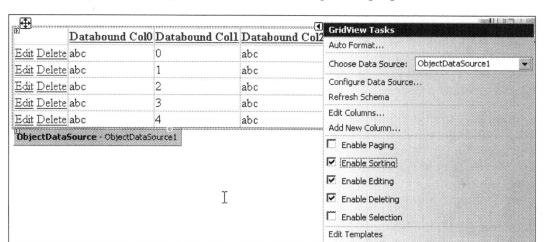

11. Using the **Properties** window provide the **DataKeyNames** property of the **GridView** as **empno**.

12. Press *F5* to test and execute the application.

Developing Smart Device Applications

Microsoft Windows Mobile Platform is now fully supported with .NET technology. We can develop and deploy .NET-based applications directly on to smart devices enabled with Microsoft Windows Mobile operating system. Before proceeding with developing smart device applications, let us discuss Microsoft Windows Mobile platform and the devices supporting it.

Introducing Microsoft Windows Mobile

There exist several types of smart devices in the market including Smart Phones, Pocket PCs, Pocket PC Phones, Tablet PCs, etc. Every smart device is installed with a mobile-based operating system with respect to the features of the device. One of such operating systems is Microsoft Windows CE.

Microsoft Windows CE is a small, embedded operating system (runs from ROM) that has a look and feel similar to Microsoft Windows 95/98. It includes scaled down versions of Microsoft Excel, Microsoft Word, Microsoft Internet Explorer, etc.

Microsoft Windows Mobile (Windows Mobile in short) is a complete software platform built on Windows CE. Unlike Windows CE, the Windows Mobile for Smart Phone or Pocket PC operating systems is specifically designed for devices that require a specialized hardware configuration. The software includes standardized interfaces and applications that ensure compatibility across hardware designs. The Pocket PC is the best example device that gets equipped with Microsoft Windows Mobile operating system.

The Pocket PC runs Windows CE as its core operating system. Pocket PCs come with mobile versions of Microsoft Office applications in addition to Microsoft Outlook Mobile. Though there are different Pocket PCs, many come with Wi-Fi to enable you to connect to the Internet when you are near to a wireless hotspot. You can compose email messages and send them wirelessly or by synchronizing with your desktop computer.

A Pocket PC Phone is a bit different from an ordinary Pocket PC. You can do everything with a Pocket PC Phone that you can do with a Pocket PC, but with the addition of cellular phone capabilities. If you have a Pocket PC Phone, you can access the Internet through the GPRS service.

A Smart Phone has phone capabilities and comes with a smaller set of applications. Though you can add third-party software titles to your Smart Phone, the smaller keypad and screen are designed to give you quick one-handed access to important data. A Smart Phone is a good choice for business users who need to check email, keep track of their calendars, and take voice notes.

Microsoft.NET enables us to develop and deploy .NET applications on Microsoft Windows Mobile-enabled smart devices like Smart Phones, Pocket PCs, Tablet PCs, etc. To develop for either Smart Phones or Pocket PCs, we need not really buy those devices. We simply need to have smart device client extensions installed as a part of Visual Studio 2005 (which automatically installs .NET Compact Edition). When the extensions are installed, we are provided with few device emulators for developing and testing .NET-based mobile applications. However, for testing and production, it is recommended to have physical smart devices.

The next section focuses on developing a simple Pocket PC application, which consumes the web service developed previously.

Consuming a Web Service from Pocket PC

We have already developed a web service previously. Now, let us make use of the same web service for the Pocket PC. You need not have a physical Pocket PC in your hands to test it.

We can simply use existing emulators available as part of Visual Studio 2005. The following are the steps:

1. Open Visual Studio 2005 Environment.
2. Go to **File | New | Project**.
3. Select and provide information as shown in the following figure:

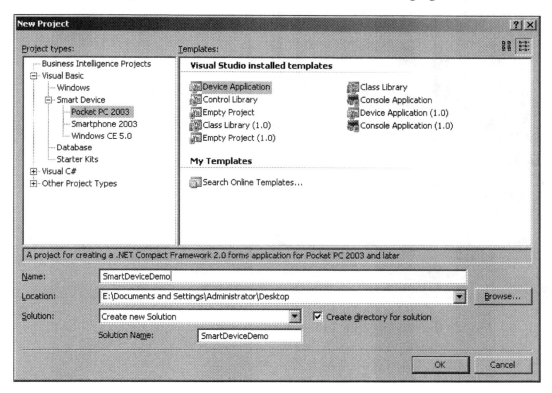

4. Add a Web Reference for the web service you created earlier.

5. Drag and drop a **DataGrid** on to the Pocket PC emulator as shown below:

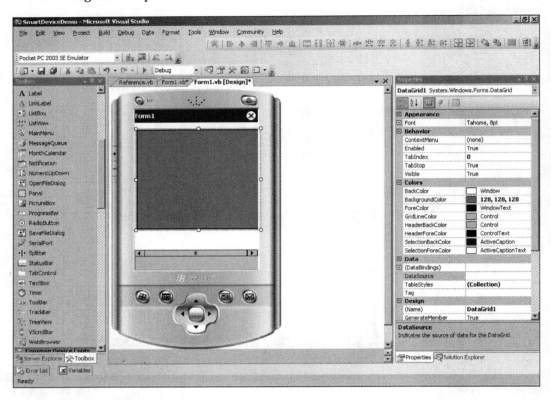

6. Modify the existing code as follows:

```
Public Class Form1
  Private Sub Form1_Load(ByVal sender As
  System.Object, ByVal e As System.EventArgs) Handles
  MyBase.Load
    Me.DataGrid1.DataSource =
        (New EmpService.Service).getList.Tables(0)
  End Sub
End Class
```

7. Press *F5*, and select any Emulator for deployment. The output should look like the following:

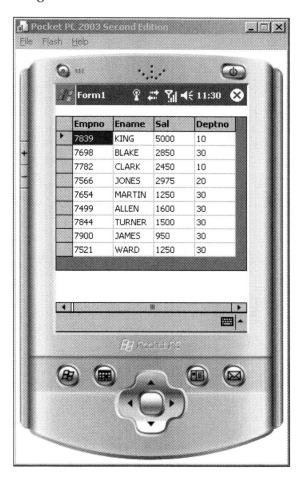

Summary

In this chapter, we concentrated on real-world application development covering the aspects of asynchronous and multi-threaded development, web applications (ASP.NET), web reporting, object-oriented development, web services development, and smart device (Pocket PC) application development.

9

Introduction to Oracle Developer Tools for Visual Studio 2005

Oracle Developer Tools for Visual Studio is an "add-in" for Microsoft Visual Studio 2003/2005, which helps developers to work with Oracle database and develop Oracle-based .NET applications without leaving the Visual Studio Environment. You can download it for free from `http://www.oracle.com/technology/software/tech/windows/odpnet/index.html`.

In this chapter, we will mainly focus on the following:

- Features of Oracle Developer Tools for Visual Studio
- Creating and debugging PL/SQL stored procedures using Visual Studio
- Developing applications using the Automatic Code Generation feature of ODT
- Developing and deploying .NET CLR stored procedures in Oracle database using Visual Studio

Features of Oracle Developer Tools

Oracle has released Oracle Developer Tools (ODT in short) for Visual Studio .NET 2003/2005 to provide integrated support for developing .NET applications that access Oracle databases.

When ODT gets installed, the most important feature we notice is the **Oracle Explorer** (available through the **View** menu of Visual Studio.NET). It allows us to browse existing Oracle objects (like tables, views, stored procedures, etc.), create or modify tables using table designer, view or edit data, execute SQL statements, etc.

Some of the other major features are the following:

- Designers and Wizards
- Automatic Code Generation
- PL/SQL Editor
- Stored Procedure Testing
- Oracle Data Window
- SQL Query Window
- Integrated Help System

In this section, we will have a glimpse at the most commonly used features along with sample screenshots.

 Before working with ODT, make sure that you configure your connection to connect to Oracle database using Oracle client.

Connecting to Oracle from Visual Studio Using Oracle Explorer

Once ODT is installed on your system, you should be able to observe the **Oracle Explorer** option in the **View** menu as follows:

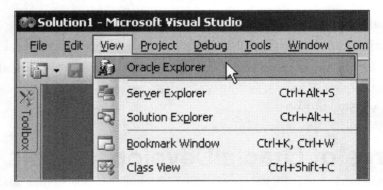

Oracle Explorer allows you to connect to and work with Oracle database from within the Visual Studio environment. It is very similar to Server Explorer (in Visual Studio) except that it works only with Oracle databases.

Once you click on **Oracle Explorer**, you should be able to see the following:

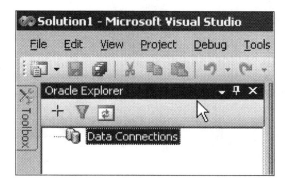

Using the **Oracle Explorer** window, you can connect to Oracle database using **Add Connection** as follows:

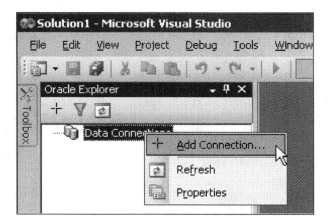

Once you are prompted with the **Add Connection** dialog box, you can provide your own connection parameters similar to following:

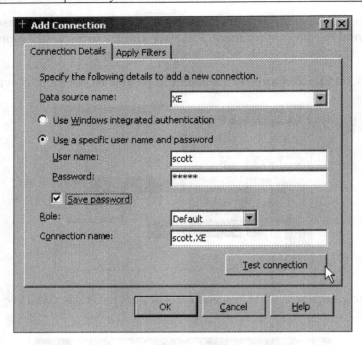

Once you hit **Test connection**, you should see the following message:

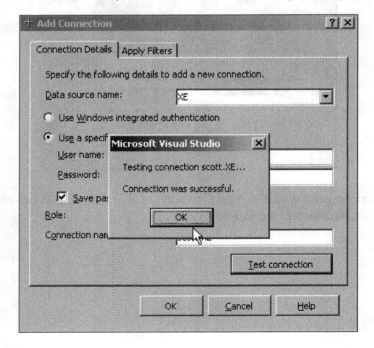

After hitting **OK** twice, you will see **scott.xe** added to **Data Connections**. Once you open the **scott.xe** tree and further open the **Tables** folder, you should be able to view the following:

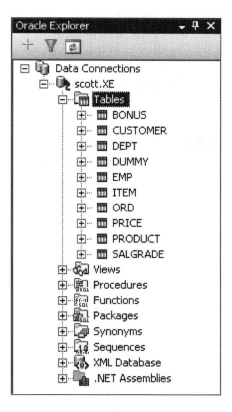

Retrieving Oracle Information from Visual Studio Using ODT

One of the easiest ways to retrieve Oracle table or column information is by using **Oracle Explorer** together with the **Properties** window. The moment we select a database object, the details will be shown in the properties as follows:

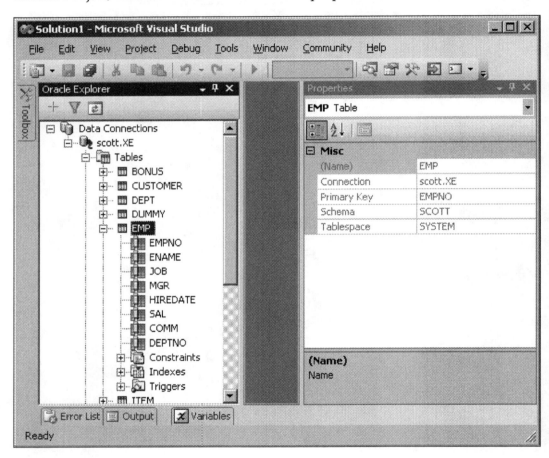

Similarly, when a column is selected, the details get pulled out as follows:

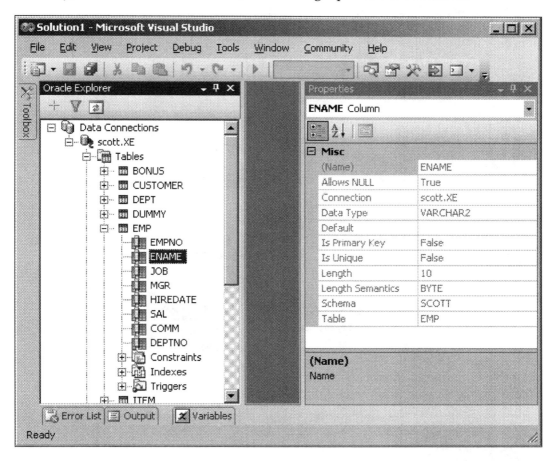

To retrieve all rows in a table, we can simply right-click on the table and select **Retrieve Data...** as follows:

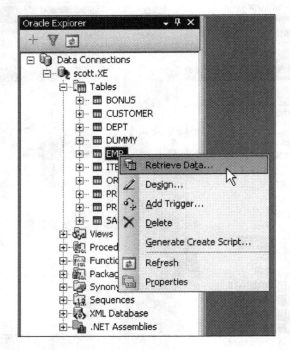

That would automatically bring all the rows into the Visual Studio environment where we can view or modify the information as follows:

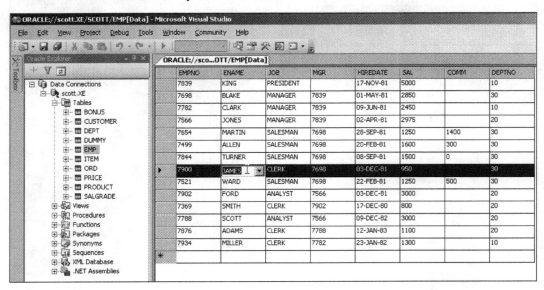

If you would like to write your own query, execute it, and view the results, you can use the **Query Window** option as follows:

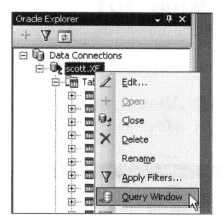

Once the **Query Window** is opened, you can provide your own query and execute it as follows:

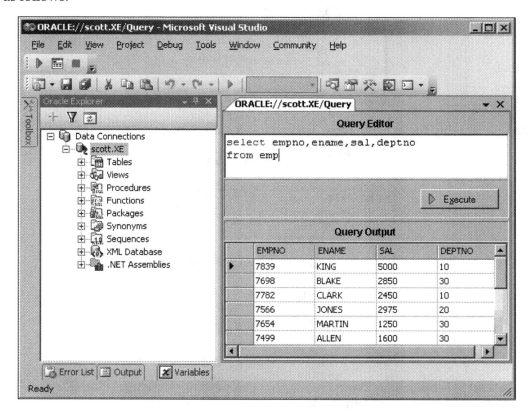

Working with Oracle Database Objects from Visual Studio Using ODT

We can create, modify, and drop different database objects from within the Visual Studio environment using ODT. All of the most important database objects that are frequently used by developers are accessible through ODT.

Dealing with Tables, Views, and Sequences Using ODT

You can create a new table by right-clicking on **Tables** and selecting **New Relational Table...** as follows:

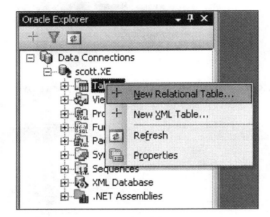

You can modify the existing table design by selecting **Design...** as follows:

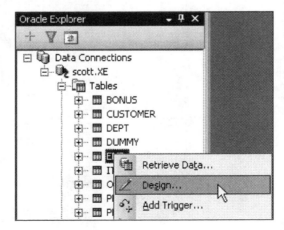

Once a table is opened in Design mode, you can modify all the information (including columns, constrains, indexes, etc.) visually as follows:

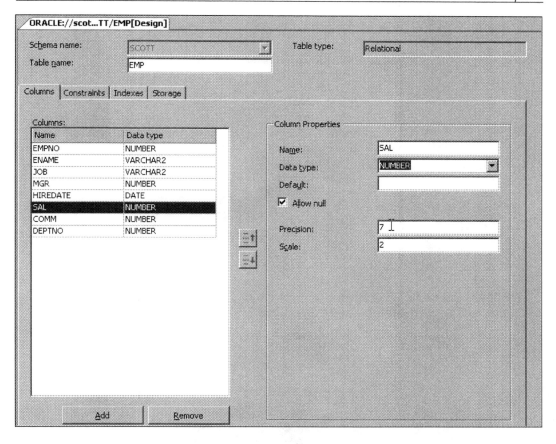

You can create or modify views in Oracle as follows:

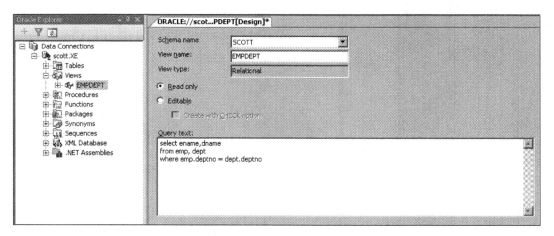

You can also create and work with sequences by right-clicking on the **Sequences** folder as follows:

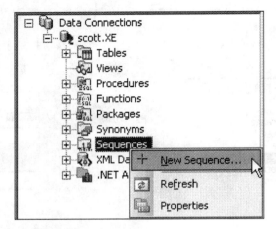

The following screenshot defines a sequence named **EMPSEQ**, which starts at **1001** and ends at **2001** with an incremental value of **1**:

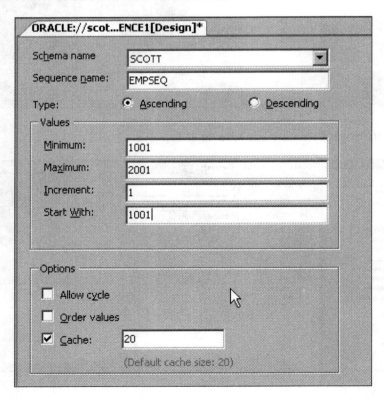

Very similar to sequences, we can even define synonyms with the following layout:

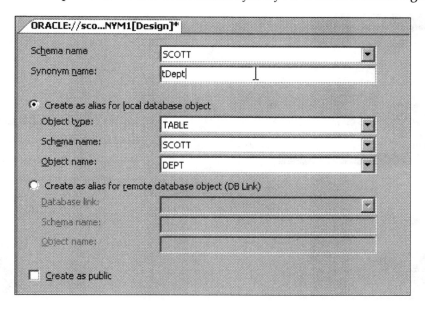

Another nice feature of ODT is the support for stored procedures, functions, and packages. We can straight away create, modify, test, and execute these objects from within the Visual Studio Environment together with other features like IntelliSense, automatic script generation, etc.

Creating Stored Procedures Using ODT

You can observe the following sequence of figures to create a stored procedure using ODT. The following initiates the creation of a new PL/SQL stored procedure:

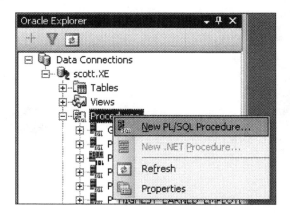

The following are the details of the stored procedure being created:

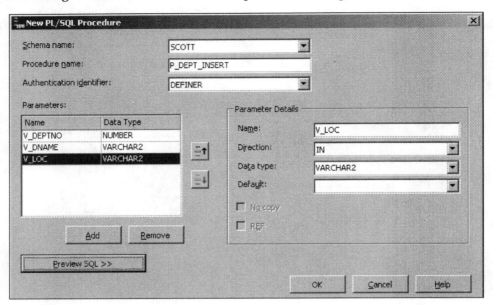

The moment **Preview SQL** is hit, you will observe the script generation as follows:

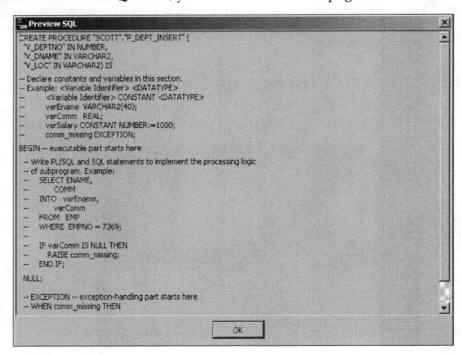

The moment we save the stored procedure, the Visual Studio environment automatically opens the stored procedure for editing (along with automatic code generation and IntelliSense support) as follows:

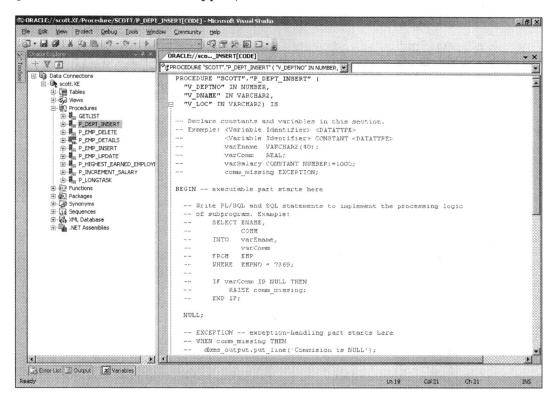

Debugging PL/SQL Stored Procedures from Visual Studio

ODT is tightly integrated with Visual Studio even to the level of debugging PL/SQL stored procedures. Before using the PL/SQL debugging feature, we need to configure the database and Visual Studio environment to enable PL/SQL debugging. Let us start configuring the database first.

We need to provide a few privileges for user Scott, to allow him to debug PL/SQL stored procedures. Once he is provided with the privileges, we will create a sample stored procedure and develop a small Windows (desktop) application, and finally debug the application together with a PL/SQL stored procedure.

Log in with DBA privileges (or log in as SYSTEM user) and execute the following two commands:

```
SQL>grant debug any procedure to scott;
SQL>grant debug connect session to scott;
```

Open your Visual Studio IDE and create a new **Windows Application** project. In the Project properties of the application, make sure that **Enable the Visual Studio hosting process** is checked off (in the **Debug** tab) as follows. This is required as the debugging process crosses beyond the Visual Studio Debugger level.

Go to the **Tools** menu and switch on **Oracle Application Debugging** as follows:

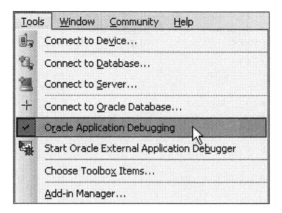

Go to the **Tools** menu again and within the **Options**, switch on **PL/SQL debugging** (of ODT) for all the necessary connections (you may have to connect to the database using **Oracle Explorer** prior to doing this) as follows:

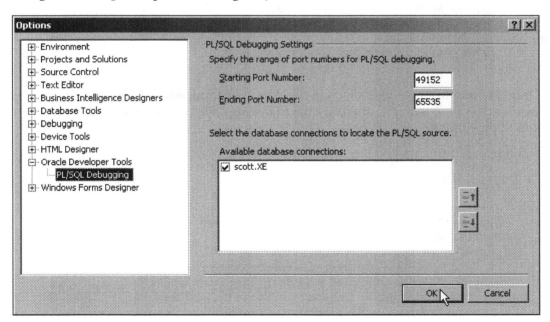

Develop a stored procedure in Oracle database (in SCOTT user) as follows:

```
CREATE OR REPLACE PROCEDURE p_emp_details(p_empno
   emp.empno%TYPE, p_ename OUT emp.ename%TYPE,
   p_AnnSal OUT NUMBER, p_deptno OUT emp.deptno%TYPE)AS
   v_Sal emp.sal%TYPE;
   v_AnnSal NUMBER(11,2);
BEGIN
   SELECT ename, sal, deptno
   INTO p_ename, v_Sal, p_deptno
   FROM emp
   WHERE empno = p_empno;
   v_AnnSal := v_Sal * 12;
   p_AnnSal := v_AnnSal;
EXCEPTION
   WHEN NO_DATA_FOUND THEN
     RAISE_APPLICATION_ERROR(-20001,
                                  'Employee not found');
   WHEN TOO_MANY_ROWS THEN
     /* this would not happen generally */
     RAISE_APPLICATION_ERROR(-20002,
          'More employees exist with the same number');
   WHEN OTHERS THEN
     RAISE_APPLICATION_ERROR(-20003, SQLERRM);
END;
```

Drag a button from the toolbox on to the Windows form, add reference to `Oracle.DataAccess.dll,` **and copy the following code, which executes the above stored procedure:**

```
Imports Oracle.DataAccess.Client

Public Class Form1

   Private Sub Button1_Click(ByVal sender As
   System.Object, ByVal e As System.EventArgs) Handles
   Button1.Click
     Dim cn As New OracleConnection("data source=xe; _
                      user id=scott;password=tiger")
     Dim cmd As New OracleCommand("p_emp_details", cn)
     cmd.CommandType = CommandType.StoredProcedure
     cmd.Parameters.Add("p_empno", OracleDbType.Double)
     cmd.Parameters.Add("p_ename", OracleDbType.Varchar2,
                20, Nothing, ParameterDirection.Output)
     cmd.Parameters.Add("p_AnnSal", OracleDbType.Double,
                            ParameterDirection.Output)
     cmd.Parameters.Add("p_deptno", OracleDbType.Int16,
                            ParameterDirection.Output)
```

```
        cmd.Parameters("p_empno").Value = 7369
        cmd.Connection.Open()
        cmd.ExecuteNonQuery()
        cn.Close()
        MsgBox(cmd.Parameters("p_ename").Value.ToString & ","
        & Convert.ToString(cmd.Parameters("p_AnnSal").Value))
    End Sub

End Class
```

This code starts with creating an `OracleConnection` and adds an `OracleCommand`, which is linked with the stored procedure `p_emp_details`. As the stored procedure accepts four parameters, all of them are added using `OracleCommand`. Once the stored procedure gets executed using the `ExecuteQuery` method, the output parameters (`p_ename`, `p_AnnSal`, and `p_deptno`) get filled with values, which are finally displayed using `MsgBox`.

Using the **Oracle Explorer**, right-click on **P_EMP_DETAILS** and click on **Compile Debug** as follows:

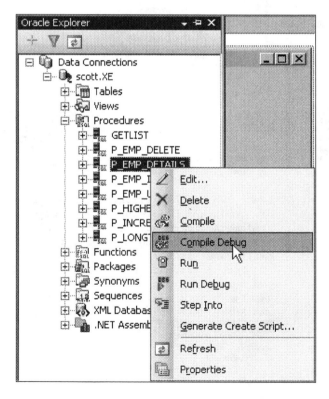

That will put the stored procedure into debug mode as follows:

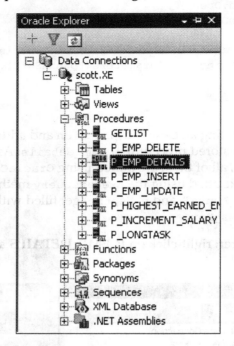

Now, place some break points in your .NET code as follows:

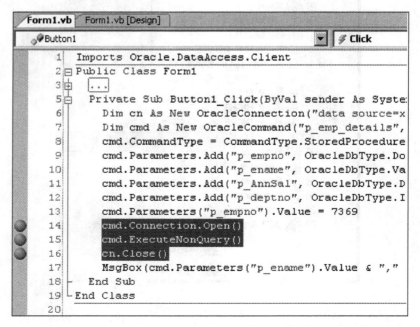

Similarly, double-click on the stored procedure (in **Oracle Explorer**) and place break points as shown in the following screenshot:

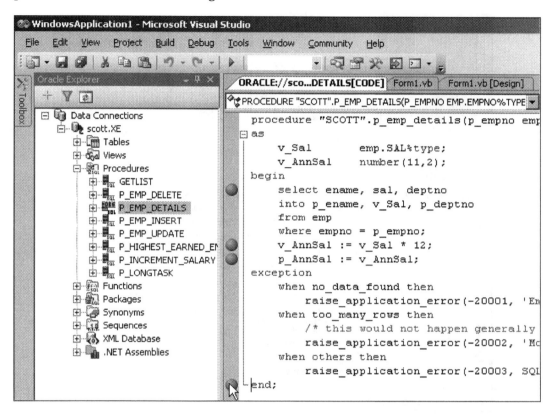

Finally hit *F5* to debug the application. It runs through each of the break points available in the .NET code as follows:

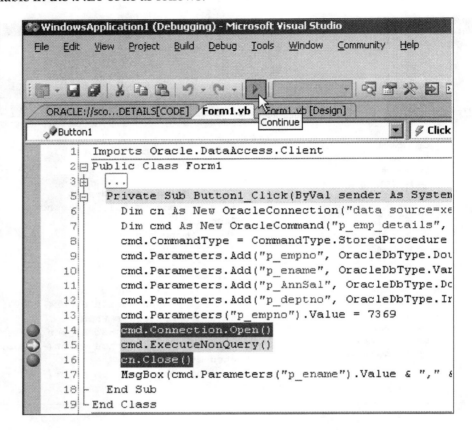

On hitting *F5* again, it starts to debug the stored procedure as follows:

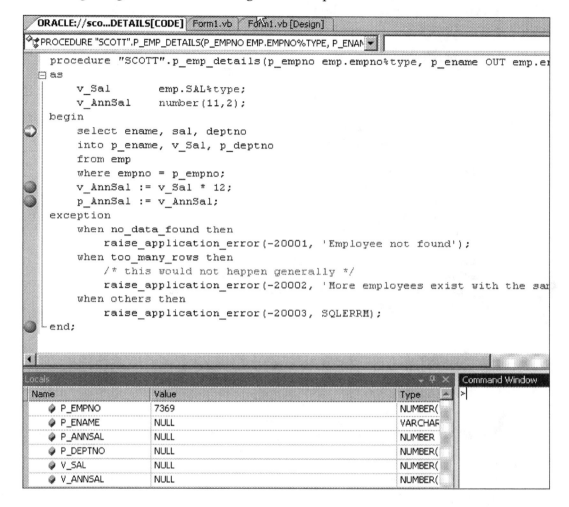

You can also observe the local variables and their values during debugging. Hitting *F5* further, you should be able to observe that the values get assigned to variables as follows:

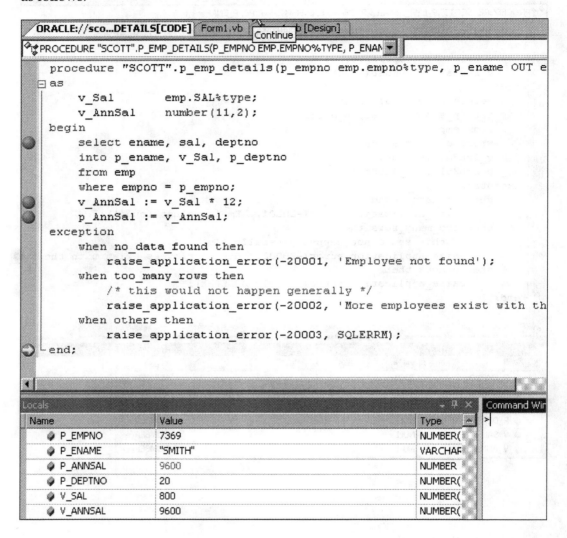

Finally, the control comes back to the Visual Studio environment (after debugging the PL/SQL stored procedure) and waits at the final break point as follows:

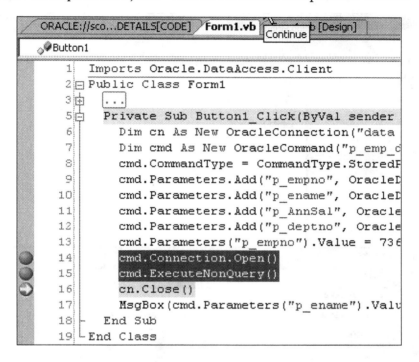

.NET CLR Stored Procedures in Oracle

Every programmer knows that Oracle database supports native stored procedures with the help of PL/SQL. The trend of "native stored procedures" expanded even to the capability of supporting external language-based stored procedures.

Oracle started supporting Java (external language) stored procedures from Oracle version 8i onwards. And now, it has further expanded its capability, even to the .NET-based CLR stored procedures (using any .NET language like VB.NET, C#, etc.) with Oracle version 10.2 onwards (Windows version). In this section, we will completely focus on working with .NET CLR stored procedures on Oracle 10.2 database.

Now, let us develop a small .NET stored procedure, which is very much a rewrite of IncrementSalary. The following are the steps to achieve this:

1. Open **Microsoft Visual Studio**.
2. Go to **File | New | Project**.

3. In the **New Project** dialog box, select **Oracle Project** as the template and provide the project name as **SampleCLR**, and click on **OK**.

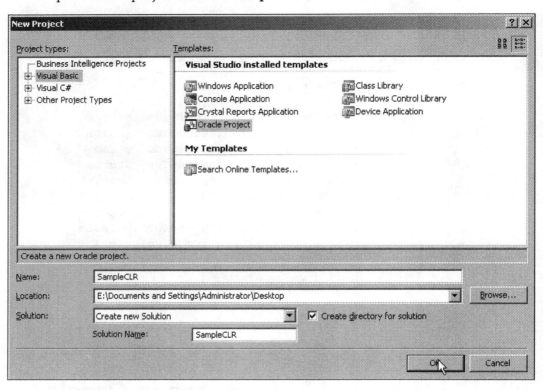

4. Delete the existing class (`class1.vb`) and add a new class named **Employee.vb**.

5. Copy the following code:

```vb
Imports Oracle.DataAccess.Client
Imports Oracle.DataAccess.Types

Public Class Employee

  Public Shared Sub IncrementSalary(ByVal empno As
  Integer, ByVal incrementValue As Double)
    ' Add code here.
    Dim conn As New OracleConnection("context
                          connection=true")
    conn.Open()
    Dim cmd As OracleCommand = conn.CreateCommand
    cmd.CommandText = "UPDATE scott.emp SET sal =
                sal + " & incrementValue & " WHERE
                empno = " & empno
```

```
      cmd.ExecuteNonQuery()
      cmd.Dispose()
      conn.Close()
   End Sub

   End Class
```

6. Rebuild the solution.

7. Right-click on the solution and click on **Deploy**:

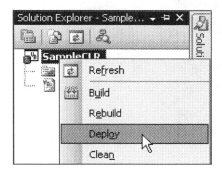

8. **Oracle Deployment Wizard for .NET** opens up; simply click on **Next**.

9. Click on **New Connection...** in the **Configure your OracleConnection** screen:

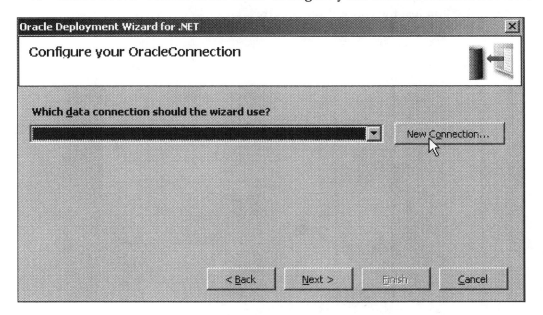

10. In the **Add Connection** dialog box, provide all the connection details as follows:

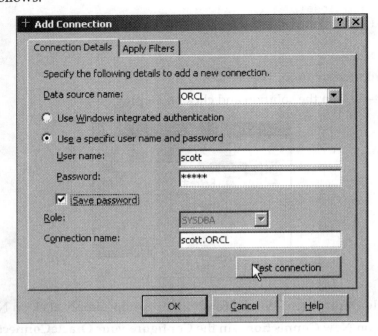

11. Once you test the connection, hit **OK**.

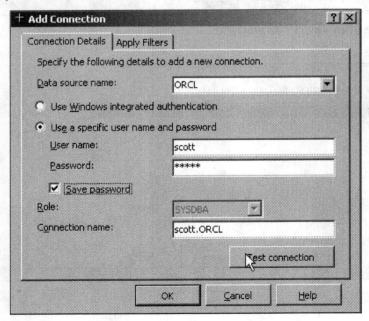

12. Click **Next**, select **Copy assembly and generate stored procedures**, and click on **Next**:

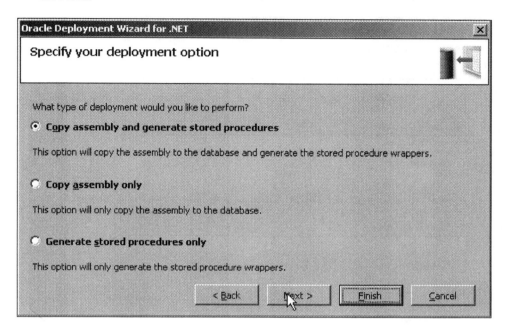

13. Leave the library name as **SAMPLECLR_DLL** and click on **Next**:

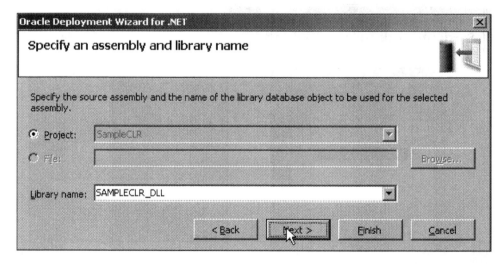

14. In the **Specify copy options** screen, you can provide the **Destination subdirectory**. At this moment, simply leave it blank and click on **Next**.

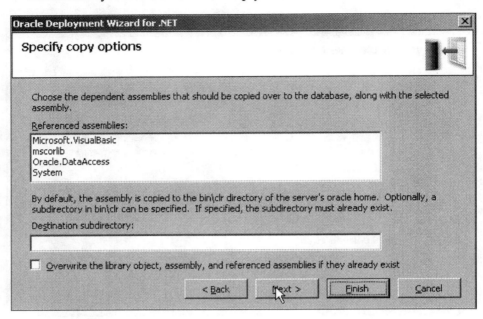

15. Select as shown in the following screenshot and click on **Next**:

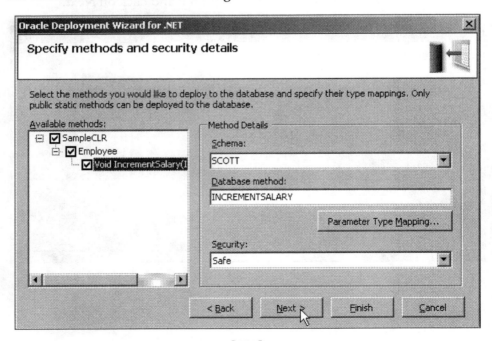

16. Check the final summary screen and hit **Finish**:

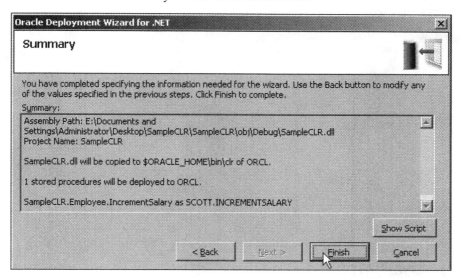

17. Once it gets deployed, it should show up in **Oracle Explorer**. Right-click on the same stored procedure and click on **Run** as shown in the following screenshot:

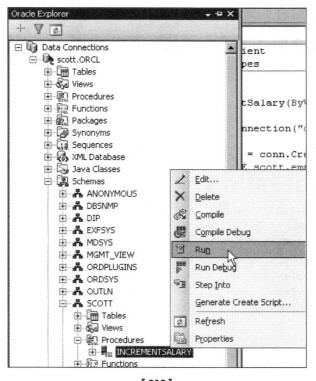

18. In the **Run Procedure** dialog box, provide parameter values as follows and click on **OK**:

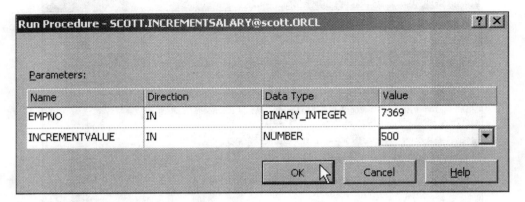

19. If it gets successfully executed, you should see the following output:

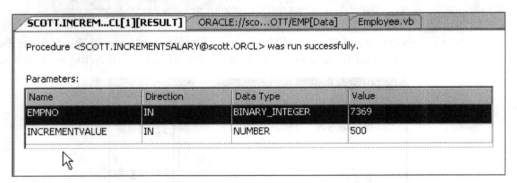

Taking Advantage of Automatic .NET Code Generation

Let us consider that we would like to develop a simple Windows form that lists out all the employees in a grid. To develop this application using ODP.NET, generally, we would need to add a reference to **Oracle.DataAccess.dll**, create objects based on `OracleConnection`, `OracleCommand`, and `OracleDataAdapter`, create a `DataSet`, fill it with data, and finally bind it to the GridView. If we need to work with a strongly-typed dataset, we would need to add a dataset to our project using Visual Studio and use the **BindingSource** tool to easily bind the dataset to the GridView.

Instead of achieving all of these steps manually, we can make use of the *Automatic Code Generation* feature available through ODT. This is a great feature, which provides a drag-and-drop facility to create all the necessary objects (including adding references) and to develop code automatically.

Let us try to develop the same application by making use of the Automatic Code Generation feature. The following are the steps:

1. Open Microsoft Visual Studio.

2. Go to **File | New | Project**.

3. In the **New Project** dialog box, select **Windows Application** as the template and provide the project name as **AutoCodeGen**, and click on **OK**:

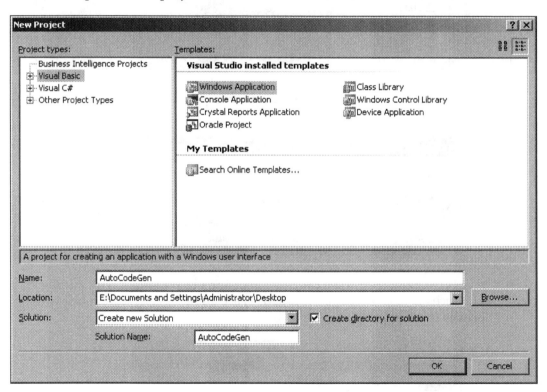

4.   With **Oracle Explorer** already opened and connected, simply drag the **Emp** table from **Oracle Explorer** on to the **Form1** as follows:

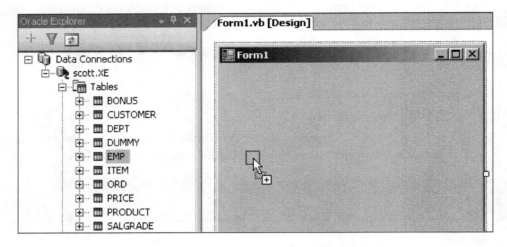

5.   You will be prompted to save the connection password in the generated code. Just press **Yes**:

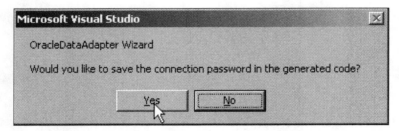

6.   `OracleDataAdapter` and `OracleConnection` objects (along with adding references to `Oracle.DataAccess.dll`) are automatically added below the form as follows:

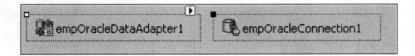

7. Using the smart tag of **empOracleDataAdapter1**, click on **Generate Dataset...** as follows:

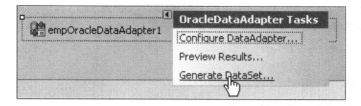

8. This brings up the **OracleDataAdapter Wizard** as follows:

9. Click on **Next** and, in the **Configure your OracleConnection** screen, select the existing connection (or create a new connection) and hit **Next**:

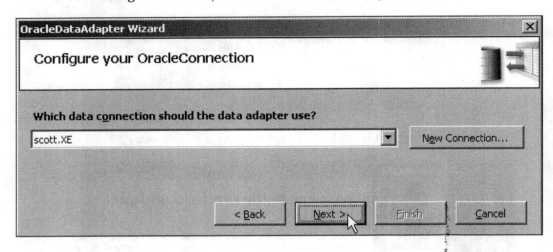

10. In the **Specify your SELECT statement type** screen, select **Create SQL SELECT statement** and hit **Next** as shown below:

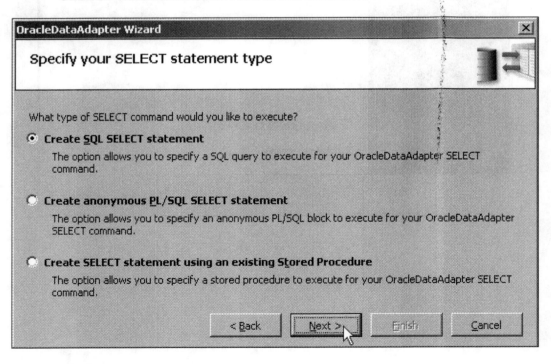

11. In the **Configure your SELECT statement** screen, you can modify the SELECT statement or simply hit **Next** as shown in the following screenshot:

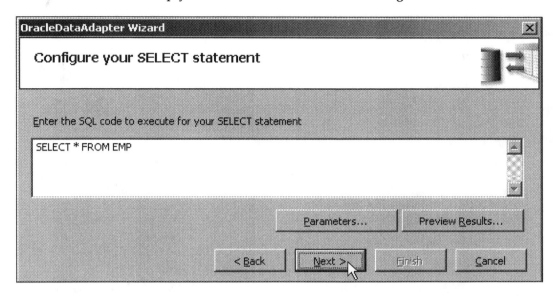

12. In the next screen simply select **Automatic** (which automatically generates all DML statements for the table) as follows and hit **Next**:

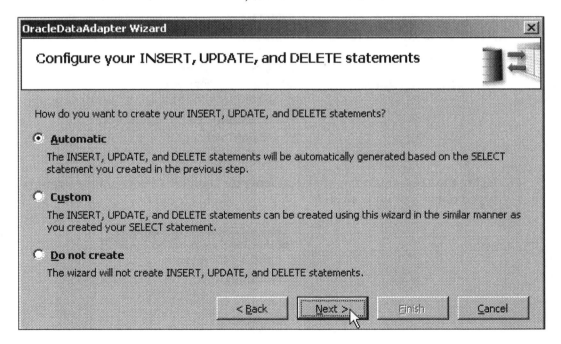

13. Make sure that the **Summary** screen looks like the following, and then hit **Finish**.

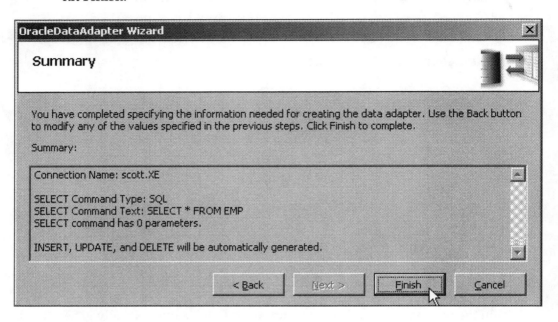

14. When it prompts for saving of the connection password, hit **Yes**.

15. Using the smart tag of the **empOracleDataAdapter1** object, click on **Preview Results...** to give you the list of employees:

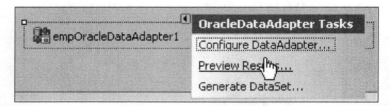

16. Using the same smart tag, click on **Generate DataSet...** to generate a strongly-typed dataset along with code:

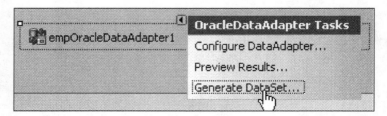

17. You should be able to see a new dataset named **Emp11** created as follows:

18. You will also see a new file named `Emp1.xsd` added to **Solution Explorer** as follows:

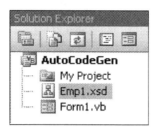

19. You can check the dataset with fields using the option **Edit in DataSet Designer...** of **Emp11** as follows:

20. The dataset designer looks like the following:

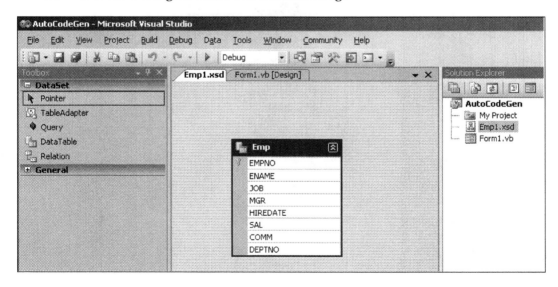

21. We can modify the attributes of each of the fields using the **Properties** window.

22. To view the automatic code generated by the designer, click on the **Show All Files** button in **Solution Explorer** as shown below:

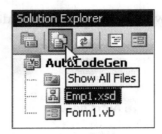

23. Go down to **Emp1.Designer.vb** and double-click on it.

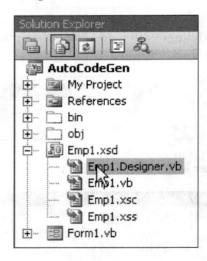

24. The code that is automatically created, looks like the following:

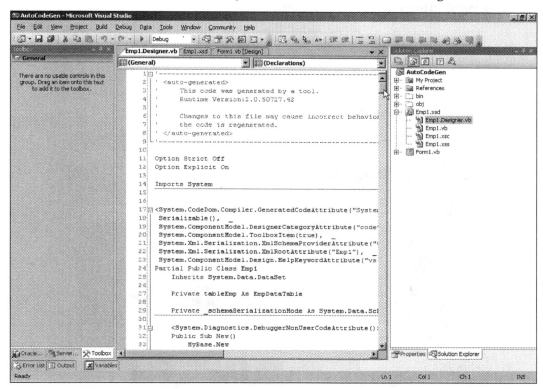

25. Now, go back to Form design, drag a GridView control onto the form and using the smart tag choose the data source as follows:

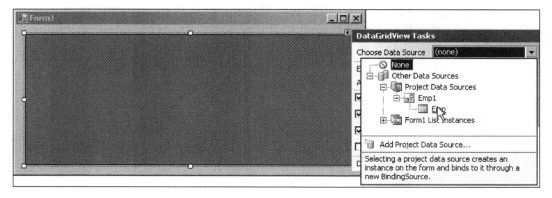

26. When the data source is selected, you can observe a new object **EmpBindingSource** at the bottom:

27. The GridView also gets automatically populated with the columns (as available in the dataset) at design time itself as shown in the following screenshot:

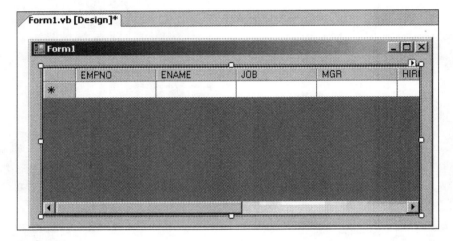

28. In the Form Load event, just add the code that simply fills the dataset, as seen in the following screenshot:

```
Form1.vb*    Form1.vb [Design]*
Form1                                                    (Declar

1  Public Class Form1
2
3      Private Sub Form1_Load(ByVal sender As Object,
4          Me.empOracleDataAdapter1.Fill(Me.Emp11)
5      End Sub
6  End Class
7
```

29. Hit *F5* to execute the application, and the output should look like the following:

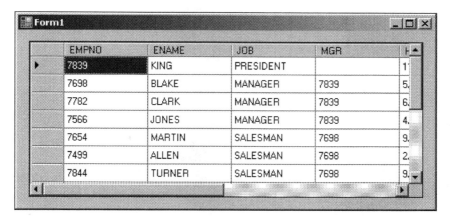

Summary

In this last chapter, we have gone through the features of Oracle Developer Tools for Visual Studio, creating and debugging PL/SQL stored procedures, developing and deploying .NET CLR stored procedures in Oracle database, and finally concluded with developing applications with the Automatic Code Generation feature of ODT.

Index

D

data, manipulating
DDL statements executing, OracleCommand used 71
DML statements executing, OracleCommand used 71
offline data, updating to database 82-84
OracleCommandBuilder, working with 84, 85
OracleDataAdapter, working with 84, 85
transaction, working with 86, 87

data, retrieving
data sets, working with 48
data tables, working with 48
from Oracle, ODP.NET used 37
fundamental classes 37
OracleDataReader used 39
performance improving techniques 67-69

database, Oracle
arrays, passing 116
arrays, receiving 116-121
arrays, sending 117, 118
changes, notifying to applications 185
CLOB information, retrieving 143
documents, retrieving 154-158
documents, uploading 154-157
images retrieving, BLOB used 153
images uploading, BLOB used 150
large objects 131
LOBs 131
text information, inserting 140, 141

data sets
master-detail information, presenting 58-61
populating, with multiple data tables 56, 57
populating, with single data table 55, 56
web reports, binding 224
working with 48

DataTableReader
working with 54

data tables
DataTableReader, working with 54, 55
filling, OracleDataReader used 51, 52
multiple rows retrieving, OracleDataAdapter used 48-50
single row retrieving, OracleDataAdapter used 52, 53
working with 48

DDL. *See* **statements, executing**
DML. *See* **statements, executing**

E

error handling
first error, displaying 88, 89
multiple errors, displaying 89-91
single error, displaying 88, 89
eXtensible Markup Language. *See* **XML**

F

factory class 15
features, ODT
Oracle, connecting to 266, 267
Oracle database objects 274-278
Oracle information, retrieving 270-273
functions. *See* **user-defined functions**
fundamental classes
for retrieving data 37

L

large objects
about 131
BFILE 131
BLOBs 131
CLOBs 131
types 131
LOBs. *See* **large objects**
long running applications
developing 193-198
multi-threading 195-198
Not Responding error 194

M

MARS
working with 126
Microsoft Windows CE 259
Multiple Active Result Sets. *See* **MARS**

N

native XML
node information, extracting 181-183
working with 175

U

user-defined functions
executing 109-111
executing, in PL/SQL package 114-116
working with 98

W

web applications
ASP.NET DropDownList control, populating 199-206
ASP.NET GridView control, linking 207, 210, 211
developing 199
developing, smart data binding used 199
rows, adding 212-218
rows, deleting 212-218
rows, updating 212-218
web control, working manually 218-220
web controls
working manually 218-220
web reports
charts, embedding 232-234
dataset, binding to 224-228
designing 224-227
developing, ASP.NET used 221
graphs, embedding 232-234
strongly-typed dataset creating, designer used 221-224
sub-totals, displaying 228-232
sub-totals, grouping 228-232

web services
.NET XML service, creating 247-254
consuming 255-259
consuming, from Pocket PC 260-263
developing 247

X

XML
about 159, 160
document generating, SELECT used 160
Oracle XML DB 159
rows. manipulating 171
SELECT statement 160
XML, generating from existing rows
ADO.NET Dataset used 163, 164
DBMS_XMLGEN used 166, 167
ExecuteXMLReader used 164-166
rows to HTML converting, XML and XSLT used 167-170

Thank you for buying

ODP.NET Developer's Guide

About Packt Publishing

Packt, pronounced 'packed', published its first book "*Mastering phpMyAdmin for Effective MySQL Management*" in April 2004 and subsequently continued to specialize in publishing highly focused books on specific technologies and solutions.

Our books and publications share the experiences of your fellow IT professionals in adapting and customizing today's systems, applications, and frameworks. Our solution based books give you the knowledge and power to customize the software and technologies you're using to get the job done. Packt books are more specific and less general than the IT books you have seen in the past. Our unique business model allows us to bring you more focused information, giving you more of what you need to know, and less of what you don't.

Packt is a modern, yet unique publishing company, which focuses on producing quality, cutting-edge books for communities of developers, administrators, and newbies alike. For more information, please visit our website: www.packtpub.com.

Writing for Packt

We welcome all inquiries from people who are interested in authoring. Book proposals should be sent to authors@packtpub.com. If your book idea is still at an early stage and you would like to discuss it first before writing a formal book proposal, contact us; one of our commissioning editors will get in touch with you.

We're not just looking for published authors; if you have strong technical skills but no writing experience, our experienced editors can help you develop a writing career, or simply get some additional reward for your expertise.

Programming Windows Workflow Foundation

ISBN: 1-904811-21-3   Paperback: 252 pages

A C# developer's guide to the features and programming interfaces of Windows Workflow Foundation

1. Add event-driven workflow capabilities to your .NET applications.

2. Highlights the libraries, services and internals programmers need to know

3. Builds a practical "bug reporting" workflow solution example app

Building Websites with VB.NET and DotNetNuke 4

ISBN: 1-904811-99-X   Paperback: 336 pages

A practical guide to creating and maintaining your own DotNetNuke website, and developing new modules and skins

1. Specially revised and updated version of this acclaimed DotNetNuke book

2. Create and manage your own website with DotNetNuke

3. Customize and enhance your site with skins and custom modules

4. Extensive coverage of the DAL and DAL+ for custom module development

5. Complete coverage of setup, administration, and development

Please check **www.PacktPub.com** for information on our titles